THE POETIC MIND

THE POETIC MIND

By Frederick Clarke Prescott

GREAT SEAL BOOKS

A Division of Cornell University Press

ITHACA, NEW YORK

To the memory of

J. H. PRESCOTT

FOREWORD

IN April 1912 the specialized audience of the *Journal of Abnormal Psychology* encountered (among the "original articles" listed) a discussion of essentially literary concern. Its author, Frederick C. Prescott, was not a psychologist but a teacher of English at Cornell, a forty-year-old Kansan who had studied and taught at Harvard. "Poetry and Dreams" was followed by a second installment, and then the two were generally ignored, even when issued separately in 1912 and 1919. By the year following the last publication, however, the original seventy pages had become a full-length study of the operation of the poet's mind, a subject described by its author as "lying halfway between psychology and literature."

When *The Poetic Mind* appeared in 1922, reviewers examined it with care but little relish, and its existence could hardly have been detected throughout the succeeding twenty years. But then rediscovery set in. Critics began to refer to Prescott as a pioneer and to his book as having been ahead of its time. Today *The Poetic Mind* is "classified"—as "one of the first notable efforts to relate Freudian theory to a theory of poetry" (Herbert J. Muller) or "the first careful adaptation of Freudian theory to literature" (William Van O'Connor).

Thoughtful consideration—of the 1912 articles in particular—casts doubt on such summary characterizations. To be sure, Prescott follows Freud's view of the unconscious (though not always: see pp. 116–117 for a Jungian deviation), and he never turns his eyes from Freud's dream interpretation in describing the mechanisms of poetic thought. But he also counts heavily on certain theories advanced by the Rev. John Keble. Indeed if *The Poetic Mind* was noteworthy for relating Freud to literature, it was even more remarkable for rescuing and emphasizing the radical ideas that Keble had ventured eighteen years before the birth of Freud.[1]

Readers who know Keble as the Anglican clergyman whose St. Mary's sermon of 1833 set off the Oxford Movement may be shocked to hear that he considered literature to be disguised wish fulfillment; poetry "a safety-valve, preserving men from actual madness"; the writer's product "unconscious" autobiography; meter and rhythm "useful in throwing a kind of veil over those strong and deep emotions which cannot endure publicity"; and so on. But to Prescott such unorthodoxies had extraordinary import, for Keble was a poet (of *The Christian Year*) and Prescott sturdily insisted that "the best evidence must come from the lives and works of the poets"—not only are they "in general excellent psychologists," but where the question concerns the working of the literary imagination "they are the best."

The Poetic Mind may therefore be said to draw on three main sources: Freud, Keble, and the testimony of poets. But readers today are interested not so much in the sources as in the insights to which they led. Of the many to be found in Prescott's writings, some have lost their freshness by having become familiar—we are no longer surprised to hear, for example, that the mental organization of the man in the street does not differ from that of the creative artist, or that it is possible to track down virtually all the germs of so "fantastic" a work as *The Ancient Mariner*. But we respond differently

[1] Interestingly enough, Keble reappeared in 1953 in even greater detail in the work of another Cornell scholar, M. H. Abrams' *The Mirror and the Lamp* (New York: Oxford, 1953).

before other passages—such as, for example, the one in which Prescott summarily explains why "the invention of the word *like* marks the birth of modern science": "the conscious and explicit recognition of likenesses, making possible classification and induction, opens the way to all rational thinking."

A brief foreword is hardly the place for taking inventory of an author's contributions; yet something should be said of Prescott's thought on myth and on meaning, if only to point to its pertinence. With respect to the first, one may simply call attention to the index entries (in *The Poetic Mind*) and to his volume *Poetry and Myth* (1927). The second involves complexities; nevertheless at this period in our literature, when criticism has become overwhelmingly concerned with "levels" of meaning, one cannot omit to cite such words as these which appeared almost four decades ago:

Whereas in true prose words should have one meaning and one meaning only, in true poetry they should have as many meanings as possible, and the more the better, *as long as these are true to the images in the poet's mind.*

Of these various meanings one may be the primary denotation, the others secondary, suggested, or connoted. One may be the apparent or surface meaning, the others latent. But often the surface meaning will be of less importance than the latent ones; the idea having true poetic significance and bearing the emotional emphasis will not be said but suggested, and *the real poetry will be between the lines;* the secondary meaning may be the one of prime importance [pp. 173, 171 below; my italics].

Did *The Poetic Mind* fail to win a large audience only because it was born too soon? There was something more, an impression taken by many that beneath its objectivities lurked a mystic. But what is a mystic? Having studied with Prescott daily for almost a year, I found him to be as scrupulous as any positivist in evaluating imaginative projections; and if he accepted Blake's proverb, "Everything possible to be believ'd is an image of truth," both *possible* and *believ'd* were taken literally. But did Prescott think that poets had access to special sources of revelation? The pages that follow will answer—yet I would add that Prescott seemed especially fond of reporting that Blake, when asked where he "saw all the fantastic things" recorded in his writings, calmly pointed to his head.

STANLEY BURNSHAW

April 1959

PREFACE

SOME of the principles presented in this book are new. This I acknowledge with misgiving, for in a subject as old as poetry, where orthodox views are particularly apt to be sound, novelty is not a recommendation. Fortunately most of the principles are old, and all, I hope, rest on old foundations. Indeed I have tried to return to and develop classical views of poetry which are now somewhat out of vogue. In the main, then, old principles at most receive new interpretation and relation. A discussion, even of the present length, dealing with many aspects of the large subject of poetry, must be somewhat superficial. It would have been easier and more satisfying to completeness to apply the principles herein developed to one or two divisions of the subject. I have thought it better to carry them through several, and apply them to poetry in most of its important aspects, with the prefatory statement, however, that the treatment is introductory and provisional. Each chapter invites correction, and also demands development. Some chapters, I hope, may lead to more thorough and sagacious inquiries.

The subject undertaken—the operation of the poet's mind— is fortunately not quite so broad as poetry itself. This limitation, however, is counterbalanced by its lying halfway between two provinces—literature on the one hand and psychology on the other. Evidently its treatment calls for a special psychological training, to which I cannot pretend, as will no doubt sufficiently appear. The subject as a whole, so far as I know, has not been attempted by the psychologists; perhaps it is a field in which they wisely fear to tread. In what follows a literary treatment is hazarded, which may in the end, I hope, prove helpful to psychology. Evidently the subject must be approached from both sides. If the student of literature lacks the much needed psychological training, the psychologist on the other hand might lack the wide reading in literature which must supply a large part of the evidence. The best evidence must in the nature of things come from the lives and works of the poets. The poets are in general excellent psychologists, and where the question concerns the working of their own minds they are the best. Psychology must obtain most of its facts ultimately from introspection. If then, instead of mind in general, the poet's mind is to be investigated, the poets are obviously in sole possession of the most important data. Fortunately also many of the poets—notably, for example, in England Dryden, Wordsworth, and Coleridge, and in America Emerson and Poe—have been disposed to introspection and self-analysis; and where they have been so disposed they have far surpassed ordinary men in subtlety of discrimination and in acuteness and depth of insight. For these reasons—because they possess in their own minds the facts to be observed and because they also have quite exceptional powers of observation—the poets must furnish the chief material in any investigation of the subject. If the psychologist may make best final use of this material, it is perhaps the business of the student of literature to collect, classify, and correlate it. I have made such constant use of these sources, and have so burdened, if not overburdened, the text with quotations from them, that the book might almost be regarded as a description of the poetic mind in the language of the poets themselves.

I may say here further that the rigorously scientific method, which would be employed by the psychologist, seems to me inapplicable to the subject of poetry in its present stage of investigation. Psychology is a science, and even promises, I am told, to become an exact one. But science is not always serviceable, and it may be the enemy as well as the friend of progress. Since the time of Bacon we have made tremendous advances; but since that time also we have been inclined to cut ourselves off from other sources of truth in our scientific preoccupation. We neglect the employment of other methods, or we employ them under the frown of science, apologetically and surreptitiously, leaving them mainly to the poets, when we ought to proclaim them as often the only methods available for our purpose. Some aspects of the large subject of poetry, as for example the mechanism of verse, are relatively simple, and may profitably be subjected to scientific analysis. Others, like the prophetic character of poetry, are as complex and difficult as any the mind is called upon to consider; indeed though poetry has long been the subject of investigation, it contains many such obscurities and mysteries. If these, which are the very matters calling most loudly for explanation, are approached by a purely scientific method the result is nil; and if such a method be insisted upon—as is too often the case in this age of science—all advance is for the present barred. For approaching these, and in general for proceeding into regions entirely new and unknown —as will, I trust, appear in the following chapters—only an intuitive method is possible. Some day, we may hope, these will be completely rationalized by the psychologist. Meanwhile if they are to be treated at all the method must be a compromise, or considerable relaxation in the direction of intuitive processes;—or, what amounts to the same thing, there must be a large use of the intuitions of the poets.

Just now when there is much talk of "scientific research" and "laboratory methods" in literary study—though there are signs that the fashion is passing—it is well to remember the advantage in older and freer methods. It is a great gain—I say this seriously—to be able to form or even state conclusions without proof. If the proofs, which are of only mediate importance, can be dispensed with there is tremendous saving. "The end of understanding," Carlyle was certainly right in saying, "is not to prove and find reasons, but to know and believe." Proving is the toilsome journey; knowing is the journey's end; and we should be ready enough to shorten the journey. Consider the poet, who instead of plodding, flies; who even has only to think earnestly on his destination in order to arrive—and with the quickness of thought. To change the figure a little, proving is like the day's labor; knowing is labor's reward at evening; and the two must not be disproportionate. Literary "research" is sometimes a hard task-master, rewarding a long and painful induction with a pittance of uncertain value—even withholding the pittance and pretending that the labor is its own reward. Think again of the profit of poetry which omits the proofs and crowds the page with valuable conclusions. In literary investigation we can gain much by using some of the conclusions the poets have already provided for us.

I have suggested for literary investigation a compromise method. Truths drawn from the poets, though entirely lacking in inductive evidence, may be checked by tests of a strictly scientific kind. If, for example, the statement of a poet on a matter of importance connected with the present subject, though standing unproved, is yet found to agree with the statement of another, it is strengthened; if further this agreement is found among many poets, of different ages and countries, the consensus is an argument of the strongest kind—stronger indeed than any single inductive proof. Right conclusions also show an agreement of another kind; they have a way of agreeing with each other, of fitting into and explaining each other, and of readily forming part of a larger structure. The test of them is whether they will "work," and this test is also entirely scientific. Finally, wrong conclusions are sterile, right ones productive; the former die when the book containing them is closed; the latter are alive and remain so, and soon gather to themselves other opinions. A little time applies the test, and however it may be in the practical sciences, in the investigation of poetry there is no hurry. One writing on the present subject, then, need not be too much afraid of promoting error.

Indeed I am convinced that proving and testing the material available in the dicta of the poets on the subject of poetry is the least difficult and most dispensable part of the work. When we consider these dicta we do not question their value or their truth. When we find Shakespeare saying that the poet is of imagination all compact, or Shelley saying that the poet is at once legislator and prophet, we take for granted—rather we feel—that these expressions are valuable and true. The task is usually not to verify them, but to understand them and to bring them into proper relation to other thought. Taken independently these statements of the poets about poetry throw a fitful light on the subject,—sometimes the only light we have. If they could be taken together, many of them, from many ages and countries; if they could be systematized and correlated so that one might confirm, interpret, and illumine another, a theory of the greatest value would result. Some day a synthesis of this kind may be accomplished. I speak here, however, of the collection and correlation of such materials only to indicate a method—a very valuable one as I believe,—which I have tried to keep before me in what follows.

This book has grown out of brief articles which I contributed to the *Journal of Abnormal Psychology* in 1912, and which were reprinted by Mr. Richard G. Badger in *Poetry and Dreams*, 1912. I have to thank Mr. Badger for his courtesy in consenting to the use from this earlier work of some paragraphs and parts of paragraphs, the most important of which, in chapters II, XIV, and XV, are indicated in the notes. I am much indebted to my brother, Mr. C. F. Prescott, and to my friends Professor J. E. Creighton and Professor William Strunk, Jr., for criticism of my manuscript; to Professor Strunk I am especially grateful for his kindly appreciation and encouragement.

F. C. PRESCOTT.

Ithaca, New York
    February 15, 1920.

CONTENTS

CHAPTER I

INTRODUCTION

CHAPTER II

EXAMPLES OF VISION

CHAPTER III

TWO MODES OF THOUGHT

CONTENTS

CHAPTER IV

THE IMAGINATION IN CHILDHOOD—THE PRIMITIVE IMAGINATION

CHAPTER V

THE SUBJECTS OF POETRY

CHAPTER VI

THE UNCONSCIOUS MIND IN POETRY

CHAPTER VII

THE UNIVERSALITY OF POETRY

CHAPTER VIII

THE DESIRES AND EMOTIONS IN POETRY

CHAPTER IX

THE IMAGINATION: INTERNAL AND EXTERNAL ELEMENTS

CHAPTER X

THE IMAGINATION: RECENT AND EARLY SOURCES

CHAPTER XI

THE IMAGINATION: CONDENSATION AND DISPLACEMENT

CHAPTER XII

THE FORMATION OF IMAGINARY CHARACTERS

CHAPTER XIII

SYMBOLS AND FIGURES

CHAPTER XIV

THE IMPULSE AND THE CONTROL

CHAPTER XV

THE POETIC MADNESS AND CATHARSIS

CHAPTER XVI

THE USES OF POETRY

THE POETIC MIND

THE working of the poet's mind, though the subject of curious interest from the time of Plato to the present, is not yet understood. The body of poetic criticism, valuable as it is, contains no discussion of the poet's imaginative creation which does not leave the reader balked and disappointed at the crucial points. The poet himself cannot explain his special faculty, as he can his ordinary mental processes; toward his own production, indeed, he is strangely impersonal as if it were hardly his own. His attitude is that of Voltaire, who, on seeing one of his tragedies performed, exclaimed: "Was it really I who wrote that?" He feels, like Milton, that inspiration comes from without: a "celestial patroness" comes "unimplored,"

> And dictates to him slumbering, or inspires
> Easy his unpremeditated verse.

Why should the poet's mind thus hesitate to acknowledge its own faculty? There is something similarly inexplicable in the action of poetry upon the reader's mind. Lovers of poetry, the most devoted and reverent on the one hand, the most expert and critical on the other, find a mystery in its effect. A poem, they may say, has *charm*, but the word itself suggests magic; and this test, though as good as any, can be applied only by the feelings, never by the reason; and it cannot be rationally explained. Poetry indeed, as Shelley believed, "acts in a divine and unapprehended manner, beyond and above consciousness."

It would be helpful to the critic, though doubtless not to the poet himself, if we could at all understand this poetic production, and find out in what this poetic charm consists.

To the ancients, as to Shelley, poetry was divine and the poetical creation a miracle of grace. The poet, like the prophet and the dreamer, was inspired,—that is, raised above his normal power by the breath or spirit of the God—of Apollo or the muse. A poetic exercise was a religious exercise also, and the poet began it by invoking the muse—quite sincerely, as the modern religious service begins with prayer. Later this invocation became a form, and when brought into modern times, an empty form—often the object of satire and parody. "Hail, Muse, et cetera"—Byron begins a canto of *Don Juan*. Phrases based upon the primitive conception are common in modern poetry; the poet is "transported," "possessed," "filled with fury, rapt, inspired"; but such expressions are either mere classical ornament and "poetic diction," or after losing all metaphorical significance are adopted as a critical terminology vaguely descriptive of the creative process. Christian poets have given the conception new life by invoking Urania or the "heavenly muse" or the "holy ghost"; even such invocation, however, is as a rule, merely "poetical," not truly religious. Here as elsewhere in his poetry, Wordsworth replaced form by sincerity and truth:

> Descend, prophetic spirit! that inspir'st
> The human soul of universal earth,
> Dreaming on things to come; and dost possess
> A metropolitan temple in the hearts
> Of mighty poets; upon me bestow
> A gift of genuine insight.[1]

Here poetical invocation again becomes true prayer. Wordsworth showed his elevation by feeling and once more recognizing the close relation between poetry and religion. In this other poets like Shelley and Emerson agree with him. They make little attempt, however, to explain rationally the nature of in-

[1] "The Recluse."

spiration; their conception shows no advance in this respect, and is still essentially that of the Greeks.

For the sake of clearness this matter may be restated somewhat differently. The Greek poet produced, by processes of which he was largely unconscious, poetry which was felt to contain beauty and truth of the highest value. This production was clearly beyond anything of which his ordinary mind was capable. As elsewhere in his mythology, a power, hidden yet beneficent, within himself, he made objective, personified, and called the God or the muse. In the same way the modern poet, Wordsworth, finds himself gifted with a faculty higher and more creative than that of his conscious mind. He dares not attribute it to himself. By a myth-making, or as we now must call it, a poetic exercise of his mind, he conceives of it as proceeding from a prophetic spirit, having the gift of genuine insight, whom he doubtless identifies with the divinity of his modern religion. His conception is that of the Greek, except that it is elevated and refined by all the intervening growth of poetic and religious thought.

To the modern rationalist Apollo is a "myth,"—a myth, however, which may embody truth. The idea of Wordsworth likewise embodies truth, but is to be accepted and understood only poetically. The philologist or psychologist regards this conception of divinity as merely a poetic figure, by which a genuine but deeply hidden faculty of the human mind is by this mind itself projected and personified through the imagination. He does not believe in Apollo, but he is ready to believe there is truth in the Apollo myth. His problem is to rationalize and express in prose the theory poetically shadowed forth in this idea of divinity.

Modern poets like the three just mentioned—Wordsworth, Shelley, and Emerson—have done much to illuminate the working of the poet's mind. Critics of less insight are apt to deal with phrases rather than with thoughts. They speak of inspiration without feeling the vital significance of the primitive term on the one hand, and without giving it definite modern denotation on the other. They speak of poetry as a heavenly gift, meaning only that poetry is at once beautiful and inexplicable. They call Shakespeare divine, because they know nothing of his life but wish to give his poetry the highest commendation. They talk of the poetic madness without believing in it. They explain poetry as the product of imagination—"the power so-called," as Wordsworth says, "through sad incompetence of human speech" —when the imagination calls as loudly for explanation as poetry itself. They refer to artistic creation, without being able to tell what or how the poet creates. Poetic criticism tends to become a repetition of vague or empty phrases.

Some readers may even feel that the matters covered by these phrases must remain mysteries. Obscurity in the subject begets superstition and leads to supine reverence and wonder. We should indeed worship our great poets, as the men of old did their bards and prophets; not abjectly, however, as savages do their medicine men, but rather with intelligent veneration. As a subject of the highest importance poetry should be studied most carefully; little by little we shall learn about it; we shall never fully understand it. Poets like Wordsworth who have esteemed it most highly have understood it most profoundly. Reverent readers may therefore be reassured, for inquiry will at best only push the mystery a little further off, analysis will only turn a simple mystery into a complex one,—and no explanation of poetry will explain it away.

The modern student of poetry is not so much frightened by mystery in the subject as deterred by its extent and difficulty— of which no one can be more conscious than I. No treatment of poetry can be adequate; no theory complete. No explanation even of a particular point can furnish a key to all the difficulties immediately involved. At most some aspects of the whole subject may be clarified and rationalized. With this understood— and any attempt at full treatment disclaimed—I may state the purpose of the present book. I wish to attempt some further explanation of poetic vision, of the poetic imagination and poetic creation, of the poetic madness, and of the prophetic nature and function of poetry. I intend, however, not so much to present any novel theories of my own on these subjects, as to bring together and systematize views which have long been held in regard to poetry,—which have been expressed, often figuratively and obscurely, by the poets themselves, in various ages and in many books,—which, therefore, have remained scattered and, to have their full value, must be brought together from a wide reading of literature,—which must be interpreted and correlated, often indeed translated from the language of poetry to that of prose. In proceeding thus I shall have often to quote at length from these sources; and I beg the reader not merely to pardon the constant quotation, but to attend particularly to the quotations as the best possible evidence and as more authoritative and usually more important than the text.

The subject of poetry is of course very large and complex, and calls first for analysis and limitation. I shall not undertake any general definition; poetry has so many aspects that a definition for one purpose is useless, even illogical for another. In what follows I wish merely to indicate limitations, not at all dogmatic, which may be helpful for the ensuing discussion.

The word "poetical" is applied, quite properly, to objects in nature, as we call a landscape or a face "poetical;" and to products of the other arts, as we may call a painting "poetry." In both cases the analogy is veracious; we may view a natural scene imaginatively or creatively, and the painter's imaginative faculty is akin to, or identical with, the poet's. In what follows, however, if only for the simplification of the subject matter, we shall deal mainly with the poetry of words. It is helpful to distinguish the poetic inspiration, an operation proceeding within the poet's mind, from the poetic product, the expressed poem, which may be heard or read. It is the former which presents most difficulties: when we understand the inspiration we shall probably understand the poem. Further the inspiration may correspond to only a part, greater or smaller, of the poem. The latter if of any length usually contains both uninspired and inspired portions—parts which are written consciously and deliberately, by artistry, and parts which are the record of true vision and are produced more profoundly—as we say by genius. "A poem of any length," Coleridge says, "neither can be, nor ought to be all poetry." Even the inspired poet is not always inspired, but often only copying the forms of inspiration. Many passages called poetry are only verse connecting the inspired portions. Further, as everyone knows, many whole poems, so-called, are not poetry at all, but only wit, satire, philosophy, or pale narrative in verse. These—the "Epistle to Arbuthnot" or the "Vanity of Human Wishes"—may be admirable productions by no means to be excluded from the anthology, and perhaps involving, so to speak by absorption, the difficulties of the higher poetry; but the mystery is not here. There certainly is a higher poetry. In some poems, at any rate in such parts as are vital and characteristic, we feel at once, instinctively or through a strange response of the feeling, that we are in the presence of this higher production; we share with the poet in his vision. This, which we sometimes call "pure poetry," I believe to be the product of a mental operation quite different from that which produces mere verse or ordinary prose. And the difference between these two operations of the mind, which we might call the prose operation and the poetic operation, is the main subject for discussion in the following chapters.

This distinction between inspired and uninspired verse has nothing to do with subjects or kinds. A lyric or an epic may belong to either class. It has little to do with length. A short poem is more apt to be pure poetry than a long one, and this perhaps led Poe to consider a long poem a "contradiction in terms." A long poem is more apt to have intercalations of mere verse. But a very long poem may unquestionably in its conception be the unified product of one effort of the genuine poetic imagination; "Milton," as Shelley says, "conceived the *Paradise Lost* as a whole before he executed it in portions." [1] Further this distinction—of inspired and uninspired—is not final as to the

---

[1] *Defense of Poetry*, ed. Cook, p. 39.

permanent value of the product. In general the inspired poem
will be superior, but the "Vanity of Human Wishes" may be of
much greater value than the product of some minor poet's
vision. Aristotle believed poetry to be "a thing inspired."
In the *Poetics*, however, he says it "implies either a strain of
madness or a happy gift of nature." [1] That is, he divides poetry
into two classes, the ἐκστατικοί and the εὔπλαστοι—the ecstatic
and euplastic—on which John Keble bases an instructive distinction between poets of primary and poets of secondary inspiration. The poet must be either a true ecstatic, or he must be
capable by a flexible assumption through conscious art, of writing as if he were inspired. Shelley was a poet of primary inspiration. Dryden, on the other hand, "had in perfection the εὐφυΐα,
the versatility and power of transforming himself into the
resemblance of real sentiment, which the great philosopher has
set down as one of the natural qualifications for poetry, but he
wanted the other and more genuine spring of the art—τὸ
μανικόν—the enthusiasm, the passionate devotion to some one
class of objects or train of thought." [2] The work of a first rate
secondary poet may be of more value than that of a poor primary
one. But the primary poetry, of original inspiration, is that requiring explanation.

For our purposes, however, the ordinary conception of poetry
must be not only restricted but broadened. Not all verse is
poetry: conversely not all poetry is in verse. Popular use identifies the two: a "piece of poetry" means a few stanzas of verse.
Even many good critics make metrical form the essential. Hegel,
for example, thinks metre "the first and only condition absolutely demanded by poetry." There is an essential difference,
says Matthew Arnold, between imaginative production in
verse, and imaginative production in prose, that will not permit
both to be called by the common name of poetry. [3] For many

---

[1] *Rhetoric*, iii, 7; *Poetics*, xvii, 2.

[2] *The British Critic*, vol. xxiv (1838), p. 438.

[3] *Mixed Essays*, p. 435.

purposes Arnold is right. The two forms, however, have much in common; and in the following inquiry, dealing mainly with inspiration and imagination, it will be well, as Walter Pater says *per contra*, "to identify in prose what we call the poetry, the imaginative power;" [1] otherwise we shall have to disregard some most interesting and typical cases. Fortunately the best critics, from Aristotle to Wordsworth and Shelley, have taken poetry broadly, and have held that its presence is not determined by the character of the language, at least of the rhythm, in which it may find expression. "It is by no means essential," Shelley says, to quote from but one authority, "that a poet should accommodate his language to the traditional form [of metre], so that the harmony, which is its spirit, be observed;" [2] and he includes Plato, Livy, and Bacon among poets.

Poetry, then, may appear in prose as well as in verse; for our purpose this is the better view; indeed—though it may not appear true without consideration—poetry will probably be found more often, or bulking more largely, in the former than in the latter. The same creative faculty which produces poetic verse produces also prose fiction, in narrative and drama, where this is original and inspired. The mind of Scott exercised the same genial power whether he wrote in prose or in verse,—exercised it indeed more fully in the prose; the *Heart of Midlothian* is a true poetical creation. Bunyan and Dickens, who saw their characters acting before them almost with their bodily eyes, furnish perfect examples of the poetic vision. The imaginative operation of the mind of Homer is recorded in the *Iliad*; it is recorded also, if less perfectly, in a translation into English prose. The essence is in the myth, the fiction, or the poetry—the three, as we shall see, come to the same thing. The death of Arthur is poetry not because it was put into verse by Tennyson or into prose by Malory, but because it was originally conceived by an imaginative operation of the human mind. There was doubtless a new and secondary creation

[1] *Appreciations*, p. 2.   [2] *Defense of Poetry*, ed. Cook, p. 8.

in the mind of Tennyson; but so there was also in the mind of Malory. By the older critics, therefore, the word poetry was often quite properly applied to fictions in prose, just as in German the word *Dichtung* (opposed to *Wahrheit*) is broadly used to cover the whole fictional subject matter that we have here to consider.

But the field of essential poetry may be still further broadened. Much prose, not fiction in the ordinary sense, is highly poetic. "Prose poetry" is described as a hybrid and frowned upon by arbitrary critics. The name is illogical and confusing, but there can be no doubt about the thing. Poetry expressed in prose rhythms is natural and omnipresent in literature; it therefore cannot be, as eighteenth century critics thought, poetry astray and intruding anomalously into a field alien to its own. Expression in verse is natural to the poet, and was especially so in primitive times; and such expression is the highest. But there can hardly have been a time when essential poetry did not find expression, at least casually, in the rhythms of prose, which are all but equally serviceable, and which in modern times are a constant poetic medium. Just as imaginative creation is the essence of the poetic substance, so rhythm, as distinguished from metre, is the indispensable feature of the poetic expression,—and this rhythm may be found in many different literary forms, to the confusion of the classifications of the critics—in ordinary verse, rhymed and unrhymed, of course, but also in the prose of our translation of the *Psalms*, in the *Leaves of Grass*, in the *vers libre*, and in many a passage in the prose of Scott or Thackeray, of De Quincey, Poe, or Carlyle. Carlyle was a poet—perhaps the truest poet of his age, as Mr. Justice Stephen called him. He had the poet's eye, as his images on every page attest, and the poet's ear, which constantly attuned his rhythms to the "eternal music." Indeed nowhere can the working of poetic imagination and its expression be studied more readily than in *Sartor Resartus* and the *French Revolution*. These are the true tests then,—the presence of imagination in the substance and of rhythm in the form; what-

ever satisfies these tests will be included as poetry in the following discussion. I shall have no objection, however, to calling the
verse alone poetry and the remainder prose, so long as it is recognized that the same phenomena requiring explanation appear
in both kinds; and I wish here only to justify at the outset the
broad treatment and the inclusiveness of the examples in the
following chapters.

Evidently an inquiry into the working of the poet's mind
should be more inclusive than an aesthetic criticism. The discussion has to do not so much with poetry as aesthetically good
or bad, as with its essence and origin. The great poets, since
they represent the poetic operation most fully and typically,
must be most instructive, but the potential poets, like Charles
Lamb and Hartley Coleridge, may be almost equally so. Even
the mute inglorious poets may be taken into account.

> But bare of laurel they live, dream, and die;
> For Poesy alone can tell her dreams,
> With the fine spell of words alone can save
> Imagination from the sable chain
> And dumb enchantment. Who alive can say
> "Thou art no Poet—mayst not tell thy dreams?"
> Since every man whose soul is not a clod
> Hath visions, and would speak, if he had loved,
> And been well nurtured in his mother tongue.[1]

Thus Keats, as elsewhere Hazlitt and Emerson, insists that
all men are poets and have their moments of inspiration. "The
dullest of clowns tells or tries to tell himself a story, as the
feeblest of children uses invention in his play; and even as the
imaginative grown person joining in the game at once enriches it
with many delightful circumstances, the great creative writer
shows us the apotheosis of the dreams of common men." [2]

The clown and the great creative writer fall psychologically
into one class; both are poets and dreamers, only with difference

---

[1] Keats, "The Fall of Hyperion," i, 7–15.
[2] Stevenson, "A Gossip on Romance."

of degree.   The fact is that all men at one moment are poets and again are not.   They use their minds in two ways, in one way when they work and in another way when they dream.   In order, then, to get to the core of the matter we shall have for the present to lose sight of the distinctions—however convenient for aesthetic criticism—between the great poets and ordinary men, between prose and verse, between play, story, and poem, and turn our attention to the distinction—perhaps more philosophical, at any rate more useful for our purpose—between these two mental operations, ordinary thinking and dreaming, the practical thought and the poetic.   An analysis of the differences between the two will help somewhat toward explaining the production of poetry.

CHAPTER II

EXAMPLES OF VISION

I

BEFORE we analyze these two kinds of thought, however, and their differences, we had better take some actual examples of them and their products—at any rate of the second, —because the practical one is constantly in use, perfectly familiar, and needs no elucidation, except as any mental process may require it. We employ the mind in this practical manner whenever we plan, work, or attend to business, and when we write in the purely prosaic or scientific way—that is, during most of our waking hours. Sometimes, however, and perhaps oftener than we think, we lapse from directed thought into a state of abstraction or meditation. The poet is apparently a man to whom such abstraction is frequent, even habitual. The poet lives, not constantly of course, but more frequently than ordinary men, in a world of his imagination; he is a seer; he has a gift of vision. What is meant by this vision we shall consider closely in the next chapter; here I shall only give some examples of it, in order that we may have before us, clearly and in the concrete, the kind of phenomena the student of poetry is called upon to explain.

We may take the following as typical. Wordsworth saw, as he tells us in a note, a "multiplication of mountain ridges . . . produced either by watery vapors or sunny haze—in the present instance by the latter cause." These he must first have observed in the ordinary prosaic way in which he thus describes them. But then he must have begun to see them in the imaginative or visionary way, transforming them, with a recollection of one of Allston's paintings, into "a kind of Jacob's ladder, leading to Heaven":

> Yon hazy ridges to my eyes
> Present a glorious scale,
> Climbing suffused with sunny air,
> To stop—no record hath told where!
> And tempting Fancy to ascend
> And with immortal spirits blend!
> —Wings at my shoulders seem to play;
> But rooted here, I stand and gaze
> On those bright steps that heavenward raise
> Their practicable way.[1]

So Wordsworth records his vision. Such an imaginative operation may affect only a mild transformation, modifying, brightening, or coloring; or it may go all the way to complete hallucination,—to a "vision" in the popular sense. The ordinary man possibly thinks of vision as a rare privilege of poets—as common in biblical times and vouchsafed to saints in the middle ages, but denied now to most of us, or at best an anomalous visitation coming once in a lifetime. He expects too much. I suppose most of us have at times shared with the poet in his visionary attitude toward objects in nature. On some evening of extraordinary splendor and beauty, or even on an ordinary one, we walk alone, become abstracted, and without looking for it, suddenly find the scene before us, fields, trees, and sky, clothed in a strange appearance, colored by a strange light, taking us back to childhood or forward to another world, we hardly know which; this strangeness hovers for a moment and then as we revert to our everyday concerns, departs, leaving an indescribable pleasure. Most of us have occasionally, with Tennyson, "followed the gleam." Such an experience is not different from the poet's vision in kind, though it may be in degree. But it is clearly different from our ordinary thought.

[1] "An Evening of Extraordinary Splendor and Beauty."

Closely allied to the visions of the poet are the mild visions which we all experience in reverie or day dream. We give up work perhaps tired, sit by the fire, see the flames catching and the smoke rising, and so far we are thinking in the ordinary way,— but presently we are gazing fixedly, and transforming the shapes and colors into whatever scenes we wish. Or we stand before the window looking out at the actual scene, and presently we are abstracted or transported; we become for the moment seers or visionaries. To illustrate we may take another familiar poem of Wordsworth—which we may regard either as describing a day dream of "Poor Susan" or as a poetic production in the mind of Wordsworth, putting himself imaginatively in her place. As often happens the illusion starts from an actual sensation—the song of the bird—lasts momentarily, and then fades.

> At the corner of Wood Street, when daylight appears,
> Hangs a Thrush that sings loud, it has sung for three years:
> Poor Susan has passed by the spot, and has heard
> In the silence of morning the song of the Bird.
>
> 'Tis a note of enchantment; what ails her? She sees
> A mountain ascending, a vision of trees;
> Bright volumes of vapor through Lothbury glide,
> And a river flows on through the vale of Cheapside.
>
> .   .   .   .
>
> She looks, and her heart is in heaven: but they fade,
> The mist and the river, the hill and the shade:
> The stream will not flow, and the hill will not rise,
> And the colors have all passed away from her eyes!

The transition thus described, from practical thought to vision and back again everyone has experienced. A careful consideration of it is therefore possible for us, though we may be unable to conceive the visions of the poet. Upon such consideration I think the reader will feel that the working of the mind during the moments of vision is entirely different in character from its ordinary operation. As the words *day dream* and *reverie* suggest, it has more in common with that producing dreams in sleep than with ordinary thought.[1]

We may next take examples of a kind of vision less familiar but common enough from the earliest times to the present—that of religious mysticism or ecstasy. The saint, like the poet, is carried by strong feeling into a new mental state, a rapture, in which the imagination is freed. To the religious excitement is sometimes added, through fasting and vigilance, a mortification of the flesh, a sensuous deadening or fatigue, which is also conducive to the mental operation in question. Sometimes there is a kind of auto-hypnotism through fixed gazing upon an object of worship. Many such visions are recorded in the Bible. In *Acts*, for example, Peter goes up upon the housetop to pray, becomes hungry, falls into a trance, and sees heaven opened. In the poetical book of *Revelation* are recorded visions which came to John in Patmos while he was "in the spirit on the Lord's day." Examples might be taken from the lives of most well known religious leaders, St. Simeon or St. Jerome, Savonarola, Luther, or Swedenborg. Indeed this kind of vision, like the poetic, is apparently universal, appearing in ancient times, when poetic and prophetic vision were one, but also in the most modern, among Christian and non-Christian, civilized and uncivilized peoples. The following from St. Julian of Norwich, of 1373, is a mediaeval example. "My curate was sent for to be at my ending, and by that time when he came I had set my eyes, and might not speak. He set the cross before my face and said: 'I have brought thee the image of thy Maker and Savior: look thereupon and comfort thee therewith.' Methought I was well (as it was) for my eyes were set uprightward unto Heaven, where I trusted to come by the mercy of God; but nevertheless I assented to set my eyes on the face of the Crucifix, if I might, and so I did . . . After this my sight began to fail and it was all dark about me in the chamber, as if it had been night, save in the image of the Cross, whereon I beheld a common light; and I wist

[1] The French word, *petit roman*, suggests a relation between this reverie and a variety of literature.

not how . . . In this moment suddenly I saw the red blood trickle down from under the garland hot and freshly and right plenteously, as it were in the time of His passion, when the garland of thorns was pressed on His blessed head. I conceived truly and mightily that it was Himself showed it me, without any mean." [1]

From the full account of this vision it is somewhat uncertain whether it appeared to the saint while awake or asleep. This, however, is of little consequence. The more one studies the literature of this subject, the more one feels that, while there is a comparatively clear distinction between ordinary thought and waking vision, there is no such line between the latter and the vision of sleep; one blends so naturally with the other that it is often impossible to tell from the record of them which is which. There is the same blending in one's own mental experience. The mind often passes into a dream-like state just before falling asleep or just after waking, giving rise to what the psychologists classify as hypnogogic and hypnopompic illusions. These are akin to day dreams, if not identical with them; on the other hand they are often confused in recollection with the dreams of sleep. Poe describes them, calling them "psychal fancies" or "impressions," as arising in the soul "at those mere points of time where the confines of the waking world blend with those of the world of dreams." They have in them a "pleasurable ecstasy" which Poe regards as "a glimpse of the spirit's outer world." He has learned to control them so far as to be able to induce them and to convey them, "or more properly their recollection, to a situation where he can survey them with the eye of analysis." They are all but beyond the power of words, but "even a partial record of the impressions would startle the universal intellect of mankind by the supremeness of the novelty of the material employed, and of its consequent suggestions." [2] Here evidently we are at one of the sources of Poe's grotesque and arabesque.

Probably much of Poe's strange material came also from the

[1] Quoted by Inge, *English Mystics*, p. 55.

[2] *Works*, Virginia ed., vol. xvi, p. 88.

dreams of sleep. In true dreams the mind is freed from all bonds—the senses are in abeyance, practical effort suspended, the world shut out—and then, in entire relaxation, the imagination creates a world completely fanciful—or fantastic—in which it ranges at will. Dream is pure vision. We may try to picture to ourselves but can probably form only some vague idea of the range, vividness, and color of the imaginings of the true poet in sleep. "What dreams," Lamb exclaims, "must not Spenser have had!"

> O magic sleep! O comfortable bird,
> That broodest o'er the troubled sea of the mind
> Till it is hushed and smooth! O unconfined
> Restraint! imprisoned liberty! great key
> To golden palaces, strange minstrelsy,
> Fountains grotesque, new trees, bespangled caves,
> Echoing grottoes, full of tumbling waves
> And moonlight; aye, to all the mazy world
> Of silvery enchantment.[1]

What dreams must not Keats have had also! But even the ordinary dreamer has visions which compared with the prose of his waking life are highly poetical and which help him to explain the poets. Even the ordinary dreamer, at some favored moment, has seen Artemis and Aphrodite, or their beautiful counterparts—not as in waking moments in the likeness of human beings, but in their appropriate ethereal and dreamlike element—as true goddesses, shedding the pervasive effulgence of divinity; and with a glorified distinctness explaining and justifying both the worship and the poetry of the Greeks. The relations between such vision and that which produces poetry proper are so interesting that we shall have to return to them in a moment, here noting further only that normal dreams are often artificially modified, heightened, or colored by the effects of alcohol or opium—as in the cases, for example, of Poe, Coleridge, and De Quincey.

[1] "Endymion," i, 453.

This, like the example from St. Julian, will suggest that the visionary operation of the mind often occurs in mental states which are more or less abnormal. Without here going into the difficult question of the sanity of the poet (which must be considered later) and of the abnormality of genius in general, we may note that the visionary operation may be either apparently natural and normal, or more or less abnormal or artificial. It always occurs when the mind is relaxed from the balance or adjustment necessary to attentive thought. This relaxation may result from various causes. In the first place it may come from strong natural feeling, as in the case of the poet or religious mystic; or in the case of the lover, who is a true visionary— "Love looks not with the eyes, but with the mind"—and who is often "beside himself," but certainly cannot be called abnormal. It may come in moments of extraordinary emotion or excitement, as when a person whose nerves are unstrung sees a ghost or turns a bush into a bear. Similarly one in a moment of great danger will see an intense picture, rather than form a plan of escape, or will see in rapid succession scenes from his past life. It may come from normal fatigue, as day dreams occur when one is resting after work, or as nocturnal dreams of course come in the rest of sleep; or from abnormal fatigue or physical deprivation— as one suffering acutely from hunger or thirst becomes light-headed and then delirious.[1] In general, however,—and this is important—though such vision may be due to temporary weakness, illness, or fatigue, it cannot be attributed to men of permanently weak or degenerate mind. Hobbes, sturdy materialist as he was, "was continually haunted by faces of the dead." So sane a man as Sir Walter Scott, on getting news of Byron's

---

[1] Thus Leonard in Wordsworth's *Brothers* in the calenture

> by feverish passion overcome
> Even with the organs of his bodily eye,
> Below him, in the bosom of the deep,
> Saw mountains, etc.,

where the vision seems poetical.

death, "suddenly saw his friend's image before him. Astonished at the natural appearance of the clothes he approached the phantom and discovered that it was an illusion, and that the clothes of the figure consisted of folds of a curtain." [1] The list of visionaries also includes men of greatness in action, like Brutus (in Plutarch), Columbus, Cromwell, and Castlereagh.

In other cases the relaxation and unbalancing is clearly abnormal, as in feverish delirium and the hallucinations of hysteria; or artificial, as in those induced by intoxication from alcohol or other drugs. This pathological field we may leave in the main unconsidered, if only to narrow the subject; noting merely, first that visions seen, for example, by persons passing under the influence of an anaesthetic, are often poetically beautiful in the description; and secondly, that the drugs are often used to induce or heighten the mental condition necessary to imaginative production. [2]

There is perhaps another reason for passing over this abnormal field,—because though it is familiar to the student of psychology or literature, it is less so to the general reader, who is loth to connect it with his poetry. Healthy and sensible persons are always a little impatient or distressed in considering such abnormal manifestations. Indeed healthy and sensible persons are apt to be impatient of the whole subject of reverie and day dream, dreamers and visionaries, illusions and hallucinations, apparitions and ecstasy. For this there are at least two reasons. In the first place the mental operations in question do certainly often imply weakness, disease, or indulgence. Secondly they all produce illusion, which is falsehood to fact; and in practice fact is usually the desideratum. The practical man naturally regards ghost-seeing as silly, day-dreaming as a waste of time,

[1] E. Parish, *Hallucinations and Illusions*, pp. 78, 81.

[2] Stevenson describes hallucinations of feverish delirium, which he connects interestingly with his dreams, and in turn with his literary imagination. See his letter to F. W. H. Myers, in the latter's *Human Personality*, vol. i, p. 301, and his "Chapter on Dreams" in *Across the Plains and other Essays*.

and the imaginings of the visionary as equally idle. If we were called upon to answer these objections we might to the first plead the strength and character of many of the visionaries; and to the second reply that if practical people have little use for the visionary, when we consult the visionary, on the other hand, or the poet, we find them setting the greatest store by their illusions and happy in a certain sense of superiority to other men. Or to put the matter differently, when we are engaged in practical thought we disparage our dreams, but on the other hand how we might regard our practical thought when we are engaged in dreaming we do not consider—and unfortunately cannot know, for on such a matter no dream has ever passed judgment. The value and function of the visionary faculty, however, must be considered later. Of its value in poetry there can be no question. Here I merely beg the reader to get rid of any prepossession arising from the sound or suggestion of the names, in order to consider the material on its merits.

All the forms of mental experience we have considered—poetic or mystic visions, day dreams, hypnogogic visions, dreams, illusions and hallucinations whether normal or abnormal,—are in character alike. In all the essence is in the visionary action of the mind. One therefore may explain another; and all may help to explain the working of the poetic imagination. It is, I think, commonly supposed that poetry is the product of our ordinary thought raised to a higher power, and that therefore the poetic thought may be followed and explained by the ordinary reason, provided the analysis be keen enough. This I believe to be an error,—and an error responsible for many mistakes of criticism. I believe the student of poetry will be on the right track if, for the time being at least, he separates it as much as possible from the products of ordinary thought, and connects it with productions of an entirely different kind; if he finds its origin in one of the group of mental operations, like each other but very different from ordinary thought, which I have enumerated above.

II

Two of these operations may now be selected for further careful consideration,—first the poetic vision as the one particularly in question, and secondly the vision of dreams. There is a striking analogy between these two, and I wish to call attention to it, not at all as a mere curiosity, but because the likeness in itself will prove instructive, and further because in later chapters it will be found possible to draw most valuable conclusions by passing from one to the other. Indeed the following discussion will depend in some degree upon establishing and utilizing a clear relation between these two.

Between the two there is of course an obvious and important difference,—namely that one takes place in waking and the other in sleep. This difference, however, may seem more significant to one who has attended little to the subject than to one who has studied it carefully, both by introspection and in the literature. The ordinary man thinks of his dreams as strange, negligible, and entirely different from his waking mental experience, from which they are separated by the sharp line drawn by his falling asleep. But if he attends to his dreams, and if he goes over what he can find in books on the subject, he learns that there are countless correspondences between certain mental experiences of the daytime and his mental experiences at night; indeed that the correspondences are much more striking than the differences; and that, as I have already said, wakeful dreaming and all its allied phenomena run indistinguishably into the dreaming of sleep. It may seem, however, that there is at least this difficulty in trying to find in dreams material for the explanation of poetry, that as dreams take place in sleep we can know little about them, while poetry, as it is produced in waking hours, can be much more readily analyzed. Certainly we know little of dreams,—only what we can remember when we awake and can infer therefrom. But do we know anything more of many of our waking mental experiences? Of a day dream we know only what we can recall after the fit of abstraction is ended. Similarly of his vision the poet knows only what he can remember when he has passed his rapture; this he may record as one may tell a dream. We shall see that all the cases of true vision already enumerated are much alike in this respect; and the disadvantage of dreams may therefore be exaggerated.

Let us now consider some of the evidence indicating a relation between poetry and dreams. In the first place language tends to identify the two, and such identification always indicates a relation—what or how close a relation we do not know until it is otherwise established. Even the uses we call metaphorical establish *some* relation. Poets have always been called dreamers, from the "dreamer Merlin" to the latest youth who "dreams" and rhymes. "The true poet," says Charles Lamb, "dreams being awake." He writes of "dreams which wave before the half-shut eye." The word *vision* is applied with equal facility to the poet and to the dreamer. We read of the visions of Daniel, of Dante, of Bunyan, or of Blake, without being sure whether they occurred in waking, when we should call them poetry, or in sleep, when we should call them dreams; it is a matter of indifference; the essential thing is the vision. So a dream is often properly called "poetical."

Poets are often, if not always, great dreamers, whether by night or by day. Goethe, Blake, Lamb, Coleridge, De Quincey, and many others recount vivid, beautiful, or horrible dream experiences, sometimes in sleep, sometimes in waking, often ambiguous between the two. This suggests that poetry and dreams are products of the same imaginative operation. Tolstoi in his Souvenirs writes of lying warm in bed and "losing himself in delicious dreams and recollections." He looks fixedly at the fold in the counterpane and sees before him his sweetheart, as clearly as when he left her an hour before. "In imagination," he says, "I talked with her, and this conversation though entirely lacking in sense, at least gave me indescribable pleasure, because it was filled with affectionate *thee's* and *thou's*. These dreams were so distinct that the pleasurable emotions prevented my sleeping," etc. The "dreams" then were in waking, but they might easily have been continued in sleep, and whether true dreams or only reverie or vision, they might equally serve as material for a scene in fiction. Thus reverie often runs into dream and dream encroaches on waking life. Poe confused the experiences of sleep and waking: "The realities of the world affected me as visions, and as visions only, while the wild ideas of the land of dreams became, in turn,—not the material of my everyday existence,—but in very deed that existence solely and in itself." [1] "To dream," he says, "has been the business of my life." [2] Such cases, of which there are many, lead Chabaneix to suppose that the poet is one in whom the dream state obtrudes anomalously into waking life. It would be better, however, in my opinion, to regard both dream and waking vision as the products of the same mental operation occurring naturally and indifferently in either sleep or waking.

Further evidence relating dreams to poetry is found in the explicit statements of many poets. In *Die Meistersinger* Wagner makes Hans Sachs speak thus of the poet's work:

> Mein Freund, das grad' ist Dichters Werk,
> Dass er sein Träumen deut' und merk,'
> Glaubt mir, des Menschen wahrster Wahn
> Wird ihm im Traume aufgetan:
> All' Dichtkunst und Poeterei
> Ist Nichts als Wahrtraum-Deuterei. [3]

---

[1] "Berenice."

[2] "The Assignation." The speech is of the hero, who, however, here more clearly than usual, is Poe himself. The story was originally "The Visionary," and the dreaming hero is also a poet. Compare Raffaelli : "If I do not sleep well at night I am rarely wholly awake in the day-time. The state of reverie, indeed the state of dream, is constant, so that often I do not answer questions until ten or fifteen minutes after,—that is to say *when I wake up*." Remy de Gourmont: "It often happens that I cannot distinguish dreams from reality, and for example confuse what a friend has told me the day before with what I have dreamed at night." Mme. Rachilde: "Sometimes I was deceived and my real life appeared to me as my dreams." —Chabaneix, *Le Subconscient chez les artistes*, pp. 91, 59.

[3] Quoted by W. Stekel, *Dichtung und Neurose*, p. 2.

Hebbel after recording in his *Journal* a beautiful but terrible dream says: "My belief that dream and poetry are identical is now more and more confirmed." Lamb believed that "the degree of the soul's creativeness in sleep might furnish no whimsical criterion of the quantum of poetical faculty resident in the same soul waking;" and advises young writers who are balancing between prose and verse "to decide the preference by the texture of their natural dreams." [1] Lafcadio Hearn gives equivalent advice: "Trust to your own dream life; study it carefully, and draw your inspiration from that. For dreams are the primary source of almost everything that is beautiful in the literature which treats of what lies beyond mere daily experience." [2]

This last statement is unquestionably true if we have in mind the dreams of both sleep and waking. But even nocturnal dreams are a constant source of poetic material and inspiration. Hearn regards them as especially the source of the supernatural in literature. "All the great effects obtained by poets and story writers, and even by religious teachers, in the treatment of supernatural fear or mystery, have been obtained, directly or indirectly, through dreams." Thus dreams are sometimes a direct, sometimes an indirect source of literary material. In Coleridge they were a direct source. The "Ancient Mariner" was founded on a dream of the poet's friend Cruikshank: "it is marvelous," as Lowell notes, "in its mastery over that delightfully fortuitous inconsequence which is the adamantine logic of dreamland." Other poems of Coleridge like the "Raven" and "Christabel" are dreamlike, if not true dreams. "Your dream," Lamb calls the former; and of "Christabel" Coleridge says that, at its first conception, he "had the whole present in his mind with the wholeness, no less than the liveliness of a vision." The famous instance, however, is of course "Kubla Khan," of which I will not take time to give the poet's familiar account. In general, Coleridge's imaginations were dream-like, vivid, fleeting, highly and artificially colored. This transitoriness, combined with a

[1] "Witches and Other Night Fears."

[2] *Interpretations of Literature*, vol. ii, p. 103.

poor memory, accounts for the incompleteness of his poetry. For other examples Klopstock's *Messiah*, De Quincey's *Confessions*, Poe's *Ligeia*, and Stevenson's *Dr. Jekyll and Mr. Hyde*, drew material directly from dreams.

More often, perhaps, the influence of dreams in literature is indirect, in the manner suggested by Lafcadio Hearn. Dreams furnish hints and glimpses, constantly recurring models and prototypes for the romantic, the supernatural, and the grotesque. They furnish especially the feeling and the atmosphere—the bright effulgence, the utter gloom, the thrill of awe, the ethereal desire, the "fear of fear"—the feelings which Poe, for example, struggled so hard with his superlatives to express, and found "no utterance capable of expressing." They are the ultimate source of "the light that never was on sea or land," the true region of the "magic casements" and "faery lands forlorn."

This influence is well expressed by an anonymous writer, quoted by Havelock Ellis, who has "precise and emotional dreams,—which sometimes remind him of the atmosphere of Poe's tales, and are occasionally in sequence from night to night." "The enormous reality and vividness of these dreams," he writes, " is their remarkable point. They leave a mark behind. When I come to consider I believe that much that I have written, and many things that I have said and thought and believed, are directly due to these dream experiences and my ponderings over how they came. Beneath the superficiality of our conscious mind—prim, smug, self-satisfied, and owlishly wise—there lies the vast gulf of a subconscious personality that is dark and obscure, seldom seen or even suspected. It is this, I think, that wells up into my dreams. It is always there—always affecting and modifying us, and bringing about strange and unforeseen new things in us—but in these dreams I peer over the edge of the conscious world into the giant-house and Utgard of the subconscious, lit by one ray of sunset that shows the weltering deeps of it. And the vivid sense of this is responsible for many things in my life." [1]

[1] H. Ellis, *The World of Dreams*, p. 277.

From the earliest times men have believed that dreams thus draw from the deeper portions of the mind which are the sources of wisdom. It is from these sources also that the poet must draw if his work is to be of any worth; he must write from long settled experience and from deep conviction. The Hebrew writers had great respect for dreams. "In a dream," says the *Book of Job*, "in a vision of the night . . . then he openeth the ears of men, and sealeth their instruction." [1] The Greeks thought dreams a source of wisdom; Synesius in his *Treatise on Dreams* declares that attention to divination by dreams is good on moral grounds alone. [2] Jonathan Edwards, who by the way was a typical mystic and seer, having trance-like states under the stress of religious feeling, especially in the presence of nature, says in his *Diary:* "I think it a very good way to examine dreams every morning when I awake; what are the nature, circumstances, principles, and ends of my imaginary actions and passions in them, to discern what are my chief inclinations, &c." [3] Kant in his *Anthropology* thinks dreams of value "in laying bare for us our hidden dispositions and revealing to us not what we are, but what we might have been if we had had a different education." [4]

These quotations represent the classical and older view. At present dreams are apt to be dismissed as trifles, or discussed as merely physiological or pathological. Unquestionably dreams may follow indigestion, but they have other bearings too; and it is well to heed Charles Lamb who takes the older view. "Some people," he says, "have no good of their dreams. Like fast feeders, they gulp them too grossly, to taste them curiously. . . . We have too much respect for these spiritual communications to let them go so lightly. . . . They seem to us to have as much significance as our waking concerns; or rather to import us more nearly, as more nearly we approach by years to the shadowy

[1] *Job*, xxxiii, 15.
[2] H. Ellis, *The World of Dreams*, p. 158.
[3] *Works* 1858, vol. i, p. 9.
[4] Cited by Freud, *Interpretation of Dreams*, p. 58.

world, whither we are hastening. . . . It is good to have friends at court. The abstracted media of dreams seem no ill introduction to that spiritual presence, upon which, in no long time, we expect to be thrown. . . . Therefore we cherish dreams. We try to spell in them the alphabet of the invisible world; and think we know already how it shall be with us." [1]

We may believe then, if we take this older view, that dreams not only reveal to us our own deeper character, but draw from these deeper sources moral wisdom, truth not ascertainable by our conscious waking minds, even truths touching the life of the spirit and immortality. But these are the truths which the poets and mystics are always seeking.

> Waking or asleep,
> They of death must deem
> Things more true and deep
> Than we mortals dream.

The dreamer, the mystic, and the poet all go to the same source. If we could raise dreams to their former high consideration, and raise poetry too, for that too has fallen somewhat from its old estate, and if we could again connect the two as they were always connected in earlier times, the relation and comparison might throw some light on those arcana of poetry which are the subject matter of the present inquiry.

I do not know that the evidence so far presented to support this relation will seem convincing. I may add to it by saying that this material is in no way exceptional or selected to make a showing. It might be increased indefinitely, and it will be added to in later chapters; indeed the difficulty is not in finding such evidence, but in deciding how much to present. What has been given may perhaps represent the more definite, obvious, and

---

[1] "Popular Fallacies," XIV. Compare J. A. Symonds's "Autobiography" in H. F. Brown, *Symonds*, vol. i, p. 55; and Havelock Ellis, *The World of Dreams*, p. viii: "Rightly understood, dreams may furnish us with clues to the whole of life."

easily presentable portion of all the evidence available; much evidence of strong probative value cannot readily be reduced to expository form. When, in the line which I have quoted at the beginning of the first chapter and shall have occasion to quote again at the end of the last, Wordsworth speaks of "the human soul of universal earth *dreaming* on things to come," he does not use the word as a "mere metaphor," but in a definite sense, congruous with the whole theory of dreams—and also with the whole theory of poetry.[1] I can only say that anyone who will take the trouble to follow the subject in his reading will find constant support for the relation in question—though it may often be between the lines. He will find literature, in one way or another, constantly referring to poets as dreamers, and to dreamers as poets, constantly describing the mental operation of the one in terms which will fit the other, and attributing to the poet's imagination modes and processes which we know belong to the dreamer, and vice versa.

III

In order to indicate what kind of material such reading would discover, to bring out the mental character of poets as visionaries and dreamers, and to emphasize their dreamlike habit of thought, I may take time to look at several well known writers from this point of view. The accounts of the poets naturally deal chiefly with the outward events of their lives, and less with that inner mental life about which we are all reticent, but which is after all our truest history. From scattered passages, however, in their lives and especially in their works, their mental character can often be reconstructed, and in cases of clear poetic genius this is always found to be highly unusual or peculiar. The poets possess characteristics belonging to common men, but some of these in such high degree or such disproportionate mixture as to form what amounts to a different psychological character. Their

[1] Compare Shakespeare, Sonnet cvii:

> Nor the prophetic soul
> Of the wide world dreaming on things to come.

mental history is as difficult to understand as their work, and for much the same reasons.[1]

Bunyan, who is the type in literature of native inspiration without culture, and who therefore illustrates with special clearness the working of poetic inspiration pure and untrammelled, constantly beheld visions under the stress of his religious emotions. As a child, he tells us, he committed terrible sins. These "did so offend the Lord, that even in my childhood he did scare and affright me with fearful dreams, and did terrify me with dreadful visions." External objects and events went by him unnoticed; while "he looked upon that which was passing through his own mind and heart as though it were something external." [2] Watching his brazier's fire, journeying alone through country roads, working mechanically in Bedford jail, he saw figures and heard voices which were as clear and vivid to him as those of objective reality. Like Dunstan and Luther he was tempted by the devil in person, and yielded; he repented, and saw Christ himself looking down at him through the tiles of the house-roof, saying, "My Grace is sufficient for thee." These appearances, says Taine, were "the products of an involuntary and impassioned imagination, which by its hallucinations, its mastery, its fixed ideas, its mad ideas, prepares the way for a poet, and announces an inspired man. . . . Powerful as that of an artist, but more vehement, this imagination worked in the man without his coöperation and besieged him with visions which he had neither willed nor foreseen. From that moment there was in him as it were a second self, ruling the first, grand and terrible, whose apparitions were sudden, its motions unknown, which redoubled or crushed his faculties, prostrated or transported him, bathed him in a sweat of agony, ravished him with trances of joy, and which by its force, strangeness, independence, impressed upon him the presence and the action of a foreign and

---

[1] The paragraphs following on Bunyan, Shelley, and Stevenson are substantially reprinted from my *Poetry and Dreams*, 1912; see Preface.

[2] *Grace Abounding*, ed. Brown, pp. 9, xxiii.

superior master." [1] Bunyan was, as his principal biographer styles him, essentially "The Dreamer;" and his books are little more than a record of his dreams. "As I walked through the wilderness of this world, I lighted on a certain place where was a den, and I laid me down in that place to sleep: and, as I slept, I dreamed a dream." Thus begins the *Pilgrim's Progress*, as the title says, "in the similitude of a dream."

Charles Lamb, though more of the world in many aspects, was in the highest degree peculiar. He was at bottom good, sensible, generous, magnanimous; but this fundamentally sound character was modified—even strangely distorted—by a strain of abnormality, morbidity, and madness. As a child he was affectionate and lovable, but "alive to nervous terrors," and like many another child of genius haunted by "night fears." "I never laid my head on my pillow, I suppose, from the fourth to the seventh or eighth year of my life without an assurance, which realized its own prophecy, of seeing some frightful spectre." He "dreamed waking" over his morbid fancies, and at night "awoke into sleep, and found the vision true." [2] At twenty-one, a little before his sister suffered the same affliction, he spent some weeks in Hoxton Lunatic Asylum. He was frequently low in spirits, formed the habit of raising them with strong drink, and as a consequence of this indulgence passed through the terrible mental experience recorded, perhaps with some exaggeration, in the "Confessions of a Drunkard." "Life itself," he says at twenty-seven, "my waking life, has much of the confusion, the trouble, and obscure perplexity, of an ill dream." Other circumstances were not conducive to normality. He was unmarried and childless, was morbidly fond of his old prints and china and of his "midnight darlings, his folios." He was "painfully introspective." He was "sanguine only in prospects of other (former) years," though conscious that this retrospec-

---

[1] *English Literature*, Book ii, chap. v, sec. 6. See the vision described in *Grace Abounding*, par. 53, with Bunyan's interpretation.

[2] "Witches and Other Night Fears."

tion might be "the symptom of some sickly idiosyncrasy." [1] Through a troubled life he always retained something of the freshness, gentleness, and "wild art" of childhood; he was conscious of being "too much the boy-man," but rightly says this and other weaknesses are the "key to explicate some of his writings." [2] He was imaginative, recorded his reveries and visions,[3] and made shrewd observations on them. His thought was not strictly rational, but freely associative—that of a strange, fanciful, mature, worldly yet still unworldly, child. Even this brief summary based on a few of the *Essays of Elia* will indicate that pyschologically their author was, in biological terms, a sport or wide deviation from type. There is the closest connection, however, between this peculiar mind and its unique expression in literature, and few cases are more instructive for the student of literary genius.

Shelley, though highly individual and unconventional, exhibits more nearly the typical poetic character. He was an imaginative child.

> By solemn vision, and bright silver dream
> His infancy was nurtured.[4]

He longed for and cherished imaginative experiences.

> While yet a boy I sought for ghosts, and sped
> Through many a listening chamber, cave and ruin,
> And starlight wood, with fearful steps pursuing
> Hopes of high talk with the departed dead.[5]

"At no period of his life," says J. A. Symonds, "was he wholly free from visions which had the reality of facts. Sometimes they occurred in sleep, and were prolonged with painful vividness into his waking moments. Sometimes they seemed to grow out of his

[1] "New Year's Eve."

[2] Preface to *Last Essays of Elia*.

[3] In "Dream Children," "A Chapter on Ears," "Amicus Redivivus," "The Child Angel," etc.

[4] "Alastor," l. 67.

[5] "Hymn to Intellectual Beauty," l. 49.

intense meditation, or to present themselves before his eyes as
the projection of a powerful inner impression. All his sensations
were abnormally acute, and his ever-active imagination confused
the borderlands of the actual and the visionary."

The account given by Hogg, of his "slumbers resembling a
profound lethargy," tells us that "he lay occasionally upon the
sofa, but more commonly stretched out before a large fire, like a
cat; and his little round head was exposed to such a fierce heat,
that I used to wonder how he was able to bear it. . . . His torpor was generally profound, but he would sometimes discourse
incoherently for a long time in his sleep." Then "he would
suddenly start up, and, rubbing his eyes with great violence, and
passing his fingers swiftly through his long hair, would enter at
once into a vehement argument, or begin to recite verses, either
of his own composition or from the works of others, with a
rapidity and an energy that were often quite painful." [1] Curiously this bodily heat was with Shelley conducive to dreams and
poetry. "The Cenci" was written in the warm sun on his roof at
Leghorn.[2] "When my brain gets heated with a thought," he
said, "it soon boils." In such a mood he wrote "The Triumph
of Life." "The intense stirring of his imagination implied by
this supreme poetic effort, the solitude of the Villa Magni, and
the elemental fervor of Italian heat to which he recklessly exposed himself, contributed to make Shelley more than usually
nervous. His somnambulism returned, and he saw visions. On
one occasion he thought that the dead Allegra rose from the sea,
and clapped her hands, and laughed, and beckoned to him. On
another he roused the whole house at night by his screams, and
remained terror-frozen in the trance produced by an appalling
vision."[3] A study of Shelley's life shows that this power of vision
is to be identified with his poetic faculty. He speaks of his writings as "little else than visions," as "dreams of what ought to be
or may be." [4]

George Sand was born to be a writer of romances. Particu-

[1] *Shelley*, pp. 91, 30.   [3] Symonds, *Shelley*, pp. 166, 177.
[2] Note by Mrs. Shelley.   [4] "Dedication" of the "Cenci."

larly notable in her case is the typical character in childhood which announces the literary genius. Aurore Dupin was a highly gifted child, but like other gifted children, as Sully observes, she seemed not less but more of a child because of her gifts.[1] She was high strung, animated, affectionate, and sensitive; she suffered the terrors and enjoyed the delights of the imaginative child. She was so carried away in her play that, for example, in playing at crossing the windings of a river, rudely marked with chalk on the floor, "I lost all notion of reality," she says, "and believed I could see the trees, the water, the rocks,—a vast country—and the sky, now bright, now laden with clouds which were about to burst and increase the danger of crossing the river." She could ever after recall the astonishment she felt upon being called back from one such hallucination to the real objects about her. Her environment—the large horizons of the Vallée Noire, the old château at Nohant, the rustic legends and superstitions, the rapidly changing events of the Napoleonic era—fostered in her an imaginative view of life. In nearly every chapter of the *Histoire de ma Vie* dealing with her childhood, she recounts reveries and dreams, visions and "nouvelles visions." The retreat from Moscow, for example, excited her imagination. "I had strange dreams, flights of the imagination which gave me a fever and filled my sleep with phantoms. . . . I imagined I possessed wings, that I darted through space, and that peering into the abysses of the horizon I discovered the vast snows and the endless steppes of White Russia," etc. This waking dream—a kind of hallucination, she calls it—of the Emperor recurred for several years.[2]

Like Walter Scott, she began very early to tell herself stories. When she was four years old her mother used to shut her "within four chairs." To lighten the captivity, "I composed aloud interminable stories which my mother called my romances. . . . She declared them terribly tiresome because of their length and the development I gave to the digressions.

[1] See Sully, *Studies of Childhood*, p. 489.
[2] *Histoire de ma Vie*, Troisième partie, chaps. v, vii.

There were few wicked characters and never any great misfortunes. Everything came out right under the influence of a thought smiling and optimistic as childhood." George Sand's mature romances show the same optimism, tedium, and digression.[1] Presently she conceived a long series of scenes and songs, with a dream-hero, "Corambé," a mixture of myth, epos, and religion, to which I shall refer in a later chapter. These imaginations were suspended during her life at the convent for the composing of two romances—her first writing—and then resumed. When finally George Sand came to write her mature novels she had only to describe, as she says, quickly, easily, and without fatigue, the train of persons, actions, landscapes presented by her imagination. Her stories were facile improvisations.

Stevenson has a "Chapter on Dreams," describing his own experience, which is so instructive that if space permitted it should be quoted here entire.[2] "He was from a child," he tells us, "an ardent and uncomfortable dreamer;" as a child he had terrible dream-haunted nights. While a student in Edinburgh he began "to dream in sequence, and thus to lead a double life—one of the day, one of the night"—which soon sent him "trembling for his reason" to the doctor. He "had long been in the custom of setting himself to sleep with tales, and so had his father before him." It is not strange, then, that he "began to read in his dreams—tales, for the most part, and for the most part after the manner of G. P. R. James, but so incredibly more vivid and moving than any printed books, that he has ever since been malcontent with literature." "But presently," he continues, "my dreamer began to turn his former amusement of story-telling to (what is called) account; by which I mean that he began to write and sell his tales. Here was he, and here were the little people who did that part of his business, in quite new conditions. The stories must now be trimmed and pared and set upon all fours, they must run from a beginning to an end and fit (after a manner) with the laws of life; the pleasure in a word had be-

[1] See Doumic, *George Sand*, p. 76.

[2] *Works*, Thistle edition, vol. xv, p. 250.

come a business; and that not only for the dreamer but for the little people of his theatre. These understood the change as well as he. When he lay down to prepare himself for sleep, he no longer sought amusement, but printable and profitable tales; and after he had dozed off in his box-seat, his little people continued their evolutions with the same mercantile designs." Thus the scenes of some of Stevenson's tales, for instance of "Dr. Jekyll and Mr. Hyde," were first enacted in this dream theatre; and these tales were, as he represents them, a collaboration between himself and what he calls his "little people"—that is, between his conscious waking intellect and his dream faculty. "Will o' the Mill" shows that Stevenson has perfectly the theory of the dream.

The characters I have thus summarized are typical rather than exceptional in the poetic class. Some poets, like Chatterton and Blake, would show more of the character we associate with the word "visionary;" others, like Tennyson and Longfellow, would show less. But even Tennyson had visions and trance-like states. This visionary thought is that which produces poetry— and that which requires explanation.

CHAPTER III

TWO MODES OF THOUGHT

I

WE think in two ways, I said at the end of Chapter I—in one way when we work and in another when we dream; and of the second of these I have given various examples in the chapter preceding. These two ways of thinking must now be considered in detail. They correspond in part to the two kinds of thought recognized by the psychologists, for which we may as well refer to one of the earliest psychologists to make this distinction. " Mental discourse," says Hobbes in *Leviathan*, "is of two sorts. The first is unguided, without design, and inconstant; wherein there is no passionate thought, to govern and direct those that follow to itself, as the end and scope of some desire or other passion: in which case the thoughts are said to wander, and seem impertinent one to another, as in dream. Such are the thoughts of men who are not only without company but without care of anything. . . . The second is more constant; as being regulated by some desire, or design." [1] The first is merely associative thought, consisting of a succession of images, one calling up another freely and spontaneously, by either contiguity or similarity. "The train of imagery wanders at its own sweet will, now trudging in the sober grooves of habit, now with a hop, skip, and jump darting across the whole field of time and space. This is reverie or musing." [2] The second is voluntary or purposive thought, which is guided by a "distinct

[1] Part I, chap. iii.
[2] W. James, *Psychology*, vol. i, p. 583; compare Th. Ribot, *Psychology of Attention*, chaps. i and ii; Titchener, *Feeling and Attention*, p. 311.

purpose or conscious interest," controlling by selection the associations spontaneously offered, to fit the end in view. The will, impelled by interest, fixes the attention, and this results in reasoning; "every kind of reasoning is nothing, in its simplest form, but attention." [1] The mind, if strong and well trained, can keep up such attentive thought for considerable stretches; when it relaxes it falls into reverie; the weak mind lapses sooner and oftener.

This voluntary thought, though perhaps not the more common, is, for reasons that will appear, the more familiar to us, and is what we ordinarily have in mind when we refer to thought. It is objective,—that is, directed toward outward reality,—or, if it deals with internal events reflectively, it treats them as objects. It is closely in touch with sensuous experience, immediately utilizing the reports of the senses and controlling them. It is active, always directed toward a conscious end, which it strives directly or indirectly to attain; and it therefore carries on the practical life—of study or of business. Its result is the knowledge which guides this work, and which is systematized in science. Associative thinking, on the other hand, has a character of withdrawal and inwardness; and has less to do with sensation—arises more readily indeed, as we shall see, when the senses are in abeyance and the feelings are uppermost. It is passive—akin to the "wise passiveness" of which Wordsworth speaks; it has no set purpose, and accomplishes no practical end. It may furnish material utilizable in practice, but this is, so to speak, only a wild harvest, the other furnishing the staple cultivated crop—and in general this kind of thinking has all the irresponsibility and unpracticality which we associate with the word *dream* used in the broad sense.

The line between these two kinds of thought seems sharply drawn,—that is, in general, we seem to be either giving attention or not giving it—to be either engaged in ordinary thought or lapsing entirely from it. There are, however, probably gradual

---

[1] S. Hodgson, quoted by James, vol. i, p. 589.

stages. Bergson refers to "the necessity of distinguishing the different degrees of tension or of tone in the psychologic life. . . . Consciousness," he says, "is better balanced the more it is directed toward action; more wavering the more it is relaxed in a sort of dream; and between these opposed planes, there are all the intermediate planes, corresponding to so many decreasing degrees of 'attention to life,' and of adaptation to reality." [1] As our interest weakens and mental fatigue increases we by stages lose this "adaptation to reality," and reasoned thought is gradually replaced by spontaneous trains of imagery.

Now our ordinary prosaic thought is of the first of these kinds, dream and poetic vision of the second. Between these two, ordinary thought and visionary thought, there are further important differences. Bergson speaks of the planes of action and of dream. In the first some desire—and later we shall see that desire is the motive force behind both kinds of thinking— leads to thought directed by a conscious interest, the representative of desire, and having its end in action calculated to secure the desire's gratification. In the second the desire, temporarily at least, gives up action and actual gratification, and dreams of them—that is, through imaginary action it secures an imaginary substitutive gratification. In the first the thought may be relatively cold and mainly intellectual; in the second it is more emotional, and the stronger the emotion the more active the thought. In the first the imagination is at work but is subordinate and controlled, working in a prosaic way: in the second it is free and works poetically. Indeed this freedom of the imagination is one of the most striking and generally recognized characteristics of the poetic thought; so that it would be well if we had a word to apply particularly to this faculty in its free, visionary, or poetic action. It would be inadvisable, however, to invent a new word for so old a thing. If the word *phantasy* were

[1] *Revue Philosophique*, Dec. 1908, p. 570; compare J. Jastrow, *The Subconscious*, p. 446: "Some thinking and some dreaming enter into all our mental procedures: the extremes are sharply contrasted, but give way to delicate transitions in the middle registers."

not in its origin and history equivalent to *imagination* it might be used to mean the imagination working thus spontaneously, and the words *phantasm* and *phantastic* might be applied to its products. These three words rightly understood would accurately express things that we shall have occasion to refer to very often in what follows. Each of the three matters mentioned in this paragraph—the desires, the emotions, and the imagination—will be discussed in later chapters.

We have now before us the two kinds of mental operation—the ordinary thought on the one hand and the phantastic thought, if I may call it that, on the other—from a comparison of which, in their characteristics, processes, sources, and products, some explanation of the poetic faculty may arise. We must remember, however, that these two kinds of thought run together by a gradation, that if we compare typical or extreme forms of the two as opposed to each other it is only for the sake of simplification and clearness, and that any given poet's thought at a given moment might conceivably stand between the two. The typical poetic vision, however, is what requires explanation.

Our ordinary thought is voluntary; we think both when, and as we will. In both respects the visionary thought is beyond control. It is of course difficult to fix the attention, easy to relax it and fall in the second mode of thought, and we are all constantly doing this. But the demands of the world are so constant upon our attention and our habit of responding to them so ingrained that it is even hard to lapse when we wish or for any length of time. And the lapsing is not all: the thought that ensues, like our ordinary thought, may be good, bad, or indifferent. It may be weak and superficial. To be of value, say to the poet, it must be active, vivid, full of feeling, and drawn from deep sources. The opportune conditions—detachment, emotion, activity—cannot be commanded, nor can the resulting train of thought. The conditions may be sought and the imagination solicited,—as a poet may seek inspiration by walking into the woods or by the seashore alone. The drinking of wine and falling in love are recommended; if they either relax the "attention to life" or

heighten the feeling it is not hard to see why. Some poets find
aid to inspiration in peculiar habits of composition, which cannot always be explained,—one, like Heine, by lying down,
another by putting his feet in ice water, another, like Shelley, by
lying with his head in the heat of the fire or of the sun. But
these are only aids, and the will is powerless. "The difficulty,"
Goethe writes to Humboldt about *Faust*, "has been to get
through strength of will what is really to be got only by a
spontaneous act of nature."

> 'Tis not every day that I
> Fitted am to prophesy;
> No, but when the spirit fills
> The fantastic panicles
> Full of fire, then I write
> As the Godhead doth indite.
>
> .   .   .   .   .   .
>
> Look how next the holy fire
> Either slakes or doth retire;
> So the fancy cools,—till when
> That brave spirit comes again.[1]

So creators complain of periods of unproductiveness, and invoke
the muse, resorting to prayer, as we all do when we are impotent. The poet can only watch for the moment and pray for it
to come.

Ordinary thought is fatiguing; the attention presently tires
and flags. The other thought appears effortless or nearly so.
Falling from one to another is like dropping the study of a
serious book and listlessly turning over the pages of an illustrated magazine or going to the moving pictures. Perhaps this
is one reason why the picture theatres are so popular; they not
only avoid the complicated symbolism of words and resemble
reality, but they tell a story, like the imagination, in fusing
pictures, and parallel this second mode of thought, above which
the popular mind rises with such difficulty and into which it so

[1] R. Herrick, "Not Every Day Fit for Verse."

readily lapses. They present a kind of poetry in the natural poetic way. At any rate the second mode of thought is easier. The energizing of the will at least is spared. Reverie is indeed apparently restful and dreams go on in the rest of sleep. Poets and mystics often speak of their moments of rapture as pleasant and refreshing in the highest degree. We may imagine indeed that in the Golden Age when man knew only this older associative thinking—for it is older as we shall presently see—his life was free and restful, and that the curse of Adam naturally fell upon him when he ate of the tree of Knowledge—that is when he began to reason. Reasoning is not only laborious but elaborate and slow, plodding conscientiously toward its wilful end; whereas the imagination is of course intuitive and quick. The poet may have to wait for his inspiration, but it is worth waiting for; when it comes it reveals the truth in a moment, as if by a flash of lightning. Thus, as Sir Leslie Stephen puts it, "Genius begins where intellect ends; or takes by storm where intellect has to make elaborate approaches according to the rules of scientific strategy. One sees where the other demonstrates." [1]

The pictures presented by the poetic imagination in its sudden vision must often be worked over and connected by the ordinary thought to take their place in the poem; and they must always at least be described. There is first the sudden inspiration, then the laborious composition. But probably a larger part of the entire work is performed by the inspiration and a smaller part by the conscious labor than is generally supposed. The inspiration or vision is ordinarily thought to furnish only particular images, at most particular scenes,—a series of situations in a play or poem. In some cases at least it furnishes much more than this. It may provide the action or plot of a long work—a fiction or poem—not in successive periods of inspiration, but in one such period—in one vision or connected series of visions lasting but a few moments. In fact nothing is more marvellous

[1] *Hours in a Library*, vol. iii, p. 5.

than the extent and sweep of the poetic power, the rapidity and success of its accomplishment. Just as a person in the stress of great excitement or danger, will see in a momentary flash a whole plan of action which, in the ordinary condition of mind, would require long processes of mental elaboration, so the creative imagination of the poet will accomplish in a few moments the work of weeks or months. It is true that this superiority of accomplishment may be only apparent; it may be that the inspired moment, the crisis, is merely the last and only visible stage in an operation which has been proceeding, perhaps for weeks or months, unconsciously—and we shall find reason to believe that this is so. But at last the inspiration comes suddenly and all together, like water from a pent-up source. "A true work of art," Carlyle says, "requires to be fused in the mind of its creator, and, as it were, poured forth (from his imagination, though not from his pen) in one simultaneous gush." [1]

The following account, however, given by Mozart of his musical composition will give a better idea of the imaginative power. "When I am feeling well," he writes, "and in good humor, perhaps when I am traveling by carriage, or taking a walk after a good dinner, or at night when I cannot sleep, my thoughts come in swarms and with marvelous ease. Whence and how do they come? I do not know; I have no share in it. Those that please me I hold in mind and I hum them, at least so others have told me. Once I catch my air, another soon comes to join the first, according to the requirements of the whole composition, counterpoint, the play of the various instruments, etc., etc.; and all these morsels combine to form the whole.

---

[1] Shelley expresses the same thought: "The toil and the delay recommended by critics can be justly interpreted to mean no more than a careful observation of the inspired moments and an artificial connection of the spaces between their suggestions by the intertexture of conventional expressions—a necessity only imposed by the limitedness [transitoriness] of the poetical faculty itself; for Milton conceived the *Paradise Lost* as a whole before he executed it in portions."—*Defense of Poetry*, p. 39.

Then my mind kindles, if nothing happens to interrupt me. The work grows,—I keep hearing it, and bring it out more and more clearly, and the composition ends by being completely executed in my mind, however long it may be. I then comprehend the whole at one glance, as I should a beautiful picture, or a handsome boy; and my imagination makes me hear it not in its parts successively as I shall come to hear it later, but as a whole in its *ensemble*. What a delight it is for me! It all, the inspiration and the execution, takes place in me as if it were a beautiful and very distinct dream. What I get in this way I do not forget any more easily, and this is perhaps the most precious gift our Lord has given me. If I then sit down to write I have only to draw from this store in my mind what has already accumulated there in the way I have described. Moreover the whole is not difficult to fix on paper. The whole is perfectly determined, and rarely ever does my score differ much from what I have had already in my mind." [1]

This seems a typical experience—the favorable conditions necessary, the inspiration, the vision of the whole, the dreamlike character of it, its delightfulness, its recording—though a very fortunate one.

II

We must now note another difference between the two modes of thought, for our purposes so fundamentally important that it cannot be overemphasized. The ordinary thought is analytical and abstract; the poetic thought purely imaginative and concrete. The first breaks up the presented images for its own purposes; the second uses the images as they come. In spontaneous reverie, according to William James, "the terms which fall together are empirical concretes, not abstractions. . . . If habitual contiguities predominate we have the prosaic mind; if rare contiguities, or similarities, have free play, we call the person fanciful, poetic, or witty. But the thought as a rule is of

[1] P. Chabaneix, *Le Subconscient*, p. 94, quoting *Mozart* by Jahn, vol. iii, pp. 424, 425.

matters taken in their entirety." Reverie, then, joins concretes
or wholes. Reasoning on the other hand is essentially analysis
and abstraction.[1] It breaks up the concrete whole and substitutes for it an abstracted property or attribute; it purposely
divides it and uses the parts as tools for a practical end. The
first is the method of poetry, for poetry deals always with concretes. I do not mean of course that an abstraction is never to
be found in what we call a poem, but only that poetry is essentially concrete, and the poetic vision which in its source is
practically always so. In other words pure poetry uses the
method of mere imagination throughout, and deals entirely
with images. "Imaging," as Dryden declares, "is in itself the
very height and life of poetry." [2]

We may turn first to the dream which is clearly concrete. The
dream represents not ideas, but persons, actions, scenes. In a
dream we take part in an action or see a situation before our
eyes with its appropriate background. A dream is a kind of
dramatic representation, a series of scenes in that theatre of the
mind of which Stevenson speaks. It may of course include
sounds, and other sensations,—that is, the images of these.
But it is properly a *vision*.

Poetry is strictly analogous; it is correctly defined by David
Masson as "the art of producing a fictitious concrete." [3] "With
abstractions," says Theodore Watts, "the poet has nothing to
do, save to take them and turn them into concretions." [4] This
in fact provides the most readily applicable test of the presence
of poetry. When the poet uses abstraction he is giving us
reflection, philosophy in verse, not poetry proper. When, as
so often Carlyle, the prose writer sees his idea before him as a
picture he becomes a poet. "The quality of mercy is not
strained," at least by itself, is not poetry, though it is Shakespeare's. But take the following of Teufelsdröckh: "His look is

[1] *Psychology*, vol. ii, pp. 325, 330.
[2] "The Author's Apology for Heroic Poetry and Poetic License."
[3] *Wordsworth, Shelley, Keats, and Other Essays*, p. 201.
[4] *Encyclopedia Britannica*, "Poetry."

probably the gravest ever seen: yet it is not of that cast-iron gravity frequent enough among our own Chancery suitors; but rather the gravity as of some silent, high-encircled mountain-pool, perhaps the crater of an extinct volcano." The whole method, especially in the "cast-iron" and the "mountain-pool," is poetic. So one evidence of Goethe's poetic mastery, according to Carlyle, was his "singularly emblematic intellect; his perpetual never-failing tendency to transform into *shape*, into *life*, the opinion, the feeling that may dwell within him, which in its widest sense we reckon to be essentially the grand problem of the poet. . . . Everything has form, everything has visual existence. The poet's imagination *bodies forth* the forms of things unseen, his pen turns them to shape." [1] Working with his conscious mind the poet may mingle the abstract with the concrete, but *as a poet*, in his involuntary inspiration, he sees nothing but images. In recording his vision in the poem he uses every device to make the reader see as he does; he employs the epithet like Homer; or the apostrophe and historical present like Carlyle; or like Byron—

I see before me the Gladiator lie—

he uses the figure the rhetoricians call "vision."

"Poetic creation," Carlyle exclaims, "what is this too, but *seeing* the thing sufficiently?" And he adds, "The *word* that will describe the thing, follows of itself from such clear intense sight of the thing." [2] It is true that the mere vividness of the poet's vision is favorable to its description. This matter, however, must be examined carefully. Voluntary thought is objec-

---

[1] *Essays*, "Goethe." With this Aristotle's theory agrees: "A work of art reproduces its original, not as it is in itself, but as it appears to the senses. It addresses itself not to the abstract reason, but to the sensibility; . . . it is concerned with outward appearances; it employs illusions; its world is not that which is revealed by pure [voluntary] thought; it sees truth, but in its concrete manifestations, not as an abstract idea."—Butcher, *Aristotle's Theory of Poetry*, pp. 127, 153.

[2] *On Heroes*, III.

tive, it is closely in touch with outward reality; it is directed toward action, and toward utterance, which is a form of action. It readily finds expression in language or otherwise. We think and then naturally we speak; and even if we do not actually speak to others, yet expression is so natural that in intensive thought, in the solution of a difficult problem, we begin to talk to ourselves, or attempt, as an aid, to note our thoughts on paper. It is even doubted whether such thought is possible without words. At least the connection between the two is so close that we seem to think in words. Visionary thought, on the other hand, is subjective, it is turned inwards, it for the time being gives up action. I believe the psychologists say that there is "no thought without expression," that "thought is a word or an act in a nascent state." [1] I have no doubt that all thought is accompanied by physical manifestations; and that it looks ultimately toward action. But a man is evidently in one relation to action when he plans to do a thing, and in another when he dreams of doing it. In the latter case the external action is largely replaced by an imagined internal action, with gratification; the consummation of the thought is, for the time being, within the mind itself. The visionary is in less need of expression or communication; and he finds communication more difficult.

Language does not seem to be proper to vision as it is to ordinary thought. According to Freud there is no true speech in dream, everything that appears as a speech being mere reproduction of what has been spoken by the dreamer in waking, or heard or read by him. An auditory or visual image of waking hours is reproduced, and felt as heard or seen; but obviously this is not true language. In waking vision also words may be merely images. Belshazzar saw the handwriting on the wall, but he may not have seen it thus for the first time. Savonarola saw the heavens opened and the appearance of a sword with the inscription "Gladius Domini super terram"; but this may not

---

[1] Ribot, *Psychology of Attention*, p. 12.

differ from Constantine's seeing a cross in the sky. Words may have the same status as other objects. This does not mean that they may not, like other objects, be modified, distorted, or fused one with another, but they would still be treated merely as objects, not, as in language, as the disposable symbols of thought. It would probably be unwise to say that the visionary never makes true use of language. Coleridge's account of the composition of " Kubla Khan " verbatim in a dream does not appear to be wholly reliable; it was written nineteen years after the dream and may have exaggerated the dream composition, which also may have merely reproduced lines composed beforehand and forgotten. Mozart's account, however, just cited, of his composing, in what seems a state of true inspiration and vision, a musical piece with all its notes and movements, suggests the possibility of extended composition in metrical language. Mystical preachers seem sometimes to see and prophesy orally at the same time. There are two questions: first whether true language is ever an integral part of vision; secondly whether the visionary thought, like the ordinary thought, expresses itself immediately in language. Does the poet, at his desk, see in the visionary way and record his vision at the same time? Did Wordsworth walking out of doors at once see and compose in words? I do not know how the poets would answer these questions. Generally they make a clear distinction between their revelation and their composition. I believe also that the spirit, so to speak, of vision is against such an immediate expression in language, and that in extreme or intense vision expression would be impossible.

Though vision while it lasts is gratifying and self-sufficient, yet when it is over the poet feels its value and the need of communicating it. If he is to be ranked with the poets he must communicate it. Then at least the work of composition begins. The poetic vision is mainly in pictures; the poetic product, the poem, is in words. The work of turning one into the other must in the nature of things be difficult. The visions of the poet are largely indescribable, like the visions of sleep. The poet is in the same position as the dreamer who attempts to recount his dream at breakfast. The dreamer is conscious of the vividness of the images and feelings of his dream, and of their strangeness—conscious also that his account of them is far short of the strange truth. So when his rapture is over the poet finds his vision vivid and strange, as different from ordinary mental experience as dream from waking; he finds it ineffable, and if he is called upon to report the whole truth this is all he can say about it. Furthermore the vision, like the dream, is transient; it fades more and more as it recedes; and, as in dream, memory retains but a pale reflection of the original. The poet also, like the dreamer, when he comes consciously to recollect and record his vision, inevitably modifies it to bring it into harmony with his ordinary waking thought. To this last point we shall return later. For these reasons, then, there is a vast difference, as of two worlds, the world of dreams and the world of "every day," between the poet's inspiration and his poem. In his composition the poet accomplishes a wonderful work of memory and translation, in bringing back this visitation of the spirit and giving it local habitation in a world of prose. To paraphrase Emerson, it is in the soul that poetry exists and our poems are poor, far-behind imitations.

We must remember too that our language in its modern development is not well suited to the expression of poetry. Language in its origin and constant extensions is largely the product of an imaginative mode of thought. Originally, in a primitive language like that of the ancient Hebrews—as we shall see in the following chapter—it was a good poetic medium, because it was almost entirely concrete in vocabulary and was without a logically organized syntax. Our modern language, however, contains many abstract words, and many words or constructions to express logical relations, which are the product of our voluntary thought or reasoning, and which are useless for the pure imagination, because for the imagination these abstractions and relations do not exist. Freud, for example, attempts to show that the dream has means of representing what in waking we should call relations of time or of cause and effect—what we express in language by a *thereupon* or a *because*. But it will be found on examination that these means all reduce to a shifting or juxtaposition of images—as in the moving pictures one picture succeeding another may intimate a *presently* or a *therefore*. To constitute a true record language must simply follow the successive concrete images; and our language, partly the product of the other thought and adapted to that, is not a satisfactory medium.

Another difference between the two modes of thought is nearly related to the one we have just discussed. Ordinary thought is closely connected with sensuous experience. It is carried on while the senses are active, uses the material they furnish, and directs them in their tasks. The visionary thought, on the other hand, derives its material only indirectly from the senses, and it works when the senses are in abeyance or at rest. In day dreams, for example, the eye first sees through the window, then loses its adaptation and stares through the window without seeing; the objective scene is replaced by a subjective one. In sleep the eyes close and the senses are mainly at rest. In poetic vision there is always such a subjection of the senses, of greater or less degree, from a state of musing—which doubtless means turning to the Muses, but is always a withdrawal from the external world—to a state of trance, in which the subjection of the senses is virtually complete.

Of the poets Wordsworth has written on this matter most definitely. He tells in the *Prelude* how at one time in his life the bodily eye, "the most despotic of the senses," held him in absolute dominion.[1] He explains how Nature thwarts this tyranny by counteracting one sense with another, and so prevents "pride of the eye." The mind becomes creative when the senses are in abeyance,—when "the affections gently lead us on" and "we are laid asleep in body and become a living soul," [2]—when

---

[1] Book xii. [2] "Tintern Abbey."

> the light of sense
> Goes out, but with a flash that has revealed
> The invisible world.[1]

Sometimes he speaks of the subjection of one sense, sometimes of another; sometimes of partial subjection, sometimes of complete.

> Oft in these moments such a holy calm
> Would overspread my soul, that bodily eyes
> Were utterly forgotten, and what I saw
> Appeared like something in myself, a dream,
> A prospect of the mind. . . .
> One song they sang, and it was audible,
> Most audible, then, when the fleshly ear
> O'ercome by humblest prelude of that strain,
> Forgot her functions, and slept undisturbed.[2]

Thus any condition in which sensuous life is intermitted will be favorable to vision: rest, solitude, sleep of course, nature—at least when it soothes rather than stimulates the senses [3]—moonlight, dawn, or twilight, particularly the last because in the evening the senses are tired and ready to rest.

> Hail, Twilight, sovereign of one peaceful hour!
> Not dull art thou as undiscerning Night;
> But studious only to remove from sight
> Day's mutable distinctions.
> . . . By him was seen

---

[1] *Prelude*, Book vi.

[2] *Prelude*, Book ii. Compare the well known sonnet:

> "Most sweet it is with unuplifted eyes."

[3] Whittier sees that nature is sometimes unfavorable:

> She will not leave our senses still,
> But drags them captive at her will:
> And, making earth too great for heaven,
> She hides the Giver in the given.

The self-same Vision which we now behold
At thy meek bidding, shadowy power, brought forth.[1]

One source of Wordsworth's strength is in the perfect naturalness and sanity of the inspiration thus described. The subjection
of the sense, however, may be brought about more artificially—
and strangely in two ways which seem opposed to each other—
first by what may be called indulgence, and secondly by as-
ceticism. Mozart, as we have seen, found composition easier
after a good dinner. Perhaps the repletion, bodily comfort,
and rest after eating tended to dull the sense. Others have
found inspiration in wine or drugs. Perhaps one reason is in the
narcotic influence and deadening of the senses. On the other
hand religious mystics have usually resorted to an ascetic life as
conducive to meditation and vision. The life of luxury and of the
senses is of course the material life; the life of self-denial is the
life of the spirit. So Paul admonishes his disciples to give themselves to fasting and prayer. The discovery of the efficacy of
fasting probably dates very far back in the history of religion.
The mediaeval mystic found that mortification of the flesh—temperance and sexual abstinence—served to promote vision. Thus
customs were established, of monkish poverty and chastity,
which became merely symbols rather than means to religion; and
our lenten fasts may be either symbolic forms or true sources
of religious refreshment. The same effort to escape from the
senses is seen in Wordsworth's notion of plain living and high
thinking and in the temperance and vegetarianism of Thoreau
and other New England transcendentalists. This ground, however, has been made so familiar by all our religious teaching that
we need not stop over it, only noticing further how the efficacy of
fasting may appear in the life of a modern man of letters. Sully
Prudhomme gives an interesting account of his composition, in
which he tells how, when suffering from dyspepsia, he resorted to
a diet of milk. "The result," he says, "was a great enfeebling
of my physical condition, but also a certain spiritualizing of my

[1] "Miscellaneous Sonnets," II, 22.

mind which was favorable to imaginative work." And he goes on
to tell how in this condition he composed two dramas with full
inspiration.[1]

Thus the poetic life, like the religious one, requires a renunciation of the life of sense—a temporary renunciation, at any rate,
for the vision comes only when the senses are in abeyance.

> Strange state of being! (for 'tis still to be)
> Senseless to feel, and with seal'd eyes to see.[2]

Though poetry must indeed be sensuous, as Milton declares,
this is largely a sensuousness brought from past experience, the
phantasy being reproductive, and presenting inward sensuous
images. But there must be a fund of images to be drawn upon,
which the poet must at some time have got from experience.
Before his moments of inspiration or between them he must go
back to nature. Indeed except in purely subjective illusion,
which would not give rise to poetry of value, there must be a reaction of the visionary mind upon nature, and a fusion of external and internal elements, as we shall see in a later chapter.

We have found, then, that the poetic vision which is the source
of true poetry is the product of a mental operation essentially
different from the one with which we are most familiar. This
operation is spontaneous, quick, and effortless. Its product is
concrete, consisting of pictures which can with difficulty be expressed in words. The pictures appear when the light of sense
goes out. The mode in which poetry is produced explains many
of its peculiarities, as we shall see more fully in later chapters.

If it may seem to the reader that poetry as we know it is not
always produced by the visionary operation of the mind I have
described, I would repeat what I said at the beginning of the
chapter, that for the sake of clearness I have described two

---

[1] Another explanation of the helpfulness of fasting to the imagination,
is that a want, even a physical want, may give the impetus; see Chapter VIII.

[2] Byron, *Don Juan*, IV, xxx.

sharply opposed modes of thought,—which, however, are not so separated, but run together by a gradation; and that in particular instances, just as reasoning may involve feeling and imagination, so poetry may lie between the two modes and partake of the nature of both. The mind is a vital unity easily misrepresented by sharp distinctions. I believe, however, that essential poetry, or the element in poetry requiring explanation, is produced by what I have called the second mode of thought. So that if anyone objects that it is produced also deliberately by the ordinary mind, I may say in answer either of two things—it matters little which; either that then it is not true poetry; or that then it contains no mystery and requires no special explanation.

In this chapter I have spoken throughout of the ordinary thought first because it is more familiar, and have referred to the other as a second mode of thought. This however is misleading, because the latter—the associative, imaginative, poetic thought —is the primary one; it is older, and was indeed presumably once our only mode of thinking. From this the voluntary thought has grown, by a specialization and adaptation, with our growth in civilization; [1] it therefore is the secondary one in the historical and scientific sense. This will appear if we now take these two kinds of thought historically—in their development first in the individual man and afterwards in the race.

[1] See Ribot, *Psychology of Attention*, p. 2.

CHAPTER IV

THE IMAGINATION IN CHILDHOOD—THE PRIMITIVE IMAGINATION

I

IN man's life the time of imagination *par excellence* is child-hood. "A poet," it is said, "has died young in the breast of the most stolid." [1] Every child thinks naturally in the way in which the poet must try to think later.

As the child is born with an unformed brain his mind, we may suppose, is in the beginning only a misty chaos. Presently light comes through the windows of sense, but at first there is no stream of thought, only a "sportful sunlit ocean." When thought begins it is entirely associative—that is, it consists of a train of images, linked by contiguity or resemblance. There is no reasoning. As the curiosity is strong, and the feelings unre-strained, the imagination has free play and takes the liveliest forms. This is too well known to need development, but we had better take a few examples. A child who has seen pansies later sees butterflies. The bright colors of the second image by asso-ciation recall the first, and result in an expression clearly poetic: "The pansies are flying." [2] Like the primitive man he is, the child through resemblances personifies almost everything with which he comes in contact. Thus a child learning to write makes an F turn the wrong way and then puts the correct form to the left, Fꟻ; he regards these two and exclaims, "They're talking together." Jean Ingelow says: "I had the habit of attributing

---

[1] Stevenson, "The Lantern Bearers,"—substantially from Ste. Beuve.

[2] Sully, *Studies of Childhood*, chap. ii, from which other examples are taken, and which anyone interested in the poet's imagination should read entire.

intelligence not only to all living creatures, the same amount and kind of intelligence that I had myself, but even to stones and manufactured articles. I used to feel how dull it must be for the pebbles in the causeway to be obliged to lie still and only see what was around about;" and so carried them on to have a fresh view.[1] These instances illustrate the first flights of imagination, and the origins of poetic metaphor and personification.

Children are fond of stories, of hearing, composing and telling them endlessly,—about themselves, about other people, about animals and objects they have personified, and about characters of their own invention. "The invention of fictitious persons," according to Sully, "fills a large space in the child's life."[2] The childhood of George Sand, already referred to, is typical rather than exceptional in this respect. The child readily invents conversations, "fitting his tongue to dialogues of business, love, and strife." He readily invents plays and games of a dramatic character. With his playmates, but quite as well or better alone—that is with persons of his own imagination—he plays store or Indian, he impersonates Robin Hood, he dramatizes the story of Pocahontas, and himself assumes his chosen part. Thus he

> Fills from time to time his "humorous stage"
> With all the persons, down to palsied age,
> That life brings with her in her equipage;
>   As if his whole vocation
>   Were endless imitation.[3]

Here are the origins, in the history of the individual, of fiction and drama—of what, using the language of childhood, we still call *story* and *play*. Our literary romances and dramas are as natural and grateful to us as the imaginations of children. "Fiction," as Stevenson puts it, "is to the grown man what play

[1] Quoted by Sully.

[2] Sully, p. 39.

[3] Wordsworth, "Intimations of Immortality;" strophe vii is on this subject precisely.

is to the child."[1] In both, grown man's fiction and child's play,
the material is nothing, the creative imagination is everything.
For the child's imagination is creative and is never happier than
when making something out of nothing.

One further example of the child's imagination I shall give
because it has interesting parallels in mythology and even in
modern literature. As recent psychologists have noted the
child is given to imagining for himself a birth or origin more
romantic than the actual one. Such assumption might suggest
that the child is dissatisfied with his parents, as where a poor
man's son imagines himself a changeling, and a prince or million-
aire's son in disguise. This, however, is doubtless putting the
matter on too low a plane and doing injustice to the child. The
fancy has more generally the purpose of all romancing—that is,
it is an effort to escape from the commonplaceness of reality to a
merely ideal existence. If mystically inclined one might imagine
that the child is conscious of a spiritual, as well as a merely
physical inheritance; the fancy may symbolize more than we
know. The following, however, is an example. A little girl of
my acquaintance, who has no reason to be dissatisfied with her
parents—both, by the way, imaginatively gifted—announced
with emphasis: "My initials are E. K. D." "What, isn't your
name Lucy Gray?" "No," she replied, "I am the Erl-King's
Daughter," and for some weeks she persisted in the fancy.
Such ascription of romantic or supernatural origin is of course
common in fairy story and mythology. Cinderella turns out to
be a princess; Moses, like all founders of religion, is given a
mysterious origin; Alexander is reputed the son, not of Philip,
but of Jove—though in this last instance the myth-making is
only half sincere. The child's mind, like the primitive man's, is
constantly producing myths and by the same processes.

The myths of children, like those of primitive man, contain at
once the germs of poetry and the germs of science. They develop
in two directions,—toward literature in the expansion of lan-

[1] "A Gossip on Romance."

guage by metaphor and in the invention of play and story, toward scientific thought in offering fanciful explanations of the environment which cannot yet be rationally explained. When the child, seeing dew on the grass, exclaims "The grass is crying," he is looking in both directions. His expression is clearly poetical, but it is also a childish explanation of the presence of the dew. Indeed here we have the exact parallel to the condition of a primitive literature in which poetry is not yet differentiated from history, philosophy, and science; all are contained in the myth. How the childish fancy may develop by reflection into a theory is illustrated by the account of George Sand. Going when she was four years old with her mother to Madrid, she there first heard an echo. "I studied this phenomenon," she says, "with the greatest pleasure. What struck me as most strange was to hear my own name repeated by my own voice. Then there occurred to me an odd explanation. I thought that I was double, and that there was round about me another 'I' whom I could not see, but who always saw me, since he always answered me." Generalizing from this experience and another, she formed a theory that everything had its double. The echo was explained to her by her mother. "This voice in the air no longer astonished me, but it still charmed me. I was satisfied with being able to name it, and to call to it, 'Echo, are you there? Don't you hear me? Goodbye, Echo!'" This has the flavor of the Greek myth and of Milton's "Sweet Echo, sweetest nymph, that liv'st unseen"; but it also shows the myth giving way to rational explanation.

The child begins with poetry but he soon has to learn prose. As practical and social life develops, as the adaptation to reality proceeds, there is a development of associative into voluntary thought. Reasoning begins and the imaginative view of life gives place to a rational one. In the ordinary grown man the imagination is relegated to second place, and held rigorously in check. In some it is atrophied; for them life becomes entirely prose. In others it retains, for a time at least, part of its old freedom and vividness. "Is there not," Lamb asks, "in the bosoms of the wisest and best some of the child's heart left, to respond to its earliest enchantments?"[1] Is there not in the wisest men, and particularly in the best women, something childlike, not perhaps in action but in expression and habit of thought? Some men, at any rate, and particularly some women fall back easily into the old imaginative view of life. I think of a lady of my acquaintance, of thirty-five years or so, who still easily personifies all inanimate things, giving them sex with *he* and *she*, and addressing them with playful made-up diminutives. As she was walking one day and passed a stone wall behind which were growing a mass of sunflowers in full bloom, she exclaimed: "See them all looking over the wall at us and smiling." I recalled Wordsworth's lines:

> Methought
> That flowers, and trees, and even the silent hills,
> And everything she looked on, should have had
> An intimation how she bore herself
> Towards them and to all creatures.[2]

She has a quick wit, a most playful fancy, and the surest intuitions; though she often reasons badly, she arrives at right conclusions. This is the character of both the child and the poet.

Children, and older persons who retain something of the habit of children, are wisest and best. This is perhaps the meaning of Christ: "Except ye be converted, and become as little children, ye shall not enter into the kingdom of heaven."[3] To minds of this kind religious truths are opened. This at least is the teaching of the poets—of Vaughan, of Wordsworth, of Hood.[4] The poems are too familiar to require quotation; we

---

[1] "The Old Benchers."

[2] *Prelude*, Book xii.

[3] *Matthew*, xviii, 3.

[4] Vaughan, "The Retreat"; Wordsworth, "Intimations of Immortality" and others; Hood, "I Remember." Compare Gray, "Eton College;" Shelley, "A Lament." Coleridge in chap. xxii of the *Biographia Literaria* calls the idea of the "Intimations" "wild and exorbitant;" I think most readers will disagree with him.

may therefore quote from prose writers instead. "The poets," says Daudet, "are men who still see with the eyes of childhood."[1] Emerson's expression is equivalent: "The lover of nature is he whose inward and outward senses are still truly adjusted to each other; who has retained the spirit of infancy even into the era of manhood."[2] Emerson's thought is that in infancy the inward vision, the imagination, is uppermost; in manhood the imagination is usually subjected to the external sense. In the truly balanced mind, in the poet, there must be an interplay or reciprocal action of the two faculties. This, however, is a favorite idea of Wordsworth's, to which we must return later. The point here is that the poet, whatever new faculty he may develop, whatever wisdom he may get from his experience with life, must above all keep something of the child's freshness and vividness of imagination. He must retain the "wild wit, invention ever new," which Gray attributes to childhood.[3] Like Walt Whitman he is "a man, yet by these tears a little boy again."[4] "The moment the poetic mood is upon him all the trappings of the world with which for years he may have been clothing his soul— the world's knowingness, its cynicism, its self-seeking, its ambition—fall away, and the man becomes an inspired child again, with ears attuned to nothing but the whispers of those spirits of the Golden Age, who, according to Hesiod, haunt and bless this degenerate earth."[5]

---

[1] *Jack*, III, i. Compare Baudelaire: "Genius is nothing but childhood recovered at will."—(quoted by Balfour, *Stevenson*, vol. ii, p. 202); Palacio Valdés: "Children are the only beings who, in our prosaic age, still keep a lively imagination."—(*El Maestrante*, chap. iii); Charles Lamb: "While childhood, and while dreams, reducing [bringing back] childhood, shall be left," imagination will not disappear.—("The Old Benchers.")

[2] *Nature*, chap. i.

[3] "Eton College."

[4] "Out of the Cradle Endlessly Rocking."

[5] T. Watts, "Poetry."

II

Let us turn now from the childhood of the individual to the childhood of the race. This very expression, the *childhood of the race*,—a poetical turn of language long in use—illustrates how the imagination may suggest a truth which is later developed by science. The biologist states the truth in the familiar law that the development of the individual is a shortened and quickened recapitulation of the development of the race. This law is strikingly illustrated in the mental development; indeed the parallel between the mental life of the child and that of the primitive man is so exact and detailed that the description of the former which has just been given may seem unnecessarily repeated in the description of the latter which is to follow.[1] Striking, also, is the fact that writers on the psychology of children, like Sully, turn constantly for analogies and illustrations to the psychology of primitive men and savages. Both the latter are childlike and have in particular the imagination of children.

The thought of primitive man, like that of the child, is at first entirely, or almost entirely, associative. Out of this grows, very gradually, purposive thought. There can hardly have been a time, at least within the period covered by human records, in which man did not reason to some extent, just as there can hardly have been a time when he did not express himself partly in true prose. The history, however, shows clearly first an almost exclusive use of the imagination and this giving way gradually to reasoning. It shows first a literature made up exclusively of poetry, and this gradually growing into literature made up for the most part of prose. That primitive man was more imaginative than the man of the present hardly needs proof when we remember that the earliest poetry, that of the

[1] See J. M. Baldwin, *Mental Development in the Child and the Race*, chap. i. "The relations of individual development to race development are so intimate—the two are so identical, in fact—that no topic in the one can be treated without assuming results in the other."—p. viii.

Bible and of Homer, has always been considered the greatest, and has always been the despair of the moderns. There is reason to believe also that the dreams of primitive men were more extended and vivid than ours. The greater attention given to them, and the greater respect for them among the ancients would suggest this; and it would be expected from the analogous case of children, in whom dreaming is more vivid and absorbing than in adults. Writers like Lamb, J. A. Symonds, and Lafcadio Hearn describe very highly colored, emotional, and terrifying dream experiences in childhood, which gradually give way with age to dreams of a comparatively commonplace character. So primitive men were probably greater dreamers, as they were certainly greater poets.

That they produced the greatest poetry is purely the result of their habit of thought. Thought, as I have said, probably began by a mere associating of images. An Indian, for example, seeing fire burning in a piece of wood, feels in the operation a vague likeness to something with which he is more familiar, and says, "The fire is eating the log." We use the same figure when we speak of an acid *eating* a metal, but for us the word has lost its vividness. When, however, we hurry to a fire, perhaps at night, and come suddenly within sight of it, and so for a moment *feel* about it instead of *think*,—as we see with awe the flames and smoke rising and the building disappearing— then we are in the state of mind of the primitive Indian, and speak quite naturally of the *devouring* flames and their *roaring*, and almost feel the presence of the *monster* who thus roars and devours. The primitive man was constantly in this state of astonishment and awe as he faced the mysteries of nature, and he saw in everything living presences. In other words personification was for him natural and constant. The sun was a god, the moon a young and beautiful goddess, the earth the "ancient mother." Shakespeare uses similar personification when he speaks of the "beauteous eye of heaven," and the "pale-faced moon," and "old beldam earth;" but even in Shakespeare the personification is much less vivid and natural than it was to the primitive Greek, who felt a person in, say, the Earth much more strongly than we can possibly feel it. The Greeks readily invented stories about their imaginary persons to describe or explain actions, movements, or operations in nature. At dawn a goddess, young and fair, drove her chariot with its horses, easily pictured by an imaginative modification of the forms and colors of clouds and sky, into the world from the East, much as she is pictured by Guido Reni, and as she is described in many a modern poem. In modern times the image only gives rise to a beautiful picture or description, but with the Greeks, as with children, it had, at least for the moment of imagining, full belief. And so the persons thus imagined, with their powers and influences, grew into a religion. There was no question among the Greeks of identifying poetry and religion, for they were born one.

This imaginative way of thinking originated not only poetry and religion but also history, philosophy, and science. That is, mythology contained the germs of all of these, though in the beginning they were entirely undifferentiated. Later there was perhaps ground for the distinction that has been made between the poetical myths, which grew into poetry, drama, and fiction generally, and the reflective or explicative myths, which answered the purpose of explaining the world, and which grew into philosophy and science. The distinction, indeed, is an arbitrary one, for all were poetical and all explicative. They looked, however, in each of the directions I have named. Let us take examples of what may be called explicative myths. The Indian, seeing the sun darkened at midday in a clear sky, imagines that a "dragon is devouring the sun." This is his explanation of the eclipse. To explain the force of the thunderbolt the Greek imagines it hurled by Jove. To explain the miracles wrought by fire he imagines it stolen from heaven by Prometheus. This Promethean myth is expanded until it becomes an extensive story—a story with all sorts of meanings and implications—so that in the *Prometheus Unbound* of Shelley it can be made almost as significant for mankind as the story of Christ and his crucifixion itself. The primitive Greek could not discuss the problem of human salvation as we can discuss it; he could not reason and could have no theological thought; but he could imagine a story which was possibly more profound than any rational system of theology.

The imaginative presentation of philosophical truth is well illustrated by the myth of the Judgment of Paris. Many people suppose that the Greeks, wishing to bring out the relative merits of the abstract qualities of wisdom, power, and beauty, invented this myth for the purpose, as a modern preacher might tell a story to illustrate and vivify his meaning. This, of course, was not at all the case. The Greeks of the time when this myth was born had no idea of wisdom in general—this is a conception of abstract thought —but only of persons embodying wisdom. So they imagined a hero—a good and experienced man—meeting three goddesses in a lone place and choosing between their gifts. It was not the abstraction first and the story to illustrate it, but the story first of all. We can now substitute the abstraction for the concrete story,—that is, explain the myth—but the Greek who imagined it had no thought of any explanation. When we come to explain it we see that the choice is really between three inclinations in the man's own mind, and that these three inclinations are projected by the imagination and personified. So Byron makes Cain and Lucifer discuss religion, but the discussion, as Nichol has noted, is really between two sides of Byron's own mind; Lucifer is Byron's skepticism objectified, tempting him as the devil tempts Christ in the wilderness (the lone place of the Paris story). Satan is merely a mythical personification of all that is evil within ourselves,—and even God we can hardly think of except as a person, whereas the true kingdom of God is within us. For when we confront the deepest problems of religion the reason is powerless; we have to resort to the old faculty of the imagination and picture truths which some day perhaps we shall understand.

This imaginative approach to religious truth is of course illustrated by the parables of the Bible. "And the Disciples came, and said unto him, Why speakest thou unto them in parables? He answered and said unto them, Because it is given unto you to know the mysteries of the kingdom of heaven, but to them it is not given." [1] Christ then wishes to foretell the growth of the religion which he teaches. He cannot do this in prose, for the idea is too large and difficult to be rationally presented. Furthermore his is a primitive mind; that is, he thinks and speaks as a Hebrew and has all the Hebrew's imagination. The prophecy, as always, is poetical. He sees before him a picture of his idea, an image suggested by similarity, and tells the parable of the grain of mustard seed, "which indeed is the least of all seeds, but when it is grown, it is the greatest among herbs, and becometh a tree, so that the birds of the air come and lodge in the branches thereof." And very likely his hearers felt the force of the parable rather than explicated it. Thus myths often have the deepest meanings, which we can feel,—but cannot always understand.

The imaginative thought of primitive men expressed itself inevitably in imaginative language. Poetry was inherent in verbal expression. Take for example the language of the Bible. The ancient Hebrews thought largely in trains of merely associated images; their expression was in a corresponding polysyndetic language. Their constantly employed conjunction, *vav*, was "hardly more definite than a gesture indicating that things somehow belonged together," [2] as of a showman pointing to successive pictures and crying "next." It is translated indifferently by *and, but,* and *so;* usually by the *ands* which appear so constantly in our Bible. The language had few of the inflections which arise from rational thought. It had two tenses of the verb, for example, and these not to express time, but only continuing and completed action, whether past, present, or future. Time is nothing to the imagination; fancy, as the psychologists tell us,[3] is the "association of images without

[1] *Matthew*, chap. xiii.

[2] J. H. Gardiner, *The Bible as English Literature*, p. 68, referring to E. Renan, *Histoire Générale des Langues Sémitiques*, 1858, chap. i.

[3] James, *Psychology*, vol. i, p. 598.

temporal order"; and the Hebrew thought was mainly fanciful. With such a syntax the language was entirely unfitted to express a highly complex and rationally organized thought such as is represented by a modern style like, for example, De Quincey's. On the other hand it was perfectly adapted to the expression of the Hebrew poetry. It is the same with the vocabulary, which had no words except for the concrete objects of sensuous experience. Any other idea had to be expressed metaphorically. Anger, for example, to quote Renan, "is expressed in Hebrew in a throng of ways, each picturesque, and each borrowed from physiological facts. Now the metaphor is taken from the rapid and animated breathing which accompanies the passion, now from heat or from boiling, now from the act of noisy breaking, now from shivering." Each word then is concrete, the symbol of a sensation or vivid figure. "In each word one still hears the echo of the primitive sensations which determined the choice of the first makers of the language." Such language is the ideal medium for poetry. Modern prose says for example, "What is the reason for this hesitation and inaction?" but Jacob said unto his sons, "Why do ye look one upon another?"— and the language presents the picture of indecision. We may note very briefly that much the same thing is true of the Greek language of the Homeric period, which, because of its simple syntax and concrete vocabulary, had a directness and vividness sought in vain by the modern poet; and that somewhat the same thing is true of Elizabethan English, which, with its looseness, concreteness, figurativeness, and consequent picturesqueness, was much better suited to poetic use than the English of the present day.

Primitive language is so strikingly different from ours that some students of mythology, Max Müller in particular, have thought that the myths were the result of a kind of figurative excess or "disease" in language. This seems putting the cart before the horse. Two other theories of the myth are more worth our consideration. The first is that all the fanciful or fantastic notions of the myths had their origin in dreams.

Hobbes was among the first to advance this theory;—from dreams "did arise the greatest part of the religion of the gentiles in time past, that worshipped satyrs, fawns, nymphs, and the like; and nowadays the opinion that rude people have of fairies, ghosts, and goblins; and of the power of witches." [1] This theory is of course based on the resemblance between dream and myth. Both, Nietzsche says, are arbitrary and confused yet accepted as true; "therefore in sleep and dreams we once more carry out the task of early humanity." [2]

This theory is closely related to the second, according to which myths had their origin not in dreams, but in the primitive dream-like way of thinking. "We can have very little doubt that in our dreams we are brought near to ways of thought and feeling that are sometimes closer to those of early man, as well as of latter-day savages, than are our psychic modes in civilization." [3] "In sleep," says Sully, "we have a reversion to a more primitive type of experience." "Dreaming," says Jastrow, "may be viewed as a reversion to a more primitive type of thought." Thus, the waking imagination of primitive men, which, however, was constantly dreamlike, produced the myths; this is doubtless an adequate explanation. This view has been developed by the followers of Freud,[4] by whom it is stated succinctly as follows: "Myth is the dream of a people; dream is the myth of the individual." This is essentially true; the parallel is perfect. We

[1] *Leviathan*, Pt. I, ch. ii. H. Ellis, *The World of Dreams*, refers to Synesius, who in the fourth century, suggested that conversations with animals in dreams may be the origin of animal fables and bestiaries. Compare Balaam's ass speaking in *Numbers*, xxii.

[2] *Human, All too Human*, vol. i, p. 23. Compare Charles Richet, in Chabaneix, *Le Subconscient*, p. 56: "I once tried to make literary use of a dream which I had had; it has been published, a little changed, in the form of a story for children."

[3] H. Ellis, *The World of Dreams*, p. 266, who quotes Sully, *Fortnightly Review*, March, 1893, and Jastrow, *The Subconscious*, p. 219, as above.

[4] See K. Abraham, *Traum und Mythus*, and other volumes by Riklin and Rank in *Schriften zur angewandten Seelenkunde*.

must remember, however, that, though the myths were anonymous and homogeneous and it is therefore convenient to assign them to a whole people, there is in strictness no such thing as folk-dreams or folk-myth or folk-poetry. That is, every myth, taken in its parts, was originally the product of some individual mind. Myths may indeed be the dreams of a people in the sense that those which embodied common thought or aspiration, though imagined by one person, would appeal to others, and would be preserved and added to by other dreamers.

Now we have seen that the products of the phantasy in sleep and in waking are so much alike that it is hardly worth while to distinguish between the two. This would be particularly true of primitive times when men spent so much of their waking hours in dreamlike thought. It is not worth while, therefore, to decide between the first theory above and the second; this would be like trying to decide whether the original inventor of the myths was at the time awake or asleep; the question is idle. The essential point is that the myths were a product of the phantasy in a period when it was much stronger than it is with us. The myths are dreams and they are poetry: all three come to the same thing.

If we keep in mind the facts which I have tried to establish in the preceding pages—that primitive man thought for the most part merely in images, and hence lived in the imagination; that his imagination gradually became weaker as his reasoning became stronger; that the modern man spends his time mainly in voluntary thought—it will explain many things in poetry which are at once familiar and puzzling. It will explain, for example, why poetry invariably precedes prose, and why prose in the end becomes predominant. It will explain why Milton complained that he was born "an age too late"—for which he was ridiculed by Johnson, and defended by Macaulay. The half dozen pages of the latter's Essay on Milton proving that "as civilization advances, poetry almost necessarily declines," and that the modern poet must "struggle against the spirit of the age" show quite remarkable insight. It will explain again why the age of Elizabeth was so prolific, why the romantic writers returned to the middle ages, and why their poetry has such magic—why, for example, a reading of "Christabel" is as refreshing as a dream of childhood. It will explain why modern poets, like modern sculptors and architects, go back to the Greeks, to the golden age of the imagination, for material and inspiration, and why modern poets, like Keats, feel the affinity and catch the Greek spirit intuitively without scholarship. In the same way the Greeks themselves of the time of Sophocles went back to and adapted legends of the age of Homer. It will explain why Homer and Shakespeare are still the greatest of poets, and why the Bible is the most inspired of books. Finally, it will explain why, as G. E. Woodberry puts it, "the poet seems to present the phenomenon of a highly developed mind working in a primitive way." [1]

Because we speak of the imaginative way of thinking, of the phantasy, as primitive we are tempted to think of it as inferior. And indeed there are other reasons why we should depreciate it. Our growth in command of voluntary thought, in power of reasoning, has been so remarkable, we have come to depend on reasoning so exclusively, and the products of our reasoning in modern science have been of such immediate and immense practical value, that we are inclined to undervalue the other faculty; the younger brother looks down upon the elder.[2] But

[1] *Inspiration of Poetry*, p. 13.

[2] The practical man of course depreciates the phantasy and its products. He calls a thing a myth or a dream, visionary or romantic, to condemn it. Even the psychologists do the same thing. C. G. Jung, *Psychology of the Unconscious*, p. 35, speaks of directed thinking as having taken the place of phantastic thinking, which, however, remains as a survival, like those physical organs, the relics of outgrown functions, which have become useless. So even as broad-minded a writer as William James depreciates imaginative thought as primitive and says that the analytic "represents the higher stage;"— *Psychology*, vol. ii, p. 363—though the context shows that he has great respect for the former. The psychologists who write in this way should explain why mankind has always preferred its poets to its reasoners, and why "a dreamer lives forever, but a thinker dies in a day." See also James, vol. ii, p. 361.

the other faculty is still as valuable as ever. The heart still sees further than the head; the poet still sees more deeply and more quickly, than the reasoner; poetry still shows the way in which science must follow. If we look at it broadly enough we shall see that the older faculty in many respects is still the better.

It is therefore a depressing thought to realize that we may be losing this older faculty, that we may have already lost it—at any rate in its maximum efficiency and power. That the oldest books are the best would suggest this. That as a race we are beyond the period of our youth would also suggest it. The analogy between the development of the individual and the development of the race is probably more valuable for explaining the past than for foretelling the future, but one is tempted to use it for prediction. The individual, then, has most vivid imagination in childhood, and most effective use of it for poetry, say, from twenty to thirty. Then he loses in imagination; but he continues to grow in his reasoning and does his best work in science perhaps from forty to fifty. It is easy to apply the analogy: the only question is as to the present age of the race. But if the analogy holds, and if we suppose that we are now in the age of science, then we can no more expect a poet of the present day to equal Shakespeare, than we can suppose that Coleridge could have written the "Ancient Mariner" at fifty. We are so accustomed to the idea of human progress and so impressed in particular with the progress of science that we take progress in all directions for granted. We expect greater poets in the future and, with Emerson's optimism, look forward "to an ever-increasing knowledge, as to a becoming Creator." It may be, however, that Homer will always be the greatest of poets. It may be that the ancient Hebrews were at once more imaginative and more preoccupied with religion than any people can ever be again. If this is the case then in this sense the Bible would be a final revelation.

We may return from this speculation to the safer ground of

the past by saying that unquestionably there has been in history an enormous development in the command of purposive thought, and that on the other hand there has been little or no development, even a falling off, in command of imaginative thought. In poetry and religion, and generally in all subjects too difficult or profound to be approached by the reason, the imagination still has sway; in philosophy and science the voluntary thought has gradually gained the preponderance. In Plato there is a happy mingling of imagination and reasoning; the philosophy is partly mythical, partly reflective. In the modern exact sciences the method is as rigorously ratiocinative as it can be made. Even here, however, old habits of thought linger in the popular mind. For example it is difficult for anyone but a trained scientist to use a word like *energy* or *inertia* without some personification, some lingering attribution of human character to material things. The work of science may be described as a gradual "depersonification of the myth," to use the expression of Ribot.[1] The concrete picture is gradually replaced by a set of abstract symbols. When this work is complete the myth has been rationalized and explained. Sometimes this translation of one kind of thought in terms of the other is easy. "Selene kisses the sleeping Endymion" in poetry clearly becomes "It is night" in prose. Oftener, however, the myth is more complex; that of Prometheus or that of Œdipus for example, has countless suggestions, implications—the more the better, for as it is the rule of prose to have one meaning, so it is the virtue of poetry to have many. A poetic myth is all condensation, and full, as we shall see later, of what the psychologists call "overdetermination." The interpretation of such myths is difficult—indeed impossible, for their significance is like that of nature—infinite.[2]

---

[1] *Creative Imagination*, p. 133.

[2] Some modern writers give us first the poetry and then the interpretation—called the "moral"—in the last stanzas (which of course are verse but not poetry). This is also the method of La Fontaine's Fables. It is

The interpretation of myths corresponds to the interpretation of dreams, which has always so fascinated the human race. Thus Daniel interpreted the dream of Belshazzer, after it had been given up by the astrologers and the Chaldeans and the soothsayers,—that is he gave the prose which lay behind the picture of the dream. In recent times this interpretation has been taken up by psychologists; the problem is to substitute for the "manifest content" of the dream, for its series of pictures, the "latent content," that is an abstract statement of the thoughts which lie behind it.[1]

pleasing to prosaic readers, but trying to poetic ones. Minerva is made by Lowell to object to it:

> "Discriminate," she said, "betimes;
>   The Muse is unforgiving;
> Put all your beauty in your rhymes,
>   Your morals in your living."

[1] The most important work on this subject is S. Freud's *Interpretation of Dreams*. Freud says, very suggestively, that dream-thinking, is "something qualitatively altogether different from waking [voluntary] thought, and therefore not in any way comparable to it. It does not in general think, judge, or calculate at all, but limits itself to transforming,"—(p. 401). To another statement, however, I shall make an objection, which I hope will be sustained by anyone who has read the chapter above. "The psychic activity in dream formation resolves itself into two functions—the provision of the dream thoughts and the transformation of these into the dream content." And so Freud writes all through as if the dreamer first contrived his abstract latent content and then translated it into the concrete manifest one. This is surely the error of those who suppose that the Greek contrived his moral and then invented a myth to embody it. The dream content is the actuality; the dream thought is a fiction of the psychologist. The fact is that the store of desires, images, and feelings in the mind may be presented in two ways: 1. in waking conscious thought, which can be expressed in abstract language; 2. in the dream, where it has concrete representation in pictures. The dream itself involves only the pictures and not the abstract thought which subsequent interpretation may find behind it.

CHAPTER V

THE SUBJECTS OF POETRY

I

WE may return now from the mainly historical treatment of the two modes of thought in the preceding chapter, to a further description of them as we have them at our disposal at the present time. If we still think in both ways—though more largely in the newly-acquired way—the question arises, when do we use one mode and when the other? When do we fall, or rise, from directed thought into merely associative thought, from reasoning into pure imagining? The choice of words, between *falling* and *rising*, is somewhat important; the word *fall* or *lapse* is the one generally employed; but this choice we may leave open for the moment. Under what conditions and for what subjects do we employ one mode of thought or the other? These questions have already been considered to some extent, but they must now be answered as carefully as possible; then we shall know something about the conditions under which poetry is produced and the proper subjects for poetry.

They have been considered in an instructive way by H. Silberer, and I may begin by referring to his discussion.[1] "I shall not differ much," he says, "from the majority of authors if I find the most important and most general condition of the formation of symbols"—that is, equivalently, of the employment of the phantasy—"a condition which will fit the phenomena, both normal and pathological, whether in individual psychology or in the psychology of the race—if I find the

---

[1] "Über die Symbolbildung," in *Jahrbuch für psychoanalytische und psychopathologische Forschungen*, vol. iii, p. 680.

condition in an inadequacy of the comprehending faculty relatively to its object, or, to use other words, in an apperceptive insufficience." The idea of a mental insufficiency is the important one, and this insufficiency is a relative matter,—that is, there are in it two factors, first the mind, and secondly the task or the subject. The insufficiency may arise either from the weakness of the mind, or from the difficulty of the task with which it is confronted. The mind may be unequal to its task for various reasons. It may be so because it is naturally weak, as in children or savages; and thus, as we have seen, children and savages think in images. It may be so because it is tired, as reverie arises most often in fatigue, or because it is sleepy or asleep, as in hypnogogic illusions or in dream. It may be so because it is in a state of emotion, preventing the adjustment necessary to attentive thought.

But the second factor, the subject, also comes in. This may be too difficult, as almost any subject is difficult for the childish or primitive mind. But many subjects are too difficult for any mind—and it is these that we should especially consider, because they are particularly the subjects of poetry. Many subjects, like the mysteries of religion, the meaning of life, the secrets of nature and its beauty, love, death, and immortality, cannot be approached by the reasoning mind. They are beyond our comprehension even when we are grown, sound of mind, and wide awake,—even in our best moments. They are beyond the power of the strongest reasoner, even of the greatest poet, though the poet is a man of insight and wisdom. Each of these subjects often presents merely an obscure total impression, with the elements of which we are not familiar, and which is therefore unanalyzable. When a man confronts such subjects it is useless for him, however strong his mind, to attempt voluntary thought. He may fix his attention upon them, but without result. The volition can only select and reject among the images spontaneously offered to the mind,[1] and here

---

[1] James, *Psychology*, vol. i, p. 589.

there is no principle of selection, no clue; it is like venturing into a wilderness without path or guide. The country must first be guessed at and spied out and surveyed from a distance before it can be traversed. It is this preliminary survey of an unknown country which the poet undertakes; he must always go first and be followed by the reasoner. Voluntary thought being useless, the only resort is purposeless or merely associative thought. In other words in approaching these unexplored subjects man cannot reason, but only feel and imagine. Here, then, is a mental insufficiency different from the first. Here it is useless to talk of weak minds reverting to an outgrown habit of thought. It is a case of the strongest mind using the only thought that is serviceable, which man must not at any cost allow to be outgrown if he can help it,—which, if he is to approach any new subject at all, is his only recourse.

It is true that this kind of thought is primitive—the thought of children and savages. But it is, and must be, the thought of man too. And if it is older it may be deeper. It is true that it is easier, and so the resort of a weak or tired mind. But this is not conclusive. It is harder to argue keenly than to lapse into meditation, but wisdom enforces meditation upon us, and meditation is thought to lead to wisdom, even more surely than argument. It is true also that this second thought comes into play when the emotions destroy the adjustment necessary to attention. But strong feeling, which is so unfavorable to "cool reason," is the very source and condition of the other mode of thought, for feeling starts and warms the imagination. And there is no reason for supposing that we are any more on the right track when we "reason coolly" than when we "feel warmly." The fact is that each state of mind has its place and function. In other words we might as well go beyond the idea of weakness and primitiveness, and recognize that there are these two operations of the mind, the reasoning one and the feeling one, the ordinary thought and the phantasy—each of which has its own function, its appropriate subjects, and its peculiar results.

I have spoken of subjects, concerning the meaning of life and nature, which are beyond our comprehension. We must realize of course that there are many such subjects. In every field of human thought there is a part of it familiar to us—a part which is, so to speak, nearest to our door and crossed by beaten paths. There is another part of it distant from us, so distant that it is beyond our ken and entirely unknown. Then there is a part between the two, between the known and the unknown, and this is always the region which most interests us, is most the object of curiosity and speculation. The first does not take our attention because it is too familiar, the second also does not, precisely because it is entirely beyond our vision, and except as a vague whole, can never enter the mind. To the third—the known-unknown—we readily attend. In every science, for example, we understand to a certain point; beyond lie the parts of the subject we are learning, and beyond these the great unknown. In going forward over this new country towards the unknown, the imagination always leads the way and the reason follows. The poet sees first and points out, the scientist then explains and demonstrates. The familiar country is the region of prose and science. The region of poetry is always just on that frontier where the known verges upon the unknown. There lies the field of greatest interest and greatest difficulty. There lie the subjects which can be approached only poetically, and the work of the poets. But since this verge or horizon of thought lies about us always, in every science and department of knowledge,—and not only here but in every matter which we may contemplate, and in all our physical surroundings, there is always work for this poetical pioneer—work which only the poet can perform. This is the true apologia for poetry—the argument which, if he can understand it, must appeal even to the most practical man, and by which all the dreams and fancies, the vision and ecstasy, of the poet are justified.

The matter may be put in another way which will make the subject matter of poetry more specific. Poetry is produced

by the imagination stimulated by emotion. Anything therefore which heightens the feeling and starts the imagination
will properly be poetized. If a thing is perfectly apprehended
in all its features it is commonplace. The multiplication table
and the rule of three with their whole vocabulary are hope-
lessly prosaic. The imagination starts only when the subject is more obscure, when it is a little more distant or dimly
seen, when in consequence it begins to have color and shadow,
when it begins to have mystery. Then begins romance. Take
the imagination of childhood. In the child, Sully says, "the
external world, so far as it is only dimly perceived, excites
wonder, curiosity, and the desire to fill in the blank spaces
with at least the semblance of knowledge." The same thing
might be said of the man, but let us take the child because he
is the more imaginative. "Here," Sully continues, "distance exercises a strange fascination. The remote chain of
hills faintly visible from the child's home, has been again and
again endowed by his enriching fancy, with all manner of
wondrous scenery and peopled by all manner of strange creatures. The unapproachable sky—which to the little one, so
often on his back, is much more of a visible object than to us—
with its wonders of blue expanse and cloudland, of stars and
changeful moon, is wont to occupy his mind, his bright fancy
quite spontaneously filling out this big upper world with appropriate forms." Taking the child's point of view, we begin
to understand the celestial mythology of the Greeks. "This
stimulating effect of the half-perceivable is seen in still greater
intensity in the case of what is hidden from sight. The spell
cast on the young mind by the mystery of holes, and especially
of dark woods, and the like, is known to all." We begin to
understand also the poetry that gathered around the chasm
at Delphi and the oak-grove at Dodona. These are the shrines
of Apollo. "This imaginative filling up," Sully continues, "of
the remote and the hidden recesses of the outer world is subject
to manifold stimulating influences from the region of feeling
. . . . The unseen, the hidden, contains unknown possibilities,

something awful, terrible, it may be, to make the timid, wee thing shudder in anticipatory vision, or wondrously and surprisingly beautiful." [1] And we begin to understand the religion of the Greeks also, with its childlike awe and love of beauty.

If we change a little the figure of the preceding page and compare what is known to a lighted space just about us—lighted we may say by the mind—and what is unknown to a more distant obscurity, then we shall find the province of the imagination and of poetry in the penumbra, first in the twilight of the physical world—and here is a reason added to that mentioned on an earlier page why dawn and evening and moonlight are poetical—or secondly, in the twilights of the mind. Irving shows his instinctive comprehension of the whole matter at the beginning of "Rip Van Winkle." The opening paragraph describes the Catskills first in plain prose, then poetically. The second begins: "At the foot of these fairy mountains the voyager may have descried the light smoke curling up from a village whose shingle roofs gleam among the trees, *just where the blue tints of the upland melt away into the fresh green of the nearer landscape.*" This is the true poetical location. In this village "there lived many years since," etc. This is the poetic time.[2]

In other words the poetical subject-matter may be found, and in the nature of things found only, in what is removed from us, either in space or in time, just far enough to be unfamiliar with-

---

[1] Sully, *Studies of Childhood*, chap. ii.

[2] Compare the following: "Lady Mary Wortley Montague has said, with equal truth and taste, that the most romantic region of every country is that where the mountains unite themselves with the plains and lowlands. For similar reasons, it may be in like manner said, that the most picturesque period of history is that when the ancient rough and wild manners of a barbarous age are just becoming innovated upon, and contrasted, by the illumination of increased or revived learning, and the instructions of renewed or reformed religion. The strong contrast produced by the opposition of ancient manners to those which are gradually subduing them, affords the lights and shadows necessary to give effect to a fictitious narrative," etc.—Scott, *Fortunes of Nigel*, "Introduction."

out being unknown. This is most obvious in what is physically at the poetic distance. The horizon is naturally poetical. The scientist, by exercise of the volition, may think of it as the circle which bounds that part of the earth's surface visible from a given point. But not the ordinary man—certainly not the poet or the child. To the child it is a platform upon which bright figures are dancing in the shimmering light. The fact of the poetic distance explains the charm of *Childe Harold* and *Les Orientales*, of Poe's out of the way geography in the "MS. Found in a Bottle," of the South Seas and the Spanish Main. The poet always makes a "journey into the blue distance." But distance in time as well as in space may lend enchantment to the view. This explains the charm of the "return to the past," in *Ivanhoe*, in *Christabel*, in the *Scarlet Letter*. No one has shown surer instinct in the choice of the poetic subject than Hawthorne. Like so many of our writers, especially of his time, he despairs of finding romance in the commonplace United States of the present. "No author," he says, "can conceive of the difficulty of writing a romance about a country where there is no shadow, no antiquity, no mystery, no picturesque and gloomy wrong, nor any thing but a commonplace prosperity, as is happily the case with my dear native land." [1] Even here, however, Hawthorne found romance also,—at least by withdrawing, as the poet always may, from the external world into the world of the mind itself. In this internal world, too, there are the known, the half known, and the unknown—and that penumbra of the mind itself, which is more poetical to us than any other. This is Hawthorne's true field. No one has portrayed better its half lights and glooms,—the figures and apparitions of this region where credulity and incredulity meet. His treatment of the so-called supernatural in fiction is a pattern for all other artists. Poe also found his best subjects in these out of the way regions of the "psyche,"—sometimes too crudely as in the "Case of Monsieur Valdemar," sometimes with the best results as

[1] Preface to the *Marble Faun*.

in the "Fall of the House of Usher." But it is useless to give examples. In *Hamlet* and every other "psychological" story the poetical location is the same.[1]

Let it not be supposed, however, that poetry can be found only in what is out of the way,—as Poe and Hawthorne found it. Though I may at first seem to contradict what I have said before, it is found perhaps oftenest in what is nearest. It is not the nearness but the familiarity that breeds contempt. And even in the things which we think we know best, in a well known landscape or in the features of a face we love, there is often the same presence of both the known and the unknown—the same horizon where the finite verges upon the infinite. In love, the most poetic of all subjects, there is always this blending; love thrives on half knowledge, on curiosity, and has always a mystery about it. When the mystery is entirely fathomed the love is over. Take for example four couplets from a poem which I should rather quote entire.

> She was a Phantom of delight
> When first she gleamed upon my sight.

The word "phantom" fits the lover's vision, which fades as he approaches.

> I saw her upon nearer view
> A Spirit, yet a Woman too.

In the third couplet the transformation is complete:

> And now I see with eye serene
> The very pulse of the machine.

The much discussed *machine* at least indicates utter prose; the eye is now serene and the vision is over. Not, however, quite:

[1] Hawthorne indicates not only the subject matter of poetry, but the spirit in which it must be read as well as composed. "The book," he says of the *Twice Told Tales*, "requires to be read in the clear brown twilight atmosphere in which it was written; if opened in the sunshine it is apt to look exceedingly like a volume of blank pages." (Preface.)

> And yet a Spirit still, and bright
> With something of angelic light.

As we might expect, Wordsworth has perfectly the theory of the poetry in familiar things. Even in the familiar there is poetry as long as there is any mystery left. But to the thoughtful mind there is curiosity and mystery in everything; so Wordsworth is the poet of the common.

> O Reader! had you in your mind
> Such stores as silent thought can bring,
> O gentle Reader! you would find
> A tale in everything.

Only, however, because the thoughtful reader sees that each thing involves all, and the mystery of all; that each subject is part of the greatest of all subjects,—which is infinite, beyond our comprehension, beyond even our power of vision, but which we must strive to see until our eyes shall at last be opened. "For we know in part, and we prophesy in part. But when that which is perfect is come, then that which is in part shall be done away. For now we see through a glass, darkly; but then face to face."

II

We have gone no great way—the reader may feel—in thus outlining the familiar subjects of poetry. But we are perhaps on the way toward establishing a principle. All the subjects are in principle alike; in each case there is, as we confront it, a mental insufficiency,—that is an inability to encompass the subject by means of reasoning. In each case there must be a mental halting and readjustment, a new focusing of the mental eye or a turning to another mode of thought. In each case, in other words, we necessarily begin to feel and to imagine—and feeling and imagination are of course the conditions of poetry. Both the feeling and the imagination must be considered in later chapters, but there is one peculiar and characteristic feeling involved in this readjustment and adoption of the second mode of thought

which must be described here. It is difficult to describe because
it is a "dream feeling," so to speak, and must be recollected and
analyzed by ordinary thought. We have a name for it, however;
it is the feeling of *awe*. What is half-known to us is always to a
greater or less degree awful. This feeling may be tinged by
others—by the feeling of sadness which Shelley and Poe thought
inseparable from the highest beauty, or by a softer feeling
which might be called "pathetic," or by the more playful and
genial feeling with which we regard a thing humorous but not
quite comprehended. The central feeling, however, is one of
awe. It is that of the boy who stops before the mouth of the
cave or at the entrance to the deep wood—with a strange feeling
impelling him to enter and another strange feeling holding him
back; it is a compound of strong fascination and less strong repulsion; that is normally, I think, the attraction should be the
stronger feeling, and the boy should venture. So when he grows
a little older and falls in love, the beauty by which he is dazzled,
is in the first place of course, an object of the strongest attraction,
but in the second place of slight fear also. "La beauté est une
chose terrible." "At first" as Lafcadio Hearn says, "the sur-
prise of the discovery leaves him breathless: instinctively he turns
away his gaze. That vision seemed too delicious to be true. But
presently he ventures to look again,—fearing with a new fear,—
afraid of the reality, afraid also of being observed,—and lo! his
doubt dissolves in a new shock of ecstasy." [1] True love, as has
often been noted, is a compound of these opposed elements. Perhaps in timid youth the fearful feeling is even the stronger. In
the same way when one walks out of doors, perhaps in the
evening, and presently ceases to observe intellectually, and
begins to feel—as the eye catches and follows the "gleam"—
the feeling is one of awe,—that is of vague fascination, as if one
were drawn to "all things" on the one hand, but of slight dis-
comfort, insecurity, apprehension, perhaps sadness on the other.
It is the feeling of Gideon, exclaiming, "Alas, O Lord God! for

---

[1] *Shadowings*, "In a Pair of Eyes."

because I have seen an angel of the Lord face to face." The religious feeling—that which we have before the highest unknown—is the same compound: we are directed to fear God and love him.

In every case the feeling of awe is precedent to an imaginative employment of the mind. The boy's fancy is started and he peoples the cave or the wood with figures or presences, more or less distinct, beautiful or fearful, robbers, giants, or fairies. The awestruck lover sees not with the eye but with the mind, and beauty is enhanced or even created. The lover of nature proceeds to recreate nature.

> From worlds not quickened by the sun
> A portion of the gift is won.

The religious feeling draws down the same gift; the mood of reverent awe is that of religious ecstasy and vision.

Now let us see what the result is, of the employment of this second mode of thought, upon the half known subject with which it deals. The second operation of the mind, like the first, has the effect of bringing knowledge, of lightening the darkness, or the penumbra, as I have called it—but in a different way. It also discovers truth, what we call poetic truth. What does this mean? But in the first place there is no doubt that it does discover truth. There is a disposition in this age of science to doubt the mystic's vision, for example, as a source of truth, as there is to doubt the dream, as such a source, which the ancients believed in—and a disposition even to doubt the poet's vision and poetry as such a source. There is a feeling that poetry is merely a thing of beauty, of art for the sake of art, and that the true poet does not bother about the truth of his art, but only about its beauty. Certainly the poet does not "bother" about truth; but still the discovery of truth is the result. It is hard to see why anyone should question the mystic's vision as a source of truth, if he looks at the matter broadly enough. There can be no doubt that the imagination of the Hebrews, who saw visions and dreamed dreams, and of other imaginative peoples who have concerned themselves with religion,—the Greeks and the Hindoos, the saints of the middle ages,—have contributed much more to our present store of religious knowledge than has come from the other source; in other words that revelation—for this is the only possible meaning of the word—has given us much more than theology. This would be expected in a subject where the mystery is greatest. Theology has been content mainly to systematize the truth got in the other way.

The reasoner reaches a conclusion which seems to him to agree with fact, external or internal, which therefore has the conscientious approval of mind, and he proclaims this as truth. When the myth or fiction produced by the imaginative mind is interpreted, the interpretation has likewise the approval of the mind, and this is proclaimed as truth also. But this is a subsequent interpretation made by the reason, with which the poetic mind itself is not primarily concerned. The imagination works spontaneously,—that is, as far as we can see, without the conscious purpose of producing truth. And furthermore the fiction as it is produced has on the face of it nothing to do with truth; it impresses us rather by its want of correspondence to actuality. But the fiction may have another quality which is apparent, and which if present wins the approval of the mind. Truth in the sphere of reason becomes in the sphere of the imagination beauty: the two are analogous. I shall not attempt a new definition of beauty, but merely suggest that we truly see beauty only in the second mode of thought, and that whatever wins our approval among the products of the second mode of thought, as truth wins it in the first—and in either case we cannot by analysis go much beyond the word approval—that we call beautiful. And further our idea and standard of beauty seem to come from this source; they are established by the productions of the second mode of thought. The agreement between the true and the beautiful has always been recognized—"Beauty is truth," says Keats, "truth beauty"; they are not synonymous only because they belong to the different orders of thought;

they are brother and sister, but not identical.[1] But whenever a fiction of the poetic mind wins us because of its beauty, we may be pretty sure that it embodies an idea which, if we could get it, would win our reasonable approval also. We can only feel the beauty of the fiction; we can perhaps by analysis demonstrate the truth of the idea; but our judgment is as much to be trusted in one case as in the other. We may indeed by a transference of the terms even call the fiction " true," and speak of the truth of poetry. Keats, therefore, is essentially right when he says: "What the imagination seizes as beauty must be truth, whether it existed before or not. . . . The imagination may be compared to Adam's dream; he awoke and found it truth." [2] Thus the poet dreams and his dream seems idle, but when he awakes he finds there is a rational conception correspondent to it, and this is an addition to knowledge. The poet looks upon that semi-obscurity which I have described as his proper field of vision, and enlightens it. In the process of enlightenment the poet performs the first if not the greatest work.

For purposes of instruction it is doubtless desirable that the poet's vision should be interpreted, that in the poem, concrete in its method, we should discover the abstract meaning which lies behind it, that the poetic beauty should be translated into the truth of reason. This of course is not at all necessary to the enjoyment of poetry, for the true reader of poetry reads, as the poet writes, with vision, and is amply satisfied with its beauty. The translation is not necessary even for instruction, because the mind can receive the truth of the poem without interpretation, imaginatively and unconsciously, as the mind of the poet has imparted it; the thought need nowhere be formulated; the fable is instructive without the moral; and the parables of Christ were edifying even though they were not rationally comprehended. But the inclination of the human mind is finally to interpret, and this is the course of progress. The scientist succeeds to the poet. " The poet picks the flowers," as Silberer expresses it,

[1] Compare Coleridge's beautiful "Time, Real and Imaginary."

[2] *Letters*, ed. Forman, 1895, pp. 52, 53.

"without knowing their names, and holds them out to us, to our joy. Then much later comes the botanist who discovers what kind of a plant it really is. What was at first prized merely for its beauty, is now disclosed as a source of knowledge." [1]

This then is the relation of poetry and science. Similarly the relation of poetry and criticism is well expressed by W. C. Brownell. "Criticism may not inexactly be described as the statement of the concrete in terms of the abstract. . . . The concrete absorbs the constructive artist whose endeavor is to give substance to his idea, which until expressed is an abstraction. The concern of criticism is to measure his success by the correspondence of his expression to the idea it suggests and by the value of the idea itself." [2] Theory thus certainly justifies not only poetry, but the criticism of poetry as well; though the merit of poetry is quite independent of any critical interpretation. We must indeed beware of supposing that the poet's intuitive thought can always be rationalized. Some deeper portions of poetic truth, particularly those arising from the unconscious mind—which we must now go on to consider—may be entirely incapable of such rationalization, and completely out of the range of the ordinary thought.

[1] *Jahrbuch*, as above, vol. iii, p. 674.   [2] *Criticism*, p. 16.

CHAPTER VI

THE UNCONSCIOUS MIND IN POETRY

I

IN the production of poetry the mental operation is partly an unconscious one and draws material partly from unconscious sources. Poetry, as Shelley declares, is "created by that imperial faculty whose throne is curtained within the invisible nature of man."[1] In the consideration of this unconscious element arise some of the chief difficulties of the subject—difficulties indeed which in the present state of knowledge are insurmountable.

We have found that poetry is produced by a mental operation different from ordinary thought; now we shall find that this operation is often entirely beyond our direct observation. Without this added element there are difficulties enough. It is impossible to use the method of introspection while the mind is engaged in poetic thought, because in dream there can be no observation or judgment. The moment investigation begins the mind is awake, the operation to be observed is over, and one can only try to recall its processes. It is like trying to analyze the processes of a dream. The waking thought and the dream thought belong to different orders. But now, in the second place, we find that the operation runs into a deeper portion of the mind where no recollection and so no direct observation is possible to ordinary thought.

The existence of what I have called the unconscious is often doubted by the ordinary person, for the good reason that in his ordinary thought he knows nothing about it and can recollect

[1] *Defense of Poetry*, p. 7.

nothing from it. It is doubted even by many psychologists who argue that the mind can deal psychologically only with what it finds within itself—with what it is conscious of—and that therefore the unconscious is at least as good as non-existent. The best recent psychologists, however, like William James and Ribot, make no question of it. "It is the organism," says the latter, "with the brain its supreme representative, which constitutes the real personality; comprising in itself all that we have been and the possibilities of all that we shall be. The whole individual character is there inscribed, with its active and passive aptitudes, its sympathies and antipathies, its genius, its talent, or its stupidity, its virtues and its vices, its torpor and its activity. The part thereof which emerges into consciousness is little compared with what remains buried, but operative nevertheless. The conscious personality is never more than a small fraction of the physical personality." [1]

The poets certainly recognize the unconscious. Emerson's whole theory, for example, is based upon a recognition of it. "The uttered part of a man's life," Carlyle observes, "bears to the unuttered, unconscious part a small unknown proportion; he himself never knows it, much less do others." [2] One who has any doubt, in order to be assured of the actuality of the thing, by whatever name it may be called, need only read a collection

[1] *Les Maladies de la Personnalité,* "Conclusion." The overlooking of the larger fraction is due to the "tendency, rooted in our nature," of which Bergson speaks, "to represent the whole of our inner life on the model of the very small part of it which is inserted into the present reality, which perceives this reality and acts upon it." Compare J. Jastrow, *The Subconscious,* p. 84. A contemporary poet expresses much the same idea. After speaking of the unconscious character of his inspiration he says: "I think the better half of everybody's daily brain work is precisely thus intuitive and subconscious, but most people, being not introspective, forget the essential revelation in the conscious labor of arrangement. So that we imagine ourselves to have worked out an idea, whereas in fact the idea has first been revealed to us and then we have thought *about* it."—*Harper's Magazine,* Jan. 1919, p. 223.

[2] *Essays,* "Sir Walter Scott."

of observations on the working of genius in poets and artists, like that of Chabaneix,—who remarks that "the participation of the unconscious in inspired creation is recognized by all who have approached the subject." [1]

Perhaps some of the disagreement is due to differences of definition. I shall not here attempt a definition or general description of the unconscious, which is a matter for the psychologist, and shall treat it of course only so far as is necessary to an understanding of poetry. But when I use the word unconscious I refer to a part of the mind which cannot be utilized or controlled voluntarily, and whose content cannot be recovered by the memory in voluntary thought—which however, does apparently often carry on a part of the operation in the second mode of thought, and whose content is drawn upon in that thought. It is important especially in furnishing material for poetry—as also for dreams and other productions of the imagination. Let us take first a simple example from a dream. Havelock Ellis records having dreamed of a large old house belonging to "Sir Peter Bryan," the dream having many particulars, all of which he says could be traced to a recognized source in the memory, except the name.[2] "I could not recall that I had at that time ever heard of any one called Bryan. I abandoned the search and made my notes of the dream and its sources. I had scarcely done so when I chanced to take up a volume of biographies of eccentric personages, which I had glanced through carelessly the day before. I found that it contained, among others, the lives of Lord *Peter*borough, and George *Bryan* Brummel. I had certainly seen these names the day before; yet before I took up the book again it would have been impossible for me to recall the exact name of Beau Brummel." This is the type of an item which cannot be recalled in ordinary thought, but which emerges when the phantasy is at work. The matter emerging here is only a trifling sample and may give a wrong general idea of the unconscious

[1] *Le Subconscient*, p. 106.   [2] *The World of Dreams*, p. 221.

material. Apparently the fund which can be thus drawn upon is very large and varied, and parts of it very valuable.

How then shall we get an idea of the resources and contents of this part of the mind—of the fund from which the imagination may draw? Not directly, of course, because the unconscious is hidden from our ordinary observation; but by inference, as we infer the power of gravitation only by its effects; or indirectly, when we find the unconscious material appearing in the products of imagination in vision or dream, and then recall them in our ordinary thought. By these methods scientists, either by experiment as in hypnotism, or by observation of the matter emerging in natural mental operations, have got some notion of this hidden part of the mind.

We can get some idea of it too from references to it which may be found throughout literature, where it has constantly been recognized. The difficulty here is that these references are often vague and poetical, and made under various names; so that we are in doubt just what is referred to, and find it difficult to rationalize the information. I may give examples, however, of some of these. Sometimes, as constantly by Carlyle, this part of the mind is referred to under the name I have used— that is, as the unconscious. More often, however, it is referred to figuratively, or under names more or less mystical. Poets for example speak of the "other world" or the "invisible world" or the "spiritual world"; of the "supernal" or the "divine in man"; of "fairyland." These vague figures are doubtless often only a projection into the exterior of faculties of the mind itself; and if carefully examined might throw light on the unconscious faculties in question. When Poe, for example, says that beauty, not that of reality but a supernal beauty, is the end of poetical creation, he doubtless has in mind a quality belonging to material derived from this unconscious source. Sometimes the mental faculties are not only externalized but personified. Socrates represented admonitions coming to him inexplicably from the deeper portions of his mind as the instructions of a demon,—his mythically constructed person representing the unconscious. So angels and spirits give warnings, perhaps in dreams; and we commonly say, to explain knowledge got not by the conscious mind but intuitively, "a little fairy told me."

Silberer remarks that an external and personal God is, psychologically regarded, a "functional" symbol; a "mythological projection" from the mind itself.[1] If to God all desires are known and from him no secrets are hid, it is because this externalization represents not only the conscious but the unconscious portions of the mind. A better form of this doctrine, however, we may perhaps find in Emerson, who is particularly careful not to personify God, but to place God within—in the mind itself. "We know," he says, "that all spiritual being is in man. . . . There is no bar or wall in the soul, where man, the effect, ceases, and God, the cause, begins." He makes a sharp distinction between the intellect, that is the mind operative in ordinary conscious thought, with the will that guides it, and the "oversoul," which certainly includes, if it is not identical with, the unconscious mind in question. Emerson's teaching is very instructive on this point. If we observe ourselves carefully, he says, "in reveries, in remorse, in times of passion, in surprises, in the instructions of dreams, wherein often we see ourselves in masquerade," we get hints of the true action of the mind. "All goes to show that the soul in man is not an organ, but animates and exercises all the organs; is not a function, like the power of memory, of calculation, of comparison, but uses these as hands and feet; is not a faculty, but a light; is not the intellect, or the will, but the master of the intellect and the will; is the background of our being, in which they lie— an immensity not possessed and that cannot be possessed." For the most part this is hardly mystical at all, but psychological. The intellect, voluntary thought, is a shallow faculty; the unconscious is the deeper and more vital mind, of which the intellect is a specialization,—a tool or instrument employed for practical purposes.

[1] *Jahrbuch*, as above, vol. ii, p. 590.

This deeper mind, according to Emerson, "flows into the intellect and makes what we call genius." A poet of genius, then, is one who draws upon these deeper sources, as distinguished from a writer of talent whose production is shallower—merely intellectual. Lowell has the same idea in "Columbus":

> And I believed the poets; it is they
> Who utter wisdom from the central deep,
> And listening to the inner flow of things
> Speak to the age out of eternity.

This is poetical figure again; if we could understand what is meant by the "central deep," and the "inner flow of things," we could explain the share of the unconscious in poetry. Here is another figure of Lowell's:

> All thought begins in feeling—wide
> In the great mass its base is hid
> And, narrowing up to thought, stands glorified
> A moveless pyramid.[1]

The feeling is the deeper foundation; thought rising from this base is solid. Changing the figure a little we may compare the unconscious mind to the base of the coral reef, hidden from sight, older, deeper, larger, than the island, of the conscious mind, which has risen from it, and which alone is visible. The ignorant man sees only the island, and has no idea of the submerged reef; the better instructed one not only knows the reef is there, but has his ways of finding out something about it.

The difficulty is that the whole subject is in what in the last chapter I called the penumbra, and can therefore with difficulty be spoken of except in figures. Indeed, this is a good example of a subject which is just partly coming out of the shadow into a steadier light. We may already get a steadier, if not a fuller light upon it from the psychologists. Bergson, for example, thus describes the dream state, which is analogous to the poetic one. "The dream state is the substratum of our normal state. Noth-

---

[1] "Incident in a Railroad Car."

ing is added in waking life; on the contrary, waking life is obtained by the limitation, concentration, and tension of that diffuse psychological life which is the life of dreaming. The perception and the memory which we find in dreaming are, in a sense, more natural than those of waking life; consciousness is then amused in perceiving for the sake of perceiving, and in remembering for the sake of remembering, without care for life, that is to say without care for the accomplishment of actions. To be awake is to eliminate, to choose, to concentrate the totality of the diffused life of dreaming to a point, to a practical problem. To be awake is to will; cease to will, detach yourself from life, become disinterested; in doing so you pass from the waking ego to the dreaming ego, which is less tense, but more extended than the other." [1] This will fit poetic vision as well as dream.

As the dream state is more diffuse and extended, so the contents of the unconscious mind would, I should think, be more extensive and varied. As the unconscious in the mass from which the conscious has grown by specialization; so it is the reservoir from which the conscious is filled. We speak of desires which are impracticable or painful as being "repressed" or driven back into the unconscious; perhaps it would often be better to say that only desires which are of practical use— capable of actual satisfaction and so pleasurable—a small part of the whole, are drawn from the larger reservoir into the practical consciousness. At any rate the unconscious seems to be the larger source. If, as some psychologists think, no impression ever made upon the mind is entirely forgotten, but is registered in the unconscious, and may under the right circumstances be secured or recovered by consciousness, then the reservoir would contain the whole of the individual experience. At least the fund is demonstrably large. I should think of it as containing countless images capable of being presented in reverie, dream, or vision; as containing its own desires, latent or

---

[1] *Revue Philosophique*, Dec. 1908, p. 574.

"repressed" in waking hours, and not motives for voluntary thought and action; as having its own strange feelings, like those of nightmare, which are indescribable in waking language. And I should think of all these as possibly utilizable by the imagination in poetic vision, as in dream—which we must remember, may draw upon the fund that is available to waking consciousness as well. That is, the material comes from both conscious and unconscious sources. It is mainly the latter, however, which gives poetry its peculiar and inexplicable character. "As the artist," according to Schelling, "is drawn involuntarily and in spite of himself to his production . . . so the materials for his work are furnished him without his concurrence, provided as it were from without."

The poet has the power of utilizing this unconscious material. Genius, according to F. W. H. Myers, should be regarded "as a power of utilizing a wider range than other men can utilize of faculties in some degree innate in all;—a power of appropriating the results of subliminal mentation to subserve the supraliminal stream of thought;—so that an 'inspiration of genius' will be in truth a *subliminal uprush*, an emergence into the current of ideas which the man is consciously manipulating of other ideas which he has not consciously originated, but which have shaped themselves beyond his will, in profounder regions of his being." [1]

We must consider also that if the unconscious fund is large, it is varied; and that though it may inspire the prophet's vision it may produce also the most trifling reverie, the feverish fancy, or the illusion of delirium. "Hidden in the deep of our being," as Myers says, "is a rubbish-heap as well as a treasure-house." [2] If it contains and holds as potentially available all of our previous experience, or anything like all, its contents must obviously be good, bad, and indifferent; and its products equally miscellaneous. Furthermore if there is what used to be called "unconscious cerebration," this operation, like that of the conscious

[1] *Human Personality*, vol. i, p. 71. William James credits Myers with having first arrived at a scientific conception of the unconscious.

[2] *Human Personality*, vol. i, p. 72.

mind, may result in good or bad, strong or weak thinking.
The result, as in the case of the intellect, will depend upon the
strength and quality of the unconscious faculty, and on the
mental store available—that is, it will vary with the individual.

But on the whole the unconscious mind is superior in insight
and wisdom, to the conscious one; and this must be insisted upon
because it will demonstrate the superiority of poetry drawing
upon this source to any merely intellectual product. That the
unconscious mind is superior is the opinion of many wise men
and the settled judgment of the race. This superiority is the
reason for the wisdom of thinking upon a thing over night before
settling it, and the reason why a lesson got over night is better
learned. This is, in part at least, the meaning of the proverb,
"the heart sees further than the head." This is the reason why
an operation so well learned that it becomes second nature, is
better done; and why, as Wordsworth insists in the "Ode to
Duty," right conduct must come not from precept, but from
deeply settled character—"non consilio bonus, sed more;"—
and must be governed by a "second will more wise." The
unconscious part of the mind is the seat of wisdom. It is the
part—so difficult to know, but so important to be known—to
which the ancient "Know thyself" particularly refers. This is
the reason why Emerson depreciates the intellect as a guide and
the reason for his self-trust. "Who is the Trustee?" he asks.
"The inquiry leads us to that source, at once the essence of
genius, of virtue, and of life, which we call Spontaneity or
Instinct. . . . Every man discriminates between the voluntary
acts of his mind, and his involuntary perceptions, and knows
that to his involuntary perceptions a perfect faith is due. . . .
My wilful actions and acquisitions are but roving;—the idlest
reverie, the faintest native emotion, command my curiosity and
respect." [1] Carlyle's expression is to the same effect. "Of our
thinking, we might say, it is but the mere upper surface that we
shape into articulate thoughts; underneath the region of argu-

_____
[1] "Self-Reliance."

ment and conscious discourse, lies the region of meditation; here, in its quiet mysterious depths, dwells what vital force is in us; here, if aught is to be created, and not merely manufactured and communicated, must the work go on. Manufacture is intelligible, but trivial; creation is great, and cannot be understood. Thus, if the debater and demonstrator, whom we may rank as the lowest of true thinkers, knows what he has done, and how he did it, the artist, whom we rank as the highest, knows not; must speak of inspiration, and in one or the other dialect, call his work the gift of divinity." [1]

Poetry then is superior to prose because the latter is merely "conscious discourse;" while poetry is created in the "quiet mysterious depths." Just as in playing a game or playing upon a musical instrument one can do by instinct or second nature what would be impossible to consciously directed action, so the poet can contrive by instinct effects beyond the power of the conscious intellect, which indeed the intellect often cannot explain. The churchyard scene in *Hamlet*, for example, is felt to be strangely effective. Upon analysis many reasons may be assigned, of contrast and congruity, for its effectiveness; many reasons have been given by the annotators,—but not all of them; Shakespeare himself could not have given all of them. Read the scene and you feel that there are subtleties in the congruities and contrasts that escape you, that are inexplicable, though you may detect new ones each time you read. They are simply *there;* and not by chance; the reasons and the devices which are so carefully noted by the analysts, with many more, must have been weighed and elaborated in some way in the unconscious mind of the poet before the scene was projected by his imagination. In the same way the materials for this scene came from many directions, many experiences,—from many images stored in the poet's mind—some of them conscious, some unconscious—and of their sources Shakespeare himself could have given little account. Sophocles cried in wonder: "Æschylus does what is right without knowing it."

[1] *Essays,* "Characteristics."

II

Scenes like this in Shakespeare—the knocking at the gate in Macbeth, the finale in Othello—are beyond our analysis. They are marvellous, we say—infinite in meaning as nature itself, divine. We can wonder but not explain; and here the present book, like every other on the subject of poetry, must stop in awe before a mystery. Marvellous and "divine" as such scenes are, however, they are the product of the human mind, and surely of the mind working, not at random, but, like all else in nature, according to laws, which observation may hope sooner or later to establish. "I hold that ecstasy will be found normal," Emerson says, "or only an example on a higher plane of the same gentle gravitation by which stones fall and rivers run. Experience identifies. Shakespeare seems to you miraculous; but the wonderful juxtapositions, parallelisms, transfers, which his genius effected, were all to him locked together as links of a chain, and the mode precisely as conceivable and familiar to higher intelligence as the index-making of the literary hack." [1] By observation of the poetic product, and by comparison of it with myths and dreams, we can already get some inkling of the laws of this mode of thought,—at least we may collect similar cases and classify them, as a first step to a formulation of principles. When, for example, we take the cases already mentioned—the myth of the judgment of Paris, the stories in the Bible of Moses communing with God on Sinai, or of Christ in the wilderness tempted of the devil, and the scene in Byron between Cain and Lucifer in the Abyss of Space, with others like them, we are struck by their similarity of method, and by a law running through them all. In each there is represented a solitary meditation, and a projection of different parts or tendencies of the mind in the form of objectively imagined characters. We are almost in a position to generalize as to a law regarding the "splitting" and "objectification" of personality in fiction. In a later chapter I hope to note other cases of this sort which will justify

[1] *Letters and Social Aims*, "Inspiration."

some generalization concerning the working of the imagination in the formation of characters in poetry. Meanwhile a ray of light is thrown on the scene in Byron. Take another instance, of the little girl's fancy of a romantic birth, and compare it with the story of Cinderella, and with the myths giving miraculous birth to heroes. It is striking to find the same fancy in Carlyle's *Sartor Resartus*, where a mysterious stranger appears and leaves "a basket overhung with green Persian silk," containing the infant Diogenes, to the astonishment of the good Andreas and Gretchen, who would of course be quite unromantic parents for such a hero—like as they are to Carlyle's own father and mother. The basket is the exact analogue of the ark of bulrushes in the second chapter of *Exodus*. We are hardly ready to formulate a law, but we are less puzzled by this incident in Carlyle's "spiritual autobiography," and have a striking example of the Scotch peasant's mythopœic power. My only point here, however, is that there is some definiteness in the unconscious working of the imagination, and that we may hope some day to understand it, even in the divine Shakespeare, if we are not too much lost in admiration, and—I may add—not too much lost also in the futilities of modern Shakespearean annotation.

Productions of the kind we have just been examining, coming from a deep unconscious source, always have two characteristics, highly esteemed in literature, first an entire naturalness, and secondly an entire originality. "For in all vital things," Carlyle says, "men distinguish an artificial and a natural. . . . Thus we have an artificial poetry, and prize only the natural." But what is the difference between the two? "The artificial is the conscious, mechanical; the natural is the unconscious, dynamical." And again, "Unconsciousness is the sign of creation; consciousness at best that of manufacture." [1] So the poets look upon the conscious thought, guided by the will, as, so to speak, only a poor human contrivance,

---

[1] *Essays*, "Characteristics."

> that false secondary power
> By which we multiply distinctions, then
> Deem that our puny boundaries are things
> That we perceive, and not that we have made;

and on its product, science, as a makeshift,

> Not as our glory and our absolute boast,
> But as a succedaneum, and a prop
> To our infirmity.[1]

They look upon the unconscious mind, on the other hand, as the whole and true man, acting, not at the will's caprice, but spontaneously, with the ease and freedom of nature herself. "This instinct of imagination," Hazlitt says, "works unconsciously, like nature." [2] Their comparisons are to things in nature. "My conceptions," says Remy de Gourmont, "rise into the field of consciousness like a flash of lightning or like the flight of a bird." "Corneille," according to Voltaire, "composed the scene between Horatius and Curiatius just as the bird builds its nest." [3] Emerson uses the same figure:

> Know'st thou what wove yon woodbird's nest
> Of leaves, and feathers from her breast?
> Or how the fish outbuilt her shell,
> Painting with morn her annual cell?
>
> . . . .
>
> The hand that rounded Peter's dome
> And groined the aisles of Christian Rome
> Wrought in a sad sincerity:
> Himself from God he could not free;
> He builded better than he knew;—
> The conscious stone to beauty grew.
>
> . . . .

[1] Wordsworth, *Prelude*, Book ii.
[2] *English Comic Writers*, ed. W. C. Hazlitt, p. 147.
[3] Letter to Diderot, April 20, 1773.

> These temples grew as grows the grass;
> Art might obey, but not surpass.
> The passive Master lent his hand
> To the vast soul that o'er him planned.

That is, this deeper part of the mind produces, not the deceptions complained of by Wordsworth, but realities corresponding to the realities of nature. And these products are original, as nature is always. Mozart, after telling of composing music in a trance-like state, as noted in an earlier chapter, says that in music like this he never had to bother about originality; it was as much his own as the features of his own face. The imagination may take plot, characters, scenes, wherever it may find them, and borrow as it will; it transforms everything and finally creates in its own likeness. The mechanical artist is like a tennis player who consciously adopts another's style and is affected and unnatural; the master plays by instinct and second nature in a style all his own. Both the substance and the style of the true poet are inimitable.

Conscious thought expresses itself readily in words, and is voluble; but its speech, like its other products, is according to the poets, shallow and deceptive. The deeper mind is silent, and for this reason, according to Carlyle, "silence is golden." Or if it must express itself, it can do so only in symbols—in significant pictures. "In a symbol there is concealment and yet revelation: here, therefore, by silence and speech acting together, comes a double significance."[1] Such expressions have the truth of the oracles of nature.

Concealment and yet revelation;—it is curious that this characteristic should run all through; that just as the subjects of poetry, as we have found, are in the region that is half revealed and half concealed, so its expression should partake of the same shadowy character; and that again it should have its origin in the region of the mind where the conscious and the known runs off, so to speak, into the unconscious and the unknown. Thus poetry

---

[1] *Sartor*, Book iii, ch. iii.

partakes inevitably of the nature of its subjects, and is itself a subject—the suggestion is clear—which can be treated only poetically. Perhaps the best one can do in prose is to collect the expressions of the poets themselves, as I have tried to do here, and so drive the obscurity a little farther off.

A further consequence of this unconscious source of poetry must be mentioned. The unconscious is the more permanent and stable part of the mind. It cannot be increased or diminished by volition; on the other hand it perhaps grows with every action and impression, and has so grown from the beginning. Upon this fund the poet is largely dependent. The lawyer can work up his case; but the poet, writing a poem, cannot work up a case; he must draw on a deeply digested experience. The inspiration, when it comes, may come suddenly, and be soon over; but it is not to be depreciated because momentary and fleeting. This moment is only the crisis in a long process; behind it is presumably an incubation, and behind that an earlier preparation. Early experiences, emotionally colored, are sources of later poetical moments, repeating the emotion; and "feeling comes in aid of feeling." Thus the great poet must be one who has had a full and fortunate life,—and particularly a rich and favorable emotional development in childhood and youth. Such was the development of Wordsworth:

> Fair seed-time had my soul, and I grew up
> Fostered alike by beauty and by fear. [1]

In inspiration, then, there is first a long preparation of the mind, then a period of incubation, and finally an emergence of the thought into the conscious mind at an "inspired moment." The conscious mind is perhaps often vaguely and uneasily aware of the process of incubation—of a burden underneath of which the mind is to be delivered, and the delivery, though sometimes accompanied by throes, sometimes by feelings of pleasure, comes as a mental relief. A simple example may be given. Poe in "Ligeia" tells of the feeling of the narrator in contemplating

[1] *Prelude*, Book i.

the eyes of Ligeia—of a meaning in them which he could never fathom. "Yet not the more could I define that sentiment, or analyze, or even steadily view it." It is an unconscious feeling, then, struggling to the surface. Poe compares this state of mind to another. "There is no point, among the many incomprehensible anomalies of the science of mind, more thrillingly exciting, than the fact—never, I believe, noticed in the schools— that, in our endeavors to recall to memory something long forgotten, we often find ourselves *upon the very verge* of remembrance, without being, in the end, able to remember." This state of mind has, by the way, been frequently noticed in the schools. It is akin to the consciousness of what I have vaguely called incubation. Sometimes after the struggle to remember, the mind becomes a little relaxed in the direction of associative thinking, we "think of something else," and the matter "saunters into the mind as innocently as if it had never been sent for," accompanied by a feeling of relief.

Curiously this emergence, this birth of thought, is often described by men of genius in figures suggesting an analogy between mental and physiological creation,—an analogy which some facts seem to support.[1] The following is an example: "On several occasions," Goethe says, "the scratching and spluttering of my pen awoke me from my somnambulistic poetizing and distracted me so that it suffocated a little product in its birth. I had a particular reverence for such pieces, like a hen for her brood of chickens pipping around her."[2] Sometimes the operation is painful, as in Alfred de Musset. "Invention annoys me and makes me tremble. Execution, always too slow to suit me, makes my heart beat awfully, and in tears, and trying not to cry aloud, I am delivered of an idea that is intoxicating me, but of which I am mortally ashamed and disgusted the next morning." And again: "It presses and tortures me, until it has taken realizable proportions, when comes the other pain, of

[1] See Ribot, *Creative Imagination*, p. 74.
[2] Quoted by Hirsch, *Genius and Degeneration*, p. 33.

bringing forth, a truly physical suffering that I cannot define." [1]

But always the operation is described as one in which the conscious mind has small share. Thus de Musset again: "It is not work, it is listening, it is as if some unknown person were speaking in your ear;" and Lamartine: "It is not I who think, but my ideas who think for me." George Eliot declared "that in all she considered her best writing there was a 'not herself' which took possession of her, and that she felt her own personality to be merely the instrument through which this spirit, as it were, was acting." [2] Sully Prudhomme, like Stevenson, looks on as if the work were another's: "In writing these dramas I seemed to be a spectator at the play; I gazed at what was passing on the scene in an eager passionate expectation of what was to follow. And yet I felt that I was author of all that was enacted and that it came from the depths of my being." [3] It is almost as if not merely two minds, but two persons were at work,—while one creates the other listens or watches; while one is in rapture, the other stands open-eyed at the performance.[4] Indeed in the fic-

---

[1] George Sand, *Elle et Lui*, I.

[2] Cross, *Life of George Eliot*.

[3] Quoted by Chabaneix.

[4] A minor writer of true inspiration, Joel Chandler Harris, gives an instructive account of his composition, showing the unconscious element, the projection of the imaginative faculty, and also the relief afforded by imaginative expression. He writes to his daughter at school:

As for myself,—though you could hardly call me a real, sure enough author—I never have anything but the vaguest ideas of what I am going to write; but when I take my pen in my hand, the rust clears away and the "other fellow" takes charge. You know all of us have two entities, or personalities. That is the reason you see and hear persons "talking to themselves." They are talking to the "other fellow." I have often asked my "other fellow" where he gets all his information, and how he can remember, in the nick of time, things that I have forgotten long ago; but he never satisfies my curiosity. He is simply a spectator of my folly until I seize a pen, and then he comes forward and takes charge.

Sometimes I laugh heartily at what he writes. If you could see me at

tion of Poe, in whom the two minds were both highly gifted, the creative and the critical, there is a splitting of personality on just this line: in several tales there are two characters, the imaginative poet and the cool narrator, who represent the two planes of Poe's own mind. A similar projection accounts for the common assumption that inspiration comes from without. Jones Very said he valued his poems, not because they were his, but because they were not,—thus expressing his feeling that they came from his deeper mind. Invocation of Apollo, Urania, or the "heavenly muse," is equivalent to solicitation of the unconscious mind by the conscious one. As the will is powerless, prayer is the only recourse.

The conscious and the unconscious, which have been discussed in this chapter, correspond in part, as has been implied in the discussion, to the two modes of thought described in the earlier

such times, and they are very frequent, you would no doubt say, "It is very conceited in that old man to laugh at his own writing." But that is the very point; it is not my writing at all; it is my "other fellow" doing the work and I am getting all the credit for it. Now, I'll admit that I write the editorials for the paper. The "other fellow" has nothing to do with them, and, so far as I am able to get his views on the subject, he regards them with scorn and contempt; though there are rare occasions when he helps me out on a Sunday editorial. He is a creature hard to understand, but, so far as I can understand him, he's a very sour, surly fellow until I give him an opportunity to guide my pen in subjects congenial to him; whereas, I am, as you know, jolly, good-natured, and entirely harmless.

Now, my "other fellow," I am convinced, would do some damage if I didn't give him an opportunity to work off his energy in the way he delights. I say to him, "Now, here's an editor who says he will pay well for a short story. He wants it at once." Then I forget all about the matter, and go on writing editorials and taking Celery Compound, and presently my "other fellow" says sourly, "What about that story?" Then when night comes, I take up my pen, surrender unconditionally to my "other fellow," and out comes the story, and if it is a good story I am as much surprised as the people who read it. Now, my dear gals will think I am writing nonsense; but I am telling them the truth as near as I can get at the facts—for the "other fellow" is secretive.—Julia C. Harris, *Life and Letters*, p. 384.

pages. For our purposes—that is, for the understanding of
poetry—the latter are still the important conceptions. Before
going on, I shall stop here to restate the principles involved in
these two modes of thought as we may now regard them. The
statement may look strange to a psychologist, but it will be a
fair summary in outline, I think, of the descriptions of the working of the mind to be found in literature,—upon which the conceptions are mainly based. The older associative or imaginative
operation of the mind is the primary thought—the function of
that whole in which we live, move, and have our being. From
this the voluntary thought is a secondary and specialized development, in the way of practical adaptation, growing from the
first, as the arm and hand grow from the body. It is governed
by the will, as the hand by the voluntary muscles. It can grasp
a subject, and handle it for practical purposes, as the other cannot—just as the hand can grasp an object which the body cannot
touch. It has had great development in deftness within the
period observable in history. But it is as far from being the
action of the whole mind as the hand is from being the whole
body. Corresponding to these two operations are the mental
funds upon which they draw and which they utilize. The fund
of the primary thought is larger, more permanent, more central
and vital. Of this a part—doubtless that adapted to practice—
is specialized and devoted to the uses of voluntary thought. It
can be drawn upon at will in memory. It is our fund of
available knowledge, while the other is nearer the whole of our
mentally recorded experience.

Now it is the secondary faculty which is ordinarily employed
—employed, for example, by me as I write and by the reader as
he reads. While we are thus engaged the operations of the other
thought are all more or less hidden from us. We can at best only
look over into them. We can now only recollect how the mind
seems to have been working as we sat absorbed in day dream.
The process, moreover, runs away into obscurity—into what we
call the *unconscious operation* of the mind. Similarly while we are
thus engaged in practical thought we can command only a por-

tion of the entire mental fund. This portion we can investigate.
But the other mode of thought commands not only this but
much besides, much that we can recall with difficulty or not at
all. Perhaps it would be of no use to us in the day's work if we
could recall it—if we could remember say a trifling experience
of childhood. But the imagination may nevertheless utilize
it in a picture. Such an experience forms part of the *unconscious
material* of the mind.

Poetry then, as a product of the more general mental faculty,
runs into the unconscious in the ways I have described. In
what follows, however, it will be less necessary to refer to the
unconscious than to keep still before us the two modes of
thought. We may go on then to inquire if any other characteristics of poetry may be explained by the peculiar mode in
which it is produced.

CHAPTER VII

THE UNIVERSALITY OF POETRY

I

IT is characteristic of the imaginative mode of thought,—of the phantasy as I have called it—and of poetry as one of its products, that, compared with voluntary thought, it is less individual and limited, more general and nearer to the universal and the absolute.

This arises in the first place from the circumstance that the phantasy is more free from the limitations of time and space. As a consequence, we may suppose, of its material embodiment the mind is fixed, and at any moment occupies one time and one place; as I am *here* and *now*. In the course of mortal life it occupies many *heres* and a long succession of *nows*, which are more or less connected by memory and hope. This series, however, is limited by the length of life, to a small number of parts of the world and a small period of time. From this physical limitation there is no escape, as we may imagine there might be for a disembodied and deathless mind, or for the perfect mind,— which would be omnipresent and eternal, as we conceive the mind of God. The limits thus put upon individual experience may be qualified somewhat by impressions got by report of other lands and other ages, an imaginary reaching of them taking the place to some extent of an actual one. But essentially the poet's experience is thus limited; and Shakespeare is the poet of Elizabethan England, not of Greece in the time of Pericles. This is obvious, but I shall presently want to return to it.

In ordinary thought we think within the forms of time and space. Considering the practical nature of such thought this is obviously necessary. Primitive man, first exercising this thought and seeking food or defense, would have found it necessary immediately to fix such relations. With the development of his senses he learned to perceive immediate duration and extent, and he presently advanced from these to the conception of general time and space. He also developed memory and hope or foresight, by which images, perhaps of different places, were properly referred as belonging to past or future. To the practical life, individual or social, these two charts of time and space, upon which all impressions may be located, are indispensable.

But while ordinary thought is thus rigorously subject to these temporal and spatial conditions, thought of the other order is not. The two charts are modified, distorted, and even, in a sense, dispensed with. It would be expected that as thought recedes from the external life of the senses and gives up its adaptation to reality, and as it becomes more subjective and free, this modification would occur. But let us see some of the particulars.

It is curious that a dreamer will weave into his dream a loud sound that he hears, like the sound of a gun, with appropriate details leading up to it. These details, one would think, must have been imagined subsequently, but they are represented in the dream as antecedent, or at least so remembered. The succession in the dream is apparently different from the succession which we call actual. This is illustrated by the celebrated dream of Maury, who, when he was awakened by a portion of the bed cornice falling on him, had dreamed that he was living in the days of the Reign of Terror, and, after many adventures, was being guillotined. This shows also that the operation of the mind in the second mode of thought is so different, so much faster, that all ordinary sense of duration must be lost. The dreamer is apparently able to form a long dream, with scenes and details, crowding it all into the moment between the perception of a waking stimulus and the awakening. The same is true of waking vision. Time is nothing to the visionary; he forgets about it, has no sense of its lapse, and is conscious only of the present images. Jacob Behmen said after moments of inspiration, "In one quarter of an hour I saw and knew more than if I had been many years together at the university."[1] John Addington Symonds describes a state of trance to which he was recurrently subject, without his volition, until the age of twenty-eight. This "consisted in a gradual, but swiftly progressive obliteration of time, space, sensation, and the multitudinous factors which seem to qualify what we are pleased to call ourself. . . . At last nothing remained but a pure, absolute, abstract self."[2] The experience is the same in ordinary day dream, if the absorption is strong; the dreamer cannot tell what time it is when he awakes. The visionary "can crowd eternity into an hour, or stretch an hour into eternity." Evidently our conception of time is based entirely upon our ordinary conscious thought. Evidently also our ordinary conception of space is lost in dream and vision. The visionary is like the poet:

Modo me Thebis, modo ponit Athenis.

In another regard there is in the second order of thought hardly sense of time and space at all. The picture presented in dream or vision has of course something like ordinary place, with visualized spatial relations, but the place as a whole is absolute, —that is, there is no conception of the relation of this place to any other. In the same way the picture has time, in that successive actions go on in it, and there are also successive pictures. But there is no conception of the relation of time. There is a succession *in* thought but no thought *of* succession, and these two things are different.[3] The time again is absolute. There is, by the way, also no notion of the relation of cause and effect between successive pictures, this being another conception of practical thought which the dream does not represent. The theory is something as follows. When an image comes into the mind in ordinary waking thought it is always at first accepted

[1] Quoted by Emerson, "Inspiration."

[2] H. F. Brown, *Symonds*, vol. i, p. 29.

[3] See James, *Psychology*, vol. i, p. 629.

in itself as an existent reality. It is then by a second operation of the mind subjected to criticism, which, for example, gives or withholds belief, assigns it to the present or to the past.[1] Now in vision much of this criticism is lacking. The imagination presents an image and it is simply accepted. This explains why the presentations of the imagination are always, at the moment, received as true and not as what we call merely "imaginary." The child playing horse is carried away, and resents the suggestion that the horse is only a broomstick. The mystical visionary believes that he sees God face to face, and, like the dreamer, often has a belief so strong that it is carried over even into waking life. The dreamer, while he is dreaming certainly, does not question his dream.[2] It is the same with the matter of time. The image is simply presented and received; there is no criticism to fix its place in time. It would be equivalent to say that in vision there is properly no memory. There is of course a presentation of images brought from what in conscious thought we would call past experience. But in dream the image has no pastness. In memory, according to James, there are two elements; first, a revival in the mind of an image of the original event; secondly, an express reference of the image to the past.[3] Now in vision this second element is absent. There is therefore only the presentation; the image from the past stands on the same basis as any other. In the same way there is no reference of the image to the future. And in the same way spatial relations are lost.

This may be too dogmatic in statement. I may here repeat that I do not think of the two modes of thought as sharply separated, but as running one into the other, by a decline or by stages. And I only mean to say here that the second mode of thought tends to do away with the criticism of the first, and that, in pure vision, there would be merely a presentation of images which are *here* and *now*—which in fact are not even here

[1] James, *Psychology*, vol. ii, p. 286; Ribot, *Creative Imagination*, p.110.

[2] We are thought indeed sometimes to dream "this is only a dream." See Ellis, *World of Dreams*, p. 65.

[3] *Psychology*, vol. i, p. 648.

and now, because these words imply relation—but which simply
are. The tendency is toward the absolute.

What I have said at any rate will bear out the original statement that when we come to the second order of thought the
charts of time and space largely go to pieces. In dream or in
reverie we see before us and intimately feel the presence of
scenes from the distant past and of persons long since dead, with
no thought that they are of the past. It is as if our whole past
experience were potentially with us in our deeper thought, with
no separating gaps of space and time. Or it is as if instead of
being fixed, as we are in waking thought, at one point in the two
charts, we might be indifferently at any point—within the region
that has been touched by our experience of course—but also
without having any knowledge that the charts exist. Memory
becomes a free reproduction of scenes past, represented however
as present; hope becomes a free picturing of what we desire in the
future, represented, however, again as present. A dim idea of the
freedom of the imagination was probably behind the belief
common among primitive peoples that in sleep the spirit was
released from the body to wander at will; the notion does not
seem grotesque if we look at it in the right way. This freedom
from time explains why Emerson, in speaking of the desire for
immortality, should say that "the soul is true to itself, and the
man in whom it is shed abroad cannot wander from the present,
which is infinite, to a future [or to a past] which would be finite." [1]
And why Carlyle should write, "Think well, thou too wilt find
that space is but a mode of our human sense, so likewise time;
there *is* no space and no time; *we are*—we know not what." [2]

The Greeks represented Pegasus, like the angels which are
pure spirit, with wings. This perhaps suggests the freedom that
poetry gains coming from this thought unconditioned by time
and space. As the poetic vision is timeless so the poetic product
tends to be so. Since the inspiration must be embodied in language, and of a period, it suffers limits also from this incarnation,

---

[1] "The Oversoul."   [2] *Sartor Resartus*, Book i, ch. viii.

but there is still something of the freedom of the spirit. The rhythm of verse, conveying the feeling, is, like pure music, time-less,—except in so far as peculiar qualities would indicate a period. A poem like "Ulalume," without thought and close to mere music, is nearly absolute in time. So all of Poe's work, like his poem "Dream-land," is "out of space, out of time;"— the action even in many of the tales might go on in any country and in any age. In Poe, as in the "symbolists" and "imagists," the substance as well as the form is universal. In this kind of art, as Ribot expresses it, "everything floats in a dream, men as well as things, often without mark in time or space. Something happens, one knows not where or when; it belongs to no country, it is of no period of time; it is *the* forest, *the* traveler, *the* city, *the* knight, *the* wood; less frequently even *He, She, It*." [1] In recent pictorial art the representations are thus often mere abstract symbols. But in all art this symbolism and abstraction are the essential method; recent experiments only try to further rid it of the trammels of its material embodiment and free it in time and space. In Sophocles also it is *the* king, *the* son, *the* city—the trammels are insignificant and the meaning universal. In Aesop's fable the wind and the sun try their strength upon the universal traveller. This explains why the scientific treatise is for a day, while poetry is for all time, and why the song of Deborah is still current and valid after thirty centuries.

Shelley expresses this most definitely: "A poet participates in the eternal, the infinite, and the one; as far as relates to his con-ceptions, time and place and number are not. The grammatical forms which express the moods of time, and the difference of persons [tenses and persons of the verb] and the distinction of place, are convertible with respect to the highest poetry without injuring it as poetry." He gives Æschylus, Job, and Dante as examples. Conversely the reasoners, according to Shelley, apply the general of the poet to the particular case. "They follow the footsteps of poets, and copy the sketches of their creations into

[1] *Creative Imagination*, p. 203.

the book of common life. They make space and give time." To summarize Shelley's example, the poet generalizes, when he gives us the character of Antigone, or Beatrice, or Juliet; they are universal. The legislator gives time and place when he passes a particular law for the enfranchisement of women. But not even in the greatest poet is the abstraction complete. The poet after all belongs himself to an age and country. Shakespeare must attempt to present the universal in terms of Elizabethan England. Shelley says again: "A poet considers the vices of his contemporaries as the temporary dress in which his creations must be arrayed, and which cover without concealing the eternal proportions of their beauty. An epic or dramatic personage is understood to wear them around his soul, as he may the ancient armor or modern uniform around his body; whilst it is easy to conceive a dress more graceful than either. The beauty of the internal nature cannot be so far concealed by its accidental vesture, but that the spirit of its form shall communicate itself to the very disguise, and indicate the shape it hides from the manner in which it is worn. . . . Few poets of the highest class have chosen to exhibit the beauty of their conceptions in its native truth and splendor; and it is doubtful whether the alloy of costume, habit, etc., be not necessary to temper this planetary music for mortal ears." [1]

At any rate this alloy amounts to little; if a poem is a true product of the imagination it will have the range and freedom belonging to its source. This is one reason why, according to Aristotle, poetry is superior to history. History is bound to record actual facts in the temporal order of their occurrence. Poetry exhibits events in an order imposed only by the imagination, "according to what is probable or necessary." [2] Indeed this freedom of poetry in time and space is closely related to Aristotle's doctrine of the universal. Further the nature of the imagination itself is probably in part behind the instinctive ob-

[1] *Defense of Poetry*, ed. Cook, pp. 6, 34, 12.

[2] James defines fancy as "the association of ideas without temporal order." —*Psychology*, vol. i, p. 598.

servance among the Greeks of the dramatic unities of time and place. The pictures presented by the imagination in poetic vision are *here* and *now*. This is properly expressed by an unbroken dramatic *here* and *now*. Conversely when, as in modern plays, there is first a scene in Paris and then another in New York "twelve years later," the tendency is toward history; and I believe an audience will instinctively feel the objection. The play is felt to be a series of five dramatic acts and a dozen scenes, historically elaborated, not like the Greek drama as one act of the creative imagination.

We find then that poetry owes its general character and wide application partly to the very nature of the thought from which it springs. Poetry always has an alloy of time and place, but the pure poetry to which this alloy clings is unqualified. It represents the past and future as present; or rather it makes the past, present, and future of our ordinary thought into a oneness which must be expressed in our language by the present tense; but which is independent of all tenses. If there were no alloy the forms of the imagination would stand "out of space, out of time"—valid for the race everywhere and always.

II

This general character of poetry follows also from other considerations, closely related to those just spoken of but requiring separate treatment. It follows from the fact that the voluntary thought is practical and hence narrow and calculating, while the imagination, freed from practical aim, is relatively indifferent and disinterested. Ordinary thought has greater immediate grasp and deftness, but obviously it must secure this advantage by a limitation and a compensating loss of freedom. It is controlled by the will, apparently the most individual of the mental powers, and hence it is not only practical, but more self-seeking than the relaxed thought. We are taught that the conscious will is a relatively shallow faculty, to be distrusted, that though a strong will is valuable in action, deeper wisdom comes only in its surrender,—for the deeper will which Emerson calls spontaneity or instinct. Hence it is with a loss of course, but with perhaps a greater gain, that we pass from attentive to free thought. The mind becomes disinterested. It is then "amused in perceiving for the sake of perceiving and in remembering for the sake of remembering, without care for life, that is to say for the accomplishment of actions." [1]

This, to take a case which is between an example and a parallel, is somewhat the state of mind in which Lamb wrote the Essays of Elia, and it explains their peculiar value. Lamb's reasoning faculty was next to nothing, his imagination constant. He makes at most "crude essays at a system," and pretends only to "hints and glimpses." Compare his whole process with that of the ordinary prose writer. Newman, for example, writes always with practical purpose, to develop, by reasoning, a preconceived thought. He gives you this thought, but no hint of the thousand others which may lie hidden in the recesses of his mind. Lamb, on the other hand, is what some one has called a "disinterested servant of literature." He has no set subject, no aim voluntarily pre-established. He is purposeless, and writes literally as the spirit moves. He follows the train of images that floats through his mind, almost as simply as a child, recording it in sentences loose, broken, almost without trace of logical organization. "Dream Children," a mere reverie, in a style of utter looseness, is after all not very different from other essays. Throughout Lamb's thinking is mainly associative rather than voluntary. As a result he does not develop one organized thought but lays before us the whole content of his mind, with many thoughts and much wisdom. The relaxation and broadening give a quite unusual effect.

Ordinary thought then in its working is bound, vision is free. There is the same difference between the funds upon which the two kinds of thought draw; the first is practical and narrow, the second broader and more indifferent. We presumably hold subject to conscious recollection what will be of use to practical

---

[1] See quotation, *ante*, p. 92.

thought. This is illustrated by the fact that we often remember a thing well as long as we have to use it, and afterwards rapidly forget it. A schoolboy remembers only until the examination is over, and the lawyer soon forgets what he has learned for a particular case. On the other hand a name will come when we *have* to use it. This fund subject to memory is doubtless held together by a more or less conscious effort. "When the use of a record is withdrawn," as R. Verdon notes, "and attention withdrawn from it, and we think no more about it, we know that we experience a feeling of relief . . . . If the . . . attention is not withdrawn, so that we keep the record in mind we know that this feeling of relief does not take place. . . . Also we are well aware, not only that after this feeling of relief takes place, the record does not seem so well conserved as before, but that we have real difficulty in attempting to remember it." [1] Considerations like this suggest that any matter is held in the conscious mind subject to memory by some effort, that when this effort is seen to be of no further practical value and is relaxed, the matter then sinks into the deeper mind.[2] Here, however, if our earlier theory is correct, it may be drawn upon by the imagination. This second or unconscious fund will be more general and indifferent; it will not be a selection from experience of what we think may help us along, but will more nearly correspond to our total experience. Poetry then draws from this larger source, and has corresponding advantage. Poetry represents not a willfully limited portion of the mind, but more nearly the whole. The poet, Emerson says, "stands among partial men for the complete

[1] Quoted by James, *Psychology*, vol. i, p. 685.

[2] This does not quite agree with the theory of the psychoanalysts, who say that unpleasant or painful matters are "repressed." Consider, however, that very painful matters are kept before the mind if it is practically necessary. But a desire which is incapable of satisfaction and hence both painful and impracticable will be repressed. The will to hold would doubtless be weaker where the matter is painful. It is this repressed matter which, according to the psychoanalysts, starts neurotic illusions, and these correspond to the poetry of the text above.

man, and apprises us not of his wealth, but of the common-wealth."[1] He expresses not our immediate and selfish desires, but the deeper feelings and aspirations which we share as members of the race. It is partly to this circumstance that poetry owes its universality.

This will perhaps show some disagreement with the Freudian conception that in dreams, and I suppose therefore also in other imaginary presentations, we "lead to the full the individual life;" that in dreams we give our animal impulses unbridled license, and satisfy our desires selfishly without altruistic thought. It is true that in dreams we are no longer bound by the laws governing our conscious action, and that in dreams there is properly no ordinary moral judgment. The morality of dreams is different from that of waking life. We are properly held responsible, by human law at any rate, not for our dreams and imaginings, but only for our conscious thoughts and actions. The point is worth bringing up because it seems to argue a general moral inferiority of the unconscious as compared with the conscious mind. The subject must not be considered too narrowly, however. For example, much of the "immorality" charged against the dream is due to the fact that it gives free reign to the sexual impulses. Now the matter of love and sexual selection is expressly assigned by nature to the instinct,—that is to the unconscious mind. A man chooses his mate not consciously and voluntarily, but in exactly the opposite way; he finds himself in love. And this perhaps because the choice is not so much an individual matter, as one which concerns the race as a whole, which cannot be left to individual volition. The deeper choice is the wiser. And in general the imaginings of the unconscious mind will represent a deeper wisdom and morality. The subject is much too large to be treated in a paragraph; but I think careful consideration might show that the responsibility of the individual to society or to morality in conscious thought and action is one thing, and the responsibility in visionary unconscious thought quite another; and that though the dreamer

[1] *Essays*, "The Poet."

is freed from social obligation in a narrow sense, he is brought into relation with the mind of the race in a larger way and thus subjected to a more profound control.

I have already suggested that the deeper thought, in which poetry has its source, is in some sense racial rather than individual. The evidence indicating this is more or less speculative but worth producing because it illustrates the breadth and depth of poetry, and supports its universality. To suggest graphically how in this view the mind may be regarded, I might extend the figure of the preceding chapter, in which the conscious mind was compared to the visible island and the unconscious mind to its submerged base. If the obscuring waters were removed we might see that this foundation runs into others, all of which at some depth merge in one continent. The visible mind is individual, even its submerged base is partly so, but the deeper foundations—the unconscious portions of the mind—may not be so isolated as they at first appear.

That they are not isolated is the point on which Emerson insists most strongly. He sees the great continent below even more clearly than the individual islands. It is the virtue of Emerson, as it is perhaps of the New England transcendentalists generally, that he treats mysteries of the soul as matters of homely interest and writes of them with corresponding plainness and distinctness. His sentences, to take their place in an exposition like the present one, often need hardly be taken as poetry at all, but almost as plain statement of fact. "The mind is one," he says then, and it knows nothing of persons. There is a general mind "within which every man's particular being is contained and made one with all other." And again, "There is one mind common to all individual men. Every man is an inlet to the same and to all of the same." Upon this we must rely; but relying on oneself, confiding in the "genius of the age," and obeying "the Almighty effort" all come to the same thing. Furthermore, as Emerson believes, revelation—in other words the inspiration which is the subject of this book—is precisely an influx into consciousness from this unique mind.

Now the "Over-Soul" and "Self-Reliance" would hardly be read so widely and so eagerly if there were not truth in sentences like these; and there is evidence, if not scientific, at least literary, indicating that Emerson is right.

The mind is one. In what possible senses? Some facts not readily observed but familiar to everyone suggest that in its deeper portions the individual mind is more closely related to other minds than is at once apparent. The peculiar sympathies established between individuals without speech, the epidemic character of large ideas and feelings, the behavior of mobs, suggest that the minds of a group of persons may to some degree act as an organism and think as one. Accumulating, if not convincing evidence indicates that there may be transference of impressions from one unconscious mind to another, or telepathic communication. The feeling which is deeper than all thought particularly may be so communicated. Moreover, the individual mind may share not merely the mind of contemporaries but also that of its ancestors. This is seen most clearly in the mind of the child. The child's mind, not yet acclimated and individualized, living over, we may suppose, the psychological history of the race in little, is nearer to the common mind than that of the adult. Like his ancestors he passes through a bow-and-arrow stage, and this can be only because their mind is his and his theirs,—because, to use the old expression, his soul is *ex traduce*. Such facts suggest that there is a large unity and continuity in the life of the mind, and that expressions like the "mind of man" and the "genius of the age" are something more than abstractions. Man must have "innate ideas" (in some sense) and sentiments which cannot be explained as arising from his individual experience. The truth thus regarded scientifically has been expressed poetically by Plato in his doctrine of pre-existence and by Wordsworth in his "Intimations."

> Our birth is but a sleep and a forgetting;
> The Soul that rises with us, our life's Star,
>   Hath had elsewhere its setting,
>   And cometh from afar.

Orthodox persons, including the later Wordsworth, have questioned this teaching, but most readers probably accept it and agree with Wordsworth the poet. From it follows all Wordsworth's doctrine of the wisdom and imagination of childhood, and of their survival in maturer years. From this unformed mind of childhood grows the conscious mind and the voluntary thought by a specialization; and with this growth comes an increased isolation and individuality. But the deeper mind is retained still, with its imaginative power; and even in manhood it is still more racial and more a sharer in the common mind. Still

> Our souls have sight of that immortal sea
> Which brought us hither.

And it is from this larger mind that poetry proceeds. Poetry looks

> To the ancestral light that glows above
> Its mirrored lights in time.[1]

To Wordsworth's familiar theory we may add the fancies of other writers; for we may (without depreciation) call them fancies until they can be more definitely and rationally regarded. Poets often fancy that they may draw upon pre-natal experience, that they have feelings, and even images coming from an experience earlier than their own. "It is thus," Stevenson says, "that tracts of young fir, and low rocks that reach into deep soundings, particularly torture and delight me." Who has not shared his feeling of torture and delight? "Something," he continues, "must have happened in such places, and perhaps ages back, to members of my race; and when I was a child I tried

---

[1] G. W. Russell, *The Candle of Vision*, who expresses the view of recent mystics that in vision and dream we do not merely refashion individual memories. "We have access to a memory greater than our own, the treasure-house of august memories in the innumerable being of earth." The spiritualists who receive communications from their ancestors, or write with the pen of Socrates or St. Paul, are apparently only symbolizing in a crude way this ineradicable belief in the common mind.

in vain to invent appropriate names for them, as I still try, just as vainly, to fit them with a proper story." [1] Lafcadio Hearn similarly fancies that fear of ghosts, the "Nightmare Touch," and other "feelings thus voluminous and dim are super-individual mostly,—feelings inherited,—feelings made within us by the experience of the dead." And he explains in the same way the magic "In a Pair of Eyes." "Not to actuality belongs the spell,—not to anything that *is*,—but to some infinite composite phantom of what has been. . . . The splendor of the eyes that we worship belongs to them only as brightness to the morning star. It is a reflex from beyond the shadow of the Now,—a ghost-light of vanished suns. Unknowingly within that maiden gaze we meet the gaze of eyes more countless than the hosts of heaven,—eyes otherwhere passed into darkness and dust." [2]

If fancies like this correspond to truth the poet draws, per-haps for his images, at any rate for his feelings, on a reservoir of experience very much larger than his own.

> So come to the Poet his songs,
>   All hitherward blown
> From the misty realm, that belongs
>   To the vast Unknown.
>
> His, and not his, are the lays
>   He sings; and their fame
> Is his, and not his; and the praise
>   And the pride of a name. [3]

The poetic vision, as compared with ordinary thought, is less individual and more racial; it becomes the organ of the com-mon mind; it embraces a much larger purview, including the past of the whole race,—and to some extent even its future. Just as the individual's foresight will be dim for his own future, so this vision will be dim for that of the race,—yet will fore-shadow it. This explains the greater wisdom of poetry. It also

---

[1] "A Gossip on Romance."   [2] *Shadowings*.
[3] Longfellow, "L'Envoi."

gives one clue to the prophetic character of poetry, which must be considered later. It puts the universality of poetry, which is the subject of the present chapter, in a new light.

We may note here further that if the poetic thought is thus the product, not of the individual mind merely, but to some extent of the common mind,—if the poet speaks for and from the race,—this fact after all justifies the mythical projection of the poetic inspiration and its assignment to external agencies,—the muses and other celestial patrons. We have hitherto thought of the poetic faculty as a hidden one but belonging entirely to the poet himself, and of Apollo as a fictional externalization of this faculty. We now see that—if this faculty of the poet is "his and not his,"—the poet is, in a deep sense, right in thinking of his inspiration as coming from without.

CHAPTER VIII

THE DESIRES AND EMOTIONS IN POETRY

I

WE have now considered in some detail the peculiarities of the poetic thought; its history in the childhood of man and of the race, its proper subjects—that is, the matters outside (or even within) the mind which arouse it and with which it deals,—its depth in the unconscious mind, and its scope or universality. We have already considered to some extent also its operation and product. We must now go on to investigate these last named matters more fully, to enquire how this "dream power" of the poet, as Emerson calls it, operates, what are its sources of material within the mind, and what the nature of its product.

The poetic thought, as we have seen, is in concrete images,—that is, the imagination is always at work. It is warmed by feeling,—that is, emotion of some kind is always an accompaniment. Its images do not represent external reality, but something parallel to this and above it,—in other words they accord with external reality but also with the demands of the mind itself. Let us take this last point first; then go on to consider the emotional side of poetry, and finally the imagination and its working in detail.

The poetic vision presents images corresponding to reality, but also to the demands of the mind,—that is to the poet's wishes, desires, or aspirations. This is parallel to the principle that dreams are the imaginary fulfillment of the dreamer's ungratified wishes. That dreams are often prompted by desire is not a new idea in psychology; it goes back at least to 1851; [1]

---

[1] Janet, *Les Médications Psychologiques*, vol. ii, p. 220, citing Maury and Charma.

and it certainly is not new in literature. Nietzsche represents a common view in supposing "that our dreams, to a certain extent, are able and intended to compensate for the accidental non-appearance of sustenance," or satisfaction for our cravings, "during the day. . . . These fictions, which give scope and utterance to our cravings for tenderness or merriment, or adventurousness, or to our longing after music or mountains,— and everybody will have striking instances at hand—are interpretations of our nervous irritations during sleep. . . . The fact that this text [of our nervous irritations] which, on the whole, remains very much the same for one night as another, is so differently commented upon, that reason in its poetic efforts, on two successive days, imagines such different causes for the same nervous irritations, may be explained by the prompter of this reason being to-day another than yesterday,—another craving requiring to be gratified, exemplified, practiced, refreshed, and uttered, this very one, indeed, being at its floodtide, while yesterday another had its turn." [1] Our cravings thus secure in dream a fictional and poetic utterance and gratification.

This view has recently been psychologically elaborated by Freud, who attempts to show that many dreams, not on their face so recognizable, are yet wish fulfillments; the wish being concealed under a symbolic or fictional representation. Indeed he holds that every dream at bottom represents the imaginary fulfillment of an ungratified wish. In dream, according to Freud, the optative of conscious thought—the *Would that*—is dropped for the present indicative, or rather for a scene in which the wish is visibly represented as fulfilled. In dreams of children it is represented openly; in those of adults it is commonly disguised or distorted in the representation. A man if he is thirsty drinks, thus securing actual gratification. A sleeper who is thirsty may dream of drinking glass after glass of water; this secures an imaginary gratification, which may in some sense serve as substitute for the actual one. Or he may dream of

[1] *The Dawn of Day*, 1903, p. 118.

hydrants or running brooks or rainbows, or anything else which will symbolize water, in which case there is some disguise, but the inspiring wish is the same. This is a simple example; the disguise may be much heavier; the wish may be conscious or unconscious; but all dreams are fundamentally of this type.

This wish theory of dreams has been much discussed. Some psychologists ridicule it; others accept it partially and with reserve; others regard it as a very great scientific discovery. Havelock Ellis, for example, agrees that many dreams are of this type, but says: "To assert that all dreams must be made to fit into this one formula is to make far too large a demand." [1] He wisely observes that in psychology "no key will unlock all doors." I suspect that many who disagree with Freud take him too narrowly or otherwise misunderstand him. Many are ignorant of the desires of the mind, especially of the unconscious ones, and of the complex symbolism by which these desires are unquestionably often expressed in a dream on its face quite irrelevant to them. Others suppose Freud to believe that all dreams are inspired by sexual desire, which is not the case. Others argue that dreams may be inspired by many feelings, by love, avarice, jealousy, fear, etc.,—and that a fearful dream, for example, surely does not appear to embody the dreamer's fondest wish.

I believe this last is misunderstanding. The feelings do not inspire dreams at all; they may accompany desire and color the dream; but they are not the inspiring force, which must be found in the desire itself. In other words, it is better to distinguish the feeling from the desire—the feeling of love, for example, from the desire of love—and to find in the desire the motivating force, and in the feeling a kind of mental friction arising from the expenditure of this force in an attempt at gratification. A desire is merely an attraction of the mind toward something we wish to have, do, or feel. Its opposite is repulsion. Except for indifference, which can accomplish nothing

[1] *The World of Dreams*, pp. 166 ff.

and may be disregarded, these two are the only fundamental states of mind possible. The feelings, sympathetic or antipathetic, accompany these. The positive desire is the agent and creative force. The repulsion, which is the polar negative or inversion of the attraction, may, as far as it is a motive of thought and action, be resolved into a positive desire. Fear implies a desire to escape from the object of fear, and escape is a positive aim. Jealousy implies love; it involves the wish to be rid of a rival and to possess the object of love. It probably would not be difficult therefore, with the necessary data, to revolve a fearful dream into a wish fulfillment.[1]

At any rate I have no doubt that Freud is right when properly understood; at least—the conclusion need go no farther than this for the present purpose—that the great majority of dreams are open or concealed expressions of the desires. Apart from the evidence adduced by the psychologists I should take this view from my own observation, and from evidence in language and literature. In language to realize one's wildest dream is to obtain one's fondest wish. In literature dreams are oftenest of the type of Isaiah: " It shall even be as when a hungry man dreameth, and, behold, he eateth; but he awaketh, and his soul is empty: or as when a thirsty man dreameth, and behold, he drinketh; but he awaketh and, behold, he is faint, and his soul hath appetite." [2] The following is typical in English literature.

> The wery hunter, sleping in his bed,
>   To wode ayein his mynde goth anoon;
> The Juge dremeth how his plees ben sped;
>   The carter dremeth how his cartes goon;
>   The rich of gold; the knight fight with his foon;
> The seke met [dreams] he drinketh of the tonne;
> The lover met he hath his lady wonne.[3]

---

[1] Observe also what Freud says, *Interpretation of Dreams*, p. 375, of the inversion of affects in dreams, which often "go by contraries."

[2] Chap. **xxix**, 8.

[3] Chaucer, *Parlement of Foules*, ll. 99–105. Compare Mercutio's "Queen

More convincing as evidence, however, are many poems of which the following sonnet by Alice Meynell is a type. If in this the reader will observe carefully how the desire, impeded from action, leads to the dream (as also to the poem itself) he will fix a relation which is illustrated again and again in literature.

> I must not think of thee; and tired yet strong,
>   I shun the love that lurks in all delight—
>   The love of thee—and in the blue of Heaven's height,
> And in the dearest passage of a song.
> Oh, just beyond the sweetest thoughts that throng
>   This breast, the thought of thee waits hidden yet bright;
>   But it must never, never come in sight;
> I must stop short of thee the whole day long.
>   But when sleep comes to close each difficult day,
> When night gives pause to the long watch I keep,
>   And all my bonds I needs must loose apart,
>   Must doff my will as raiment lay away,—
> With the first dream that comes with the first sleep,
>   I run, I run, I am gathered to thy heart.

In literature, then, dreams, when they are genuinely portrayed, are made wish fulfillments.

If we consider the whole matter now more broadly we shall see that there is a very great presumption in favor of Freud's theory. All conscious thought—our ordinary voluntary thought whether immediately practical or theoretical, with the action to which it leads, and also our thought of the second order, including the poetic thought—seems to be prompted by the desires and look toward their gratification. Sometimes thought is intended to secure gratification but is unsuccessful. Sometimes it is intended to secure only indirectly a very remote gratification. But the desire is the only and sovereign agent. "All invention," as Ribot expresses it, "presupposes a want, a craving, a tendency, an unsatisfied impulse." And "the

Mab" speech in *Romeo and Juliet* (I, iv), in which each dreamer dreams according to his waking desire.

origin of all imaginative creation is a need, a desire." [1] "Magster artis ingenique largitor venter;" [2] necessity is the mother of invention, whether in the useful or in the imaginative arts. The wish is always father to the thought. Freud's only contribution—a sufficient one—is in showing that dream thought is not lawless in this respect. In the only sense in which his theory can possibly apply to dream thought it applies to all thought. The theory is, presumably, right and obviously so.

Voluntary thought is often part of a very complicated structure, in which the ultimate desire is represented by a highly specialized mediate one, and in which the satisfaction is immensely deferred. In thought of the second order the structure is less complex: the desires are more immediately operative, and the gratification is more immediate as well. But we are always busy in satisfying our desires and in nothing else. We partly secure their actual satisfaction: in case we do not, we imagine them satisfied, and the imaginary is to some extent a substitute for the real. Poetry and dreams, in general, represent such an imaginary gratification.

The poetic thought we have found to be a form of associative thought. In association the wish principle enters in what is called the "law of interest," the operation of which is thus described by Hodgson: "Two processes are constantly going on in redintegration. The one is a process of corrosion, melting, decay; the other is a process of renewing, arising, becoming. No object of representation remains long before consciousness in the same state, but fades, decays, and becomes indistinct. Those parts of the object which possess an interest resist this tendency to gradual decay of the whole object . . . This inequality in the object—some parts, the uninteresting, submitting to decay; others, the interesting parts, resisting it— when it has continued, ends in its becoming a new object." [3] The *interest* represents the demand of the desires; and the *new object* is a fiction which replaces reality. In the poetic thought

[1] *The Creative Imagination*, pp. 32, 260.   [2] Persius, *Prologue*, l. 10.

[3] Quoted by James, *Psychology*, vol. i, p. 572.

this law of interest operates very strongly; and the process of "decay" on the one hand and of the much more important "becoming" on the other, goes on very rapidly. This operation extended explains the difference between reality and fiction. We shall presently have examples of this poetical making over.

The function of poetry, according to the writers on the subject, is to represent the imaginary fulfillment of our ungratified wishes or desires. The poet, according to Bacon, "submits the shows of things to the desires of the mind." Poetry is written always in a mood of dissatisfaction. The lover, separated from his mistress, who falls to scribbling verses, is typical of all poets; as, if he dreams of her, he is typical of all dreamers. The poetic desire may be a mere personal want of this kind, or it may rise to the highest aspiration of which the mind is capable, like that, for example, which inspired the vision of St. John's Apocalypse. So poetry is well defined by Sully Prudhomme, as "le rêve par lequel l'homme aspire à une vie supérieure." [1] It is not actual life, but the better life which he desires of which the poet dreams. "It is no mere appreciation of the beauty before us," says Poe, which inspires the poet, "but a wild effort to reach the beauty above. It is the desire of the moth for the star." [2] The historian must, if he can, represent reality, and as far as it is humanly possible resist the natural tendency of the mind, with its " decay " and " new object "; but the poet gives it free rein. The use of poetry, Bacon says again, contrasting it with history, " hath been to give some shadow of satisfaction to the mind of man in those points wherein the nature of things doth deny it." [3]

The poet subjects the shows of things to the desires of the mind. Perhaps no key will unlock all doors, but I have no

[1] *La Grande Encyclopédie;* see also *Revue des Deux Mondes*, Oct. 1, 1897, "Qu'est-ce que la Poésie?"

[2] "The Poetic Principle."

[3] *Advancement of Learning*, Book ii. Compare Addison, *Spectator*, No. 418; Byron, *Childe Harold*, iv. 5.

doubt that this sentence of Bacon applies to practically all poetry—at least to all poetic vision, as to all dreams. The desires are the motive force and stand at the beginning of the poetic process. Though the establishing of this principle is not essential to the following discussion, it is so fundamental that I shall have constantly to recur to it; and it will find much confirmation in what follows, particularly in the two final chapters. Though the principle is very old in literature, it is so new in theory that I had better stop to meet obvious objections to it, and so prevent misunderstanding in what follows.

Would not a lyric of pure joy stand as an exception? It would, as far as such a lyric is possible. As an inspirer of poetry the mood of joy or exultation—that is, of satisfied desire—would be the one exception, though not an important one, to the general rule. But poems of this class will generally be found mixed and still containing the desire. Shelley's joyful "Skylark" ("Teach me half the gladness") and Deborah's song of exultation in *Judges* ("So let all thine enemies perish") are not exceptions. In the human heart new desire springs up at once in the midst of satisfaction; and not satisfaction, but dissatisfaction is the productive mood. Even in joy the heart is not entirely satisfied, but still feels, as Poe says, "a petulant impatient sorrow at our inability to grasp now, wholly, here on earth, at once and forever, those divine and rapturous joys of which . . . we attain to but brief and indeterminate glimpses." [1] So Poe, like Shelley, thought a "taint of sadness" inseparable from the highest poetry. The highest lyrical note occurs in

> a half heard strain
> Full of sweet desolation,—balmy pain.

But can a trifling, selfish, or base desire inspire poetry? Should we not distinguish and say that only certain kinds of desire may inspire it? In the first place the principle does not

[1] "The Poetic Principle."

require that all desires should inspire poetry,—only that all poetry should be inspired by desire. But secondly any desire whatever, may, if impeded, start a visionary action of the mind, which if recorded will stand as poetry in a broad sense. The desire, the visionary thought, and the product are of all qualities. A shallow or selfish desire may produce poetry,—even an insane one may produce something analogous to it, as we shall see. But to be valuable, to be what we ordinarily include under the term, poetry must be the product of high desire; to be communicable it must be the product, not of merely selfish but of shared desire. The greatest poetry is inspired by our highest and most nearly universal desires. It is inspired particularly by the deeper desires arising from the unconscious mind which are significant to the race. Sometimes, as in the case of Burns separated from his mistress, the great poet's song will seem to be started by a merely temporary and selfish desire, but even in this case the desire is a common and universal one, giving to the song a representative character. Usually the great poet is inspired by deep, unconscious yearnings, by universal or racial aspirations, pointing to an ideal or coming reality, so large that it virtually becomes objective to the individual mind. Thus indeed the great poets taken together establish a new ideal objective reality, above the reality of nature,—the perfected and universal nature of which Aristotle speaks. Between this perfected nature and our desires there is a pre-established harmony. This matter, however, may be left for later chapters.

To state one further objection, may not the poet, instead of improving nature in accordance with his desires, simply describe it with more insight and imaginative penetration into its true character than the ordinary man? Does not Shakespeare, for example, merely see and describe character, the springs of action, life, with a heightened insight—but life as it is? Such a mere description of present reality in verse might certainly be called poetry; and in this case the gratification might be thought to go no further than that derived from the expression, versified and so necessarily heightened in diction and form, and therefore an

idealization of the imperfect and inhibited utterance of ordinary
life. But thought and style are inseparable, and a heightening
of expression involves a heightening of substance. The only
medium for mere description is prose. I can only say further
that the poet seldom or never merely describes nature; he
inevitably beautifies and glorifies it. The moment he modifies
he does so not at random, but in accordance with his desires.
Instead of describing the present reality he looks through his
desires to a coming one. Shakespeare is valuable as a profound
historian and psychologist; but immensely more valuable as a
poet and prophet. He holds the mirror up to nature, but it is a
magic mirror, in which the reflection always shows a nature
perfected and beautified in accordance with our heart's desire.
And as will appear in the final chapter, nature in turn even
attempts to mould herself into harmony with this perfected
image.

II

The poet is called creative; he is essentially what the name
signifies, ποιητής, a maker or creator.   Byron says of poetry:

> 'Tis to create, and in creating live
> A being more intense, that we endow
> With form our fancy, gaining as we give
> The life we image, even as I do now.[1]

And Shelley of the poet:

> But from these create he can
> Forms more real than living man,
> Nurslings of immortality.[2]

The poet is called a creator because he creates in an ideal world,
according to our desires, what is lacking in the world of reality.

This is the ordinary explanation of poetical creation, but
there is apparently more to it than this. We have already seen
that there is a possible analogy between imaginative and phys-

---

[1] *Childe Harold*, III, 6.   [2] *Prometheus Unbound*, Act I, sc. i.

iological creation.[1] It is curious that the poets so often speak of
their work in terms suggesting this—from the birth of Minerva
to the present time. They speak of the birth of thought, of
begetting, conceiving, and giving birth to their fancies, of the
children and nurslings (like Shelley above), of their imagination.
The following from Keats is typical:

> And up I rose refreshed, and glad, and gay,
> Resolving to begin that very day
> These lines; and howsoever they be done,
> I leave them as a father does his son.[2]

The paternal attitude may seem "mere poetic figure"; but this
book will be useless if it does not show that such figure is the
poet's very means of expressing truth. It is always well to look
behind the figure to see what it may represent. In the following
from Schopenhauer the figure is more ample: "Beneath my
hand, and still more in my head, a work, a philosophy is ripening,
which will be at once an ethic and a metaphysic. . . . The
work grows, and gradually becomes concrete, like the foetus
in the mother's womb. I do not know what will appear at last.
I recognize a member, an organ, one part after another. I write
without seeking for results, for I know that it all stands on the
same foundation, and will thus compose a vital and organic
whole. I do not understand the system of the work, just as a
mother does not understand the foetus that develops in the
womb, but she feels it tremble within her. My mind draws its
food from the world by the medium of intelligence and thought;
this nourishment gives body to my work; and yet I do not know
why it should happen in me and not in others who receive the
same food. O Chance! Sovereign of the world, let me live in
peace a few years yet, for I love my work as a mother loves her
child." [3] The figure here touches several points and becomes an
analogy. "If active bodies," Plato says, "have so strong a
yearning that an endless series of lovely images of themselves

---

[1] See page 101.   [2] "Sleep and Poetry;" ll. 401-404.
[3] Quoted by Lombroso, *The Man of Genius*, p. 93.

may constitute, as it were, an earthly immortality for them when they have worn away, how greatly must creative souls desire that partnership and close communion with other souls as fair as they may bring to birth a brood of lofty thoughts, poems, statutes, institutions, laws,—the fitting progeny of the soul?" The soul, like the body, has its begetting and its children, "Homer's offspring." The *Symposium* is such a perfect treatment of this subject that it is better to refer to it, instead of carrying the discussion further here. I may add only that the emergence of the generative powers, accompanied by an increase of the emotional life and a flowering of the imagination, in youth, with the corresponding weakening of all these together in age, shows at least that they are concomitant.

The comparison in literature of poetical to divine creation is also striking. "God without any travail to his divine imagination," says Puttenham, expressing the older critical view, "made all the world of naught. . . . Even so the very poet makes and combines out of his own brain both the verse and matter of his poem." [1] The poet's work, according to Coleridge, is "a repetition in the finite mind of the eternal act of creation in the infinite *I am*." [2] If this is to be taken literally then there is actual relation between poetical and divine creation,—the relation being that of the finite to the infinite. Froschammer has the metaphysical theory that "imagination is the basic principle of the world-process," that there is a cosmic imagination at work in nature, producing the innumerable animal and vegetable forms, and evolving all life. This cosmic imaginative production is, when summed up, the divine creation. How did God create the world? Not surely in six days—for the biblical myth must be interpreted—but by a gradual evolutionary process. If we conceive that each man wishes something higher and better than reality, that his imagination represents his wish, and that this representation is then realized; that he then wills, imagines, and realizes something still higher and better,

[1] *Arte of English Poesie*, ed. Arber, p. 19.
[2] *Biographia Literaria*, chap. xiii.

and so on; and if further we conceive all minds, and all mind, doing the same progressively and *ad infinitum*: then these finite acts of creation, taken together, will make up an infinite series, and form an entire evolutionary process, which will give us an intelligible view of the creation of God. The wish, the imagination, the creation of man are finite, but they share in the will, the imagination, and the creation of God which are infinite. This at least gives Coleridge's dictum, quoted above, a meaning. Of the cosmic process physiological creation is merely an incident;—and it becomes the familiar example by referring to which poetic simile may convey to us a glimpse of the higher truth. The conception just stated is obviously not scientifically established fact, but it is possibly something more interesting,— namely poetic truth;—at any rate it is in this direction that by poetry the thought is led. We may return, however, to points less speculative.

III

The motive force in the poetic process, as we have seen, is in the desires. Of these desires the emotions are always an accompaniment. The desires when in action naturally produce feeling; they are the nuclei of feelings, of different qualities; if they are impeded they produce a greater friction, a passion or suffering, which is the inevitable effect of unsatisfied desire. So poetry, according to Wordsworth and Coleridge, always implies passion. "No literary expression," says Theodore Watts, "can, properly speaking, be called poetry which is not in a certain deep sense emotional." [1] The emotion, says Ribot, "is the ferment without which no creation is possible;" [2] as the feelings, it has been said, form the mother-mood of dreams. The feelings in poetry may be of very different qualities and degrees of intensity, from either conscious or unconscious sources, and either immediately felt or recalled.

[1] *Encyclopedia Britannica*, "Poetry."
[2] *The Creative Imagination*, p. 31.

Sometimes feeling seems to be immediately expressed in poetry, as in the case of a lover like Burns singing. This is apparently Byron's idea of poetry; the motor force which might be expended in action is at once diverted to expression in verse:

> Thus to their extreme verge the passions brought
> Dash into poetry, which is but a passion.[1]

"Poetry," he wrote to Miss Milbanke, "is the lava of imagination whose eruption prevents the earthquake." [2] But he said also, "As for poesy, mine is the dream of the sleeping passions;" and this is more in accord with Wordsworth, who believed indeed that "poetry is the spontaneous overflow of powerful feelings," but believed also that it "takes its origin from emotion recollected in tranquillity." [3] Coleridge considered passion "the all in all in poetry;" but probably thought also that poetry arises in the subsidence and control of passion. Poe believed that "poetry and passion are discordant," and that while passion may start the imagination, the true poetic mood arises only when the latter has triumphed.[4] Theoretically I should think Poe right. Strong feeling naturally first expresses itself in action, or attempt at action; and only when this attempt must be given up and as an afterthought, solaces itself through the imagination. This is perhaps why we do not dream of recent events filled with strong emotion; we do not poetize such events either. This subject will come up again later.

Generally, therefore, the emotion will be one recalled from the more or less distant past. "It is contemplated," as Wordsworth says, "till by a species of reaction, the tranquillity gradually disappears, and an emotion, kindred to that which was before the subject of contemplation, is gradually produced, and does itself actually exist in the mind." We must remember, however,

[1] *Don Juan*, iv, 106.
[2] F. I. Carpenter, *Selections from Byron*, pp. xxxii, xxxiv.
[3] Preface to the *Lyrical Ballads*.
[4] *Critical Writings of Poe*, ed. F. C. Prescott, pp. xxxvii, 344.

that this emotion, instead of being consciously recalled, may
simply emerge from the unconscious mind. Such an emotion
will probably be best suited of all to inspire poetry. It may also
have quite different quality or coloring, as compared with conscious ones, difficult for the poet to express in language,—like
the strange feelings of nightmare and vivid dream which we
find so indescribable on waking. The unconscious mind has
its desires, its emotions, and its images which may have play
in the poetic process. I should suppose, first, that the emotions
may be drawn into consciousness without the desires and the
images with which they were originally associated in experience,
and appear alone; and secondly, that such emotions may often
be transferred from these original associations to quite different
images, objects, which serve for the emotions as substitutes or
symbols for the originals. A poem about the beauty of a present
rose, for example, may be colored by feelings coming from quite
another forgotten past experience. This also will come up
again. The feelings are deeper than the thoughts, and more the
common property of conscious and unconscious mind. They
will therefore more often "come through," retaining something
like their original tone and intensity, while the images with
which they originally belonged will be distorted by the imaginative operation into strange forms. In other words, the feelings
are the more stable feature of the process. This has been
often noted in dreams. "When we awake," says Jastrow, "we
know at once that the terrifying creatures of our imagination are
purely fictitious, though the fear to which they gave rise was
a genuine psychological experience." [1] Freud has the corresponding principle: "im Traume ist der Affect das einzig Wahre."
Thus the most stable feature of poetry is its underlying feeling;
this may attach itself to the wildest fiction, but the fiction still
appeals to us as essentially truthful, because it is animated by
true feeling.

The feeling appearing in poetry may be of various kinds in

[1] *The Subconscious*, p. 226.

other respects. It may be strong, personal and transient; or more mild and continuing—what we call a mood; or still more general, diffused, and permanent. It may correspond to the wish of the moment, or to the settled desires of a life-time. As John Keble observes, "the mind has its ἤθη as well as its πάθη,—its permanent tastes, habits, inclinations, which, when directly checked, are as capable of relief by poetical expression as the more hidden and violent emotions." [1] Such a permanent inclination or "ruling passion" may run through all of a man's imaginative work, as one tone will be discovered again and again in Goldsmith, in poetry and in prose. More often it will color a whole book like the *Vicar of Wakefield* or *Madame Bovary*, where a long story in all its parts vibrates harmoniously with a controlling emotion, quite as obviously as may a shorter one, like, say, the *Eve of St. Agnes* or the *Merry Men*.

Such a feeling may be the primary and distinctive element in the story, determining the plot and characters. "You may take a certain atmosphere," says Stevenson, "and get actions and persons to realize it. I'll give you an example—The Merry Men. There I began with the feeling of one of those islands on the west coast of Scotland, and I gradually developed the story to express the sentiment with which that coast affected me." This pervasive unity of tone he considered the highest merit in a short fiction, and the one most difficult to secure. As it appears generally in literature it is what Walter Pater calls "soul" as distinguished from "mind in style." It is not, like "mind," mechanical, not the result of a conscious logical synthesis, but organic, and therefore a truer unity,—the result of a deeper and more vital force. "And this, too," Pater says, "is a faculty of choosing and rejecting what is congruous or otherwise, with a drift toward unity—unity of atmosphere here, as there of design,—soul securing color (or perfume, might we say?) as mind secures form, the latter being essentially finite, the

[1] *The British Critic*, vol. xxiv, p. 439.

former vague or infinite." [1]   This is the power of which Lamb speaks, "which draws all things to one,—which makes things animate and inanimate, subjects and their accessories, take one color, and serve to one effect." [2]   This is that "right feeling" which, according to Lowell, "heightens or subdues a passage or a whole poem to the proper tone, and gives entireness to the effect." [3]   "For always," as Carlyle says, "of its own unity, the soul gives unity to whatsoever it looks on with love." [4]   Such harmony will be due to the vivifying emotion more than to any other cause. As the feeling is the most obvious prerequisite of poetical production, so it is perhaps in fact the most vital and characteristic feature, and almost, as Coleridge declares, the "all in all of poetry." If the feeling is right, if it is vivid and sincere, and especially if it is a deeper and more unconscious one, coming, in Pater's words, not from the *mind* but from the *soul*, then the whole product will be right, will grow and organize itself, taking what is its own by true affinity, passing over or rejecting what does not by nature belong to it. It will have unity, as a tree or a flower will have, because it is alive.

[1] "Style."
[2] "On the Genius and Character of Hogarth."
[3] *Literary Essays*, vol. i, p. 245.
[4] *Sartor Resartus*, Book ii, chap. vi.

CHAPTER IX

THE IMAGINATION: EXTERNAL AND INTERNAL ELEMENTS

I

IT is time now to say something specific of a thing which has been often referred to in the preceding chapters and which has necessarily been left more or less indefinite—namely of the capital poetic faculty of the imagination. The imagination is, in a word, the eye of the mind—the mental or ideal counterpart of the bodily eye; and it is employed most readily when the bodily eye is in abeyance or at rest. For the mind also sees—but it sees in its different way, and it beholds its own ideal objects. This eye of the mind is the characteristic organ of the poet and visionary. "I assert for myself," Blake says, "that I do not behold the outward creation, and that it is to me hindrance and not action. 'What,' it will be questioned, 'when the sun rises do you not see a round disc of fire something like a guinea?' Oh! no, no! I see an innumerable company of the heavenly host, crying, 'Holy, holy, holy, is the Lord God Almighty!' I question not my corporeal eye any more than I would question a window concerning a sight. I look through it, and not with it." [1]

> We are led to believe a lie
> When we see with, not through the eye.

The true poet is gifted with a kind of "second sight," higher and freer than the ordinary sense, and with this gift he becomes a "seer." This ideal seeing, or seeing of the ideal, is the first and indispensable work of the poet.

[1] *A Vision of Judgment.*

Imagination, as is universally agreed, is a *sine qua non*, and its presence or absence a true test of poetry. And since this seeing is a gift, and not at all an acquirement, and since it is not at command but comes, so to speak, when the spirit moves, there is a tendency and constant temptation for would-be poets, and even at times for the true poets themselves, to dispense with it,—to try to do with the conscious mind, and coldly, what can be accomplished only when there is the gift. The bane of poetry, in other words, is the offering of spurious substitutes for the true products of the imagination—of base metals for the true gold. This spurious poetry is often tuneful, graphic, figurative—in many ways ingeniously like the genuine product; but it leaves its readers cold—"embarrassed," as Poe says, "between a half-consciousness that they ought to admire the production and a wonder that they do not." In general such simulation is the origin of the false and banal in poetry. But even the better poets—so rare and precious is the true gold—will fill in and eke out and connect their inspired passages with mere verse in the manner of inspiration; or, like Tennyson in the *Idylls of the King*, fall back on the images and inventions of earlier poets with fuller or more genuine vision. Even in Shakespeare much of the poetry is derivative; that is, the images— stories or characters—were first truly seen by some earlier, perhaps nameless poet. As Plato long ago noted, Homer comes first and is followed by other poets depending upon him, like the successive iron rings on the magnet. On the other hand the imagination is a perennial ever-present human faculty, and its newest product, in the midst of however many imitations, is still valuable and unmistakable.

Our theory of imagination goes back to Aristotle, who made this faculty, φαντασία, responsible for poetry, and also for dreams and other similar illusions. His treatment is not very clear; he seems inclined to regard the faculty in question as in the main a merely reproductive one. It is "the movement which results upon actual sensation,"—in other words it is "the after effect of a sensation, the continued presence of an impression after the object which first excited it has been withdrawn from actual experience." [1] The poetic imagination, as we now understand it, would be less closely bound to the reality of sensation than this definition would imply. But Aristotle's general theory of imitation in literary art would show that he did not consider the imagination merely reproductive of the images of sense. The earlier English theorists, following Aristotle and perhaps taking his imitation too narrowly, are inclined to relate imagination too closely to sensation. Thus Hobbes: "For after the object is removed, or the eye shut, we still retain an image of the thing seen, though more obscure than when we saw it. And this is it the Latins call imagination, from the image made in seeing . . . . Imagination, therefore, is nothing but decaying sense." [2] Bacon gives it more freedom; as history belongs to the memory, so poetry belongs to the imagination, "which, being unrestrained by laws, may make whatever unnatural mixtures and separations it pleases." [3] Addison makes imagination "the very life and highest perfection of poetry." "We cannot, indeed, have a single image in the fancy that did not make its first entrance through the sight; but we have the power of retaining, altering, and compounding those images, which we have once received, into all the varieties of picture and vision that are most agreeable to the imagination." The imagination thus "has something in it like creation; it bestows a kind of existence, and draws up to the reader's view several objects which are not to be found in being. It makes additions to nature." [4]

Thus down to the end of the eighteenth century English writers have a definite conception of an image-making faculty in the Aristotelian meaning, forming pictures directly or indirectly related to the pictures of sense,—and this faculty is the life of poetry. They call the faculty indifferently by the Latin name of the *imagination*, or by the Greek one of the *fancy*

---

[1] E. Wallace, *Aristotle's Psychology*, p. lxxxvii.

[2] *Leviathan*, Part I, chap. ii.

[3] *Advancement of Learning*, Book ii, chap. xiii.

[4] *Spectator*, Nos. 411, 421.

(with its different spellings, *fantasy* or *phantasy*, and its adjectives *fanciful* and *phantastic*); one is merely a translation of the other.[1] Even into the nineteenth century the words are often employed in this original sense, as when Lowell speaks of "fantasy, the image-making power, common to all who have the gift of dreams." [2]

In the nineteenth century, however, the theory, in its application to poetry, was revolutionized by Wordsworth and his contemporaries, who attempted to make a sharp distinction between fancy and imagination. Perhaps the best way to give an idea of the distinction will be to quote some of the many antitheses in which effort was made to express it. "Fancy," Wordsworth says, "is given to quicken and to beguile the temporal part of our nature, imagination to incite and to support the eternal." [3] "Imagination," according to Leigh Hunt, "belongs to tragedy or the serious muse; fancy to the comic." [4] "Fancy," Emerson thinks, "is related to color; imagination to form." [5] According to Sir Leslie Stephen, "the distinction between fancy and imagination is, in brief, that fancy deals with the superficial resemblances, and imagination with the deeper truths that underlie them." [6] Other familiar oppositions might be quoted. The main value of this Wordsworthian theory perhaps has been to call attention to the high importance of the imagination in poetry—to its complexity and profundity. I cannot help feeling, however, that, widely accepted as this famous distinction has been, it has not helped greatly in the explication of the whole subject, and that its introduction into the theory has been unfortunate; and this for three reasons. First, it does some violence to the etymological meanings, and to the previously accepted theory, particularly in case of the

[1] "I shall use them promiscuously," Addison says in No. 416.

[2] *Works*, vol. iii, p. 32.

[3] *Preface of 1815.*

[4] *Imagination and Fancy.*

[5] *Letters and Social Aims*, p. 29.

[6] *Hours in a Library.*

word *fancy*, which should after all mean something pretty close to the φαντασία of Aristotle. Secondly, and I shall leave this to the judgment of those who have read carefully the famous passages in the Preface of 1815 and in the *Biographia Literaria*— it is not really definite or intelligible; in other words you may read the passages without being able to say just where the distinction lies, and without being able to decide in the case of poems of Wordsworth, for example, which display one faculty and which the other. According to Wordsworth the imagination is both a modifying and a creative power; but the fancy, he says, modifies and creates also; and at best the distinction seems one of degree rather than of essence. Thirdly, it has made our conception of the imagination more vague rather than more definite, and therefore has not helped to advance our analysis of the poetic process. The imagination is now defined, for example, as a "fusion or unification of the powers of the mind, a blending of all the mental capacities in the intuition or the reconstruction of the ideal." Such a definition, as far as it is intelligible, would better fit the entire poetic process, of which the imagination, in the strict sense, is but a part. In other words the tendency is to make the words *imaginative* and *poetical* synonymous, with loss of hard-won analytical distinctions.

At any rate for the purposes of our discussion it will be better to go back to the older, narrower, and more definite conception— to the imagination as merely that eye of the mind, of which I have spoken—or as that mental power of forming images, actual or ideal, which it has been from the time of Aristotle, and which, in spite of the interruption noted above, it has to some extent continued to be to the present time. We may if we like call the lighter and more insignificant manifestations of this power fanciful, and the more profound imaginative—with the understanding that, as far as the forming of the images is concerned, the mental operation is in the two cases the same. And when Romeo says:

> Night's candles are burnt out, and jocund day
> Stands tiptoe on the misty mountain tops,

we need not try to apply the Wordsworthian distinction and decide whether this is merely fanciful or truly imaginative. I do not know whether Matthew Arnold ever objected to these "candles," as he did to Pope's "effulgent lamp of night," that Romeo did not have his "eye on the object,"—and that the stars are not strictly like candles any more than the moon is like a lamp. In any case "Night's candles are burnt out" makes a very pleasing combination of images, fanciful or imaginative, and is an excellent example of the faculty now before us in its poetic exercise.

We may go on, then, to inquire more particularly what this image-forming power is, and how it works in the production of poetry. We shall not of course be able to answer these questions satisfactorily; but we may note some of its characteristics, and give some typical examples of its working.

In the first place the image-forming faculty, or imagination—henceforward let us use the word in the strict sense—is employed in both the kinds of thought mentioned in the earlier chapters, in the voluntary as well as in the merely associative. In the first—in ordinary reasoning, as it is used by the business man or the scientist—it is subordinate and under control. In the second—in all the activities of the mind belonging to the second order, particularly in the visions of the poet, the dreamer, or the seer—it has free play and becomes the master faculty. In the first it is like the instrument on which one plays at will; in the second it is like the harp set in the window, which at first is silent, and then, as the breeze sweeps over it, is roused to strange music—as the soul receives "Aeolian visitations." Or to state this matter more rigorously; in each case the desires are the originating or motive element; in the first they suggest a conscious end, which will presumably lead directly or indirectly to their satisfaction, and this end, established by the will, governs the imaginative presentations; in the second the desires work their own will and find direct satisfaction in the pictures presented by the imagination, which are lawless except in so far as they are bound thus to furnish satisfaction to the desires which prompt them. This is the faculty of imagination, in a poet "wild and lawless" and "like a high-ranging spaniel," of which Dryden speaks.

From their etymology both *fancy* and *imagination* apply properly to the sense of sight alone, and in using the words (as in the preceding paragraphs) we usually think first and mainly of the sense of sight. This is because, as Addison says, "our sight is the most perfect and most delightful of all our senses." The presentations of the imagination are naturally first thought of in terms of visual images or pictures. We must remember, however, that they may be auditory images also—sounds previously heard or combinations of these. And so of the other senses;— that is, I should judge both from the analogy and from experience, that we may form images of smell, taste, and touch. Whether this be true or not the image from an actual sensation of, say, smell will call up and combine with other ideal images. So "a particular smell . . . is able to fill the mind on a sudden, with the picture of the fields or gardens where we first met with it, and to bring up into view all the variety of images that once attended it." [1] The presentations of the imagination, then, may be of different sorts—visual, auditory, etc.—or combinations of these; and if in considering them we refer to them as images or pictures it is, first, because it is necessary from convenience and limitations of our vocabulary, and, secondly, because the visual presentations are most numerous and important. The imagination is mainly a matter of *seeing*.

II

The imagination has been divided into two kinds, the reproductive, which merely presents to the mind actual images, as they are remembered; and the productive, which makes over actual images, combining them with earlier experiences, to form new ones, ideal in nature. The first is merely a visual memory; "this decaying sense," Hobbes says, "when we would

[1] *Spectator*, No. 417.

express the thing itself . . . we call imagination; but when we would express the decay it is called memory." This reproduction, as far as it is possible, we may pass over, because, as it applies to poetry, it presents no difficulties. But we must notice particularly that, except in a relative sense, there is no such thing as imaginative reproduction. Imagination is, at best, "decaying sense"; the decay sets in at once, the moment the actual sensation is over, and is in general rapid and continuous. Some features fade at once; others with which we are more concerned are kept alive. "This inequality of the object," to repeat the expression of Hodgson,[1] " some parts, the uninteresting, submitting to decay; others, the interesting parts, resisting it—when it has continued, ends in its becoming a new object." In other words, every imagination is, not a reproduction, but to some extent a "new object;" and it is this newness with which we are concerned.

Let us now look at the matter from a slightly different angle. In the formation of a mental image evidently two factors may enter; first the objective reality—that is a sensation or a recollection of one,—this being always subject to immediate modification; and secondly, as modifying it, the mind itself—in its content, that is, of desires, feelings, and previously acquired images. These two factors would enter in every case except that of pure illusion (as distinguished from hallucination)— where the mind is absolutely cut off from the stimulus of external sensation and the presentation is entirely ideal; here the first factor would be absent. But in the common case there would be at least a starting-point in sensation. In day dreams, for example, the fancies come most readily with gazing into the fire or into the crystal; the shapes or colors are first seen and then modified by the mind. So in dreams, though the mind is largely insulated by sleep, there are some sensations from outside; and there are also the somatic feelings which, as is well known, often furnish the first impulse. And so in

[1] See p. 127.

poetic vision, the sight of a present object, or a sound, or a smell, perhaps a most ordinary one, will start the associations, forming the nucleus, and becoming phantasmogenetic. But the external experience may be much more than a starting-point; it may be the larger element, while the subjective modification is relatively slight. And so there may be all degrees in the combination of the two factors, from a very slight making over of the external reality to a complete one, amounting to a new subjective creation.

To make this more clear we may take examples of imaginative modification of different kinds and in different degrees—beginning with one in which the difference is slight. The painter Fromentin, cited by Ribot,[1] presumably a man trained to close observation, and priding himself, indeed, on his ability to recall with exactness after the lapse of two or three years things barely seen in travel—that is on an imagination approaching the "reproductive"—describes his faculty as follows: "My recollection of things, though very trustworthy, by no means has the exactness and general validity of an absolute record. The more it fades, the more it is modified as it is possessed by the memory and *the more it is worth for the purpose for which I intend it*. As the exact form goes on changing it gradually becomes a new form, half real, half imaginary, which I consider *more advantageous*." The italicized words indicate the subjective element, and the direction the modification takes. A faculty of this description would be objectionable in a court witness, but by so much the better for an artist. The artist's mind with its previously acquired notions of form, color, proportion, etc., consciously or unconsciously modifies the sensory data and shapes the actual scene to something slightly different, more beautiful, better suited to his artistic purpose.

In somewhat the same way the lover, beholding his mistress, sees first what any bystander might see or what the camera would show; but secondly, since he is, as Plato believed, a

[1] *The Creative Imagination*, p. 17.

kind of poet, he "looks not with the eye but with the mind;" he has a preconceived and perhaps inherited notion of ideal beauty, with which under stress of emotion, he supplements and heightens the beauty before him, adding to form and feature every charm that love can give, and surrounding all with quite preternatural glamor. He sees Helen's beauty in a brow of Egypt. Here what the camera would show corresponds roughly to the first factor in the imaginative complex; the charm and the glamor to the second. It would be useless to decide which is the larger and more important. The first we call reality, the second illusion. But the illusion is the reality "that launched a thousand ships." And it is of the illusion that the poet writes.

> Io mi son un che, quando
> Amor mi spira, noto, ed a quel modo
> Che ditta dentro, vo significando.

To take another example in which the external sensation is hardly more than a starting-point and the main factor is the illusion,—I suppose an experience like the following is not uncommon. I am walking home on a dark night when I am stopped suddenly before a dark figure standing just off my path. I see it is a man. He has a hat and long coat; he makes a slight movement; I am apprehensive, and I wait for him to speak. But then, as this is a walk I take every day, I recall that just at this spot there is a bush, which now I remember well, and so I see instead of a man, a bush—and I recall the peculiar texture of the leaves as I see them in the daytime. Thus a slight apprehension will start the imagination; the imagination will in turn increase the fear, and so on; until in a moment a large structure is raised on a very small foundation. And this experience I should think quite typical of the imagination in general,

> That if it would but apprehend some joy
> It comprehends some bringer of that joy;
> Or in the night imagining some fear
> How easy is a bush supposed a bear!

This is precisely the working of the imagination in poetry. "Poetry," Hazlitt says, "is strictly the language of the imagination; and the imagination is that faculty which represents objects, not as they are in themselves, but as they are moulded by other thoughts and feelings, into an infinite variety of shapes and combinations of power."[1] When Shakespeare has Iachimo say of Imogen:

> The flame o' th' taper
> Bows toward her, and would under-peep her lids
> To see the enclosed lights,

he makes "this passionate interpretation of the motion of the flame to accord with the speaker's own feelings." The flame seen coldly is one thing; seen dramatically, by the poet looking through the lover's eyes, another. When he makes Romeo say, "Night's candles are burnt out," he has first perhaps an image of the stars disappearing at daybreak, with the associations that go with the end of a night of watching; and then perhaps an image of a room of feasting with the candles going out one by one, as the night of pleasure is ending; the first image is combined and fused with the second, with quite magical effect; the candles gain a kind of largeness from the stars, and the stars a tinge of humanity from the candles; and further (with the context) there is a suggestion of slight irony and slight pathos. The fact (as we may call it) that the light of the stars is obscured by that of the coming sun, is transformed by the imagination,—by the introduction of the second image from the mind itself— into the purest poetry.

The images formed by the imagination, therefore, as the preceding examples are intended to illustrate, are the products of the interplay of two elements, entering in different degrees; in the first place the external experience, and secondly the mind, quickened and heightened by emotion, modifying this experience little or much, abstracting, endowing, shaping,

[1] "On Poetry in General."

and creating, to suit its own purposes. Thus is formed a new
world, related to the world of the senses and above it,—

> A new world—a world, too, that is fit
> To be transmitted, and to other eyes
> Made visible; as ruled by those fixed laws
> Whence spiritual dignity originates,
> Which do both give it being and maintain
> A balance, an ennobling *interchange*
> *Of action from without and from within;*
> The excellence, pure function, and best power
> *Both of the objects seen, and eye that sees.*[1]

The *Prelude* furnishes further excellent examples of this
interchange. Wordsworth describes, for example, in Book
XIII how "once among the wilds of Sarum's plain," through
whose "wide waste three summer days he roamed alone," he
saw "fair trains of imagery" one after another, made up of
both sights and sounds; how he "saw our dim ancestral past
in vision clear;" and how, among the Druid circles, he was
charmed

> Into a waking dream, a reverie
> That, with believing eyes, where'er I turned
> Beheld long-bearded teachers, with white wands
> Uplifted, pointing to the starry sky,
> Alternately, and plain below, while breath
> Of music swayed their motions, and the waste
> Rejoiced with them and me in those sweet sounds.

And these visions do not come merely in solitude, because in
Book VII he tells how in the streets of London he looked
upon the crowd

> Until the shapes before my eyes became
> A second-sight procession, such as glides
> Over still mountains, or appears in dreams.

[1] Wordsworth, *Prelude*, Book xiii.

Sometimes, as Wordsworth tells us, in these imaginings the mind contributed much, sometimes little.

> Though reared upon the base of outward things
> Structures like these the excited spirit mainly
> Builds for herself; scenes different there are
> Full formed, that take, with small internal help,
> Possession of the faculties,—the peace
> That comes with night; the deep solemnity
> Of nature's intermediate hours of rest, etc.

And sometimes an external scene will repulse the imagination,— like the fair of St. Bartholomew,

> A work completed to our hands, that lays,
> If any spectacle on earth can do,
> The whole creative powers of man asleep.

In these passages and many others of the *Prelude*—which every student of poetry should read entire, and re-read, because it is the best treatise on the poetic mind—Wordsworth gives examples of the vision which he recorded in his poetry, and makes observations on the working of the imagination. His conception of the imagination is that its visions are the product of a reciprocal action between the internal and the external, between the individual mind of the poet and his outward experience, or, since Wordsworth, like Emerson, evidently believes that "the mind is one," between the mind of humanity on the one hand and nature on the other.

> How exquisitely the individual Mind
> (And the progressive powers perhaps no less
> Of the whole species) to the external World
> Is fitted:—and how exquisitely, too—
> Theme this but little heard of among men—
> The external World is fitted to the Mind;

> And the creation (by no lower name
> Can it be called) which they *with blended might*
> Accomplish:—this is our high argument.[1]

The imagination, then, to be of value, must proceed from a healthy reaction of the mind upon nature. Either element taken alone is impotent; nature, until subjected to the mind, is but an "inanimate, cold world;" the mind, without its start and base in nature, will produce only empty and disordered dreams. But when there is proper "balance" and "interchange," when the mind works upon nature to transform it, the result is happy. The transformation may be a slight one, in which common things are lightened and glorified, or it may go further and produce centaurs, witches—all the strange dreamlike combinations of images found in mythology or romance. Of the imagination both are natural products.

> Paradise, and groves
> Elysian, Fortunate Fields—like those of old
> Sought in the Atlantic Main—why should they be
> A history only of departed things,
> Or a mere fiction of what never was?
> For the discerning intellect of Man,
> When wedded to this goodly universe
> In love and holy passion, shall find these
> A simple produce of the common day.[2]

Poetry, as Pater says, "exercises two distinct functions: it may reveal, it may unveil to every eye, the ideal aspects of common things; . . . or it may actually add to the number of motives poetic and uncommon in themselves, by the imaginative creation of things that are ideal from their very birth." [3] The two functions are well illustrated in the programme of the *Lyrical Ballads*, in which the poems are of two sorts. One

---

[1] "The Recluse." Wordsworth perhaps discussed this theme with Coleridge; the latter has the same thought in "Dejection," iv.

[2] "The Recluse."

[3] *Appreciations*, p. 242.

"chooses incidents and situations from common life," throwing "over them a certain coloring of the imagination, whereby ordinary things should be presented to the mind in unusual aspect." In the other the incidents are supernatural; and "the excellence aimed at was to consist in the interesting of the affections by the dramatic truth of such emotions, as would naturally accompany such situations, supposing them real. And real in this sense they have been to every human being, who from whatever source of delusion, has at any time believed himself under supernatural agency." In the two cases there are differences of subject and degree; the external and internal elements enter in different proportions; but the imaginative action is the same in both.

CHAPTER X

THE IMAGINATION: RECENT AND EARLY SOURCES

I

THE imagination, then, as we have seen in the preceding chapter, accomplishes a fusion of images from without, and images and feelings, or images colored by feelings, already stored in the mind, from within. But this fusion is still unexplained, and to make our understanding of the actual working of the imagination at all clear we must evidently go on to answer a good many further questions. In the first place what images from without are available?—what kind of images from without "take the fancy" or start the imagination, and become phantasmogenetic? To these questions some answer has already been given in Chapter V. In the second place what images from within are utilized? What part do the feelings play? And how is the fusion accomplished? These questions are very difficult, and will doubtless be the subjects of investigation for a long time to come. In this chapter I cannot attempt to answer them; but can only call them to the attention of students of poetry; and then go on to make a few observations that may be helpful in future investigation. Some light may be thrown upon them from two sources; first from the analogous imagination in dreams which have perhaps been more fully investigated; and secondly from the expressions of the poets, particularly of Wordsworth in the *Prelude*.

The images utilized by the imagination, with the feelings which accompany them, may come from two sources, either from contemporary or recent, or from older and more settled experience. Images from the first source may be combined with images from the second; and likewise the images may come from one source and the feelings from the other,—that is, an image drawn from recent experience may have transferred to it a feeling which first belonged to an experience much older. While impressions may come from both sources there is no question of the paramount importance in poetry of impressions from the second,— that is of those that are older, and have been stored in the mind over a long period, extending even as far back as childhood.

If we take the material from these two sources in turn, beginning with the recent, it seems to be the case, in dreams at any rate, that the imagination often draws upon recent experiences which are trivial and indifferent rather than vital and significant—upon those we care nothing about rather than those in which our feelings are deeply engaged. Thus Havelock Ellis says it is "a well-known fact that our most recent and acute emotional experiences . . . are rarely mirrored in our dreams, though recent occurrences of more trivial nature, as well as older events of more serious import, easily find place there." [1] And Hildebrandt: "It is a remarkable fact that dreams do not, as a rule, take their elements from great and deep-rooted events or more powerful and urgent interests of the preceding day, but from unimportant matters, from the most worthless fragments of recent experience or of a more remote past." [2] Thus we may dream of a person of whose death we read casually in the newspaper, but not as a rule of a dear friend who is just dead. Delage, who corroborates the authors just cited, says of the dreams of persons newly married: "S'ils ont été fortement épris, presque jamais ils n'ont rêvé l'un de l'autre avant le mariage ou pendant la lune de miel; et s'ils ont rêvé d'amour c'est pour être infidèles avec quelque personne indifférente ou odieuse." [3] Freud thinks that we may dream of both significant and insignificant recent events, but that the latter case is apparently the more common. [4]

[1] *The World of Dreams*, p. 173.

[2] *Der Traum*, p. 11, quoted by Freud, *Interpretation of Dreams*, p. 13.

[3] Quoted by Freud, p. 67.

[4] Freud, p. 153.

He believes, however, that whenever we dream of an insignificant matter this stands for another matter which is significant, by a "displacement;" that is, the two matters are connected by a series of associations, more or less long and more or less obscure, by means of which the insignificant one comes to stand as representative or symbol for the one of true importance. Thus, if, after picking mushrooms on the golf course, I dream of picking up golf balls, one after another and then a great many; these are soft and edible, and I indicate to the caddy, who is a girl, that the different kinds have various botanical names; the dream seems ordinary enough, made up of indifferent elements from the preceding day's experience; but there is an eagerness and emotional emphasis connected with the picking up of the mushroom-like balls which would suggest a deeper subject matter; and this, according to Freud, might be discovered by an unravelling of the associations in analysis. If this theory be correct then all dreams deal, at least indirectly, in spite of appearances, with psychic material of vital concern.

I do not know how far this theory would apply to poetry. I have no doubt, however, that the poetic imagination also does not, except in appearance, deal with indifferent material, that it is actually concerned always with what is emotionalized and vital, and that if it involves indifferent matter this is always connected, by intellectual or emotional resemblances, with deeper and more settled experience, for which it stands as a "surrogate." Examples showing how this may occur will be given later in this chapter. The imagination, then, may draw upon recent indifferent matters, but it usually goes farther back for its true inspiring source. Fundamentally it can not care for matters which arouse no emotion.

But, in the next place, what is the case with recent experience of emotional value? I am convinced that as a rule the imagination does not at once poetize important matters with which the emotions are deeply engaged; and that it does not dream of such matters either; in other words that Delage and the other authors cited a moment ago are right about dreams, and that a corresponding principle applies to poetry. The reason for this is that immediate strong feeling produces a tension in the mind driving it to action or other practical discharge, and excluding a state of dream, reverie, or vision. Only when this tension is relaxed, and action must be given up, is the matter turned over to the imagination. It is impossible to dream while the house is on fire, or for some hours or days thereafter, because there is no relaxation. It is impossible to poetize the death of a dear friend in the first moment of grief for the same reason. When these matters have become settled and mentally adjusted we may look back and dream about them. This principle, however, may not always hold. Miss Hallam gives instances of dreams of the dead expressing immediate sorrow.[1] Byron thought that the passions might "dash into poetry." But in general Wordsworth was doubtless right in thinking that poetry "takes its origin from emotion recollected in tranquillity."[2]

II

Considerations like the preceding lead to the belief that while recent experiences, trivial or vital, may be treated or utilized by the imagination, these are at best of less value than older ones. The world *older* here is indefinite—necessarily so, for the experience may be only settled by the passing of a few days or weeks, or it may have lain in the mind for a much longer period and be drawn say from the earliest impressions of childhood. Any imaginative activity of value will go back to many roots in the poet's mind—some recent, some remote—in many cases to roots that have been growing since the very beginning of the mental life. The images from the different sources will be fused, the recent will be connected by recondite associations with the more remote, one will be substituted for another by means of resemblance, and all will be colored by a feeling which may go back to the earliest time.

[1] *American Journal of Psychology*, April 1896.
[2] See Chapter VIII, p. 135.

In many respects the older the better; that is, quite early experiences have many advantages for the imagination. Everyone has found in his own experience some confirmation of Freud's description of the dream as "a modified substitute for the infantile scene produced by transference to recent material." [1] Everyone knows that in dreams

> Sometimes forgotten things long cast behind
> Rush forward in the brain and come to mind;
> The nurse's legends are for truth received,
> And the man dreams but what the boy believed. [2]

Similarly everyone knows that a visit to a haunt of childhood— to the house in which you were born, to your first school or playground—will start the imagination, will induce a mood of abstraction, musing, free association, and day dream. It will be apt to lead to poetry, something on the order of Whittier's "In School Days."

> Still sits the school-house by the road,
>   A ragged beggar sleeping:
> Around it still the sumachs grow
>   And blackberry vines are creeping.

A similar condition of the mind will occur if such a spot be merely recollected. I find that college students, ordinarily perhaps matter of fact, will grow quite poetical in writing their compositions on such recollections; they select the right details, or the memory automatically makes the right selection, their style rises, and the result is often surprisingly effective. How often too in literature the same kind of subject will result in the same heightening—as in Whittier or Wordsworth, in Lamb or Carlyle.

Reminiscences of this kind have several advantages for the imagination. First, they are thoroughly "tranquillized": the feelings are settled and the fancy may play with them as it

---

[1] *The Interpretation of Dreams*, p. 434.
[2] Dryden, *The Cock and the Fox*, ll. 333–336.

pleases.   Secondly, they are emotionally colored, else they would probably not be recollected, for the memory apparently retains just those experiences which have received some emotional emphasis, and drops the rest.   In other words among early recollections there is no such thing as the trivial; what may seem so as it is recalled is closely related, in fact or in feeling, to matters of heartfelt importance.   In the third place, these recollections go back, as we have already seen, to the period in life of keenest imagination; they have therefore already been regarded imaginatively, and they carry with them always the "light" and "glory" which belong to their source.

But here we are coming to the thought, expressed in "Intimations of Immortality," which will always be associated with the name of Wordsworth; and so we may turn again to the *Prelude* and other poems of his to find both the best statement of the theory and the best examples; and from these I must quote at some length.

At the end of Book XII of the *Prelude* Wordsworth gives two examples of moments or "passages of life" significant for his imagination; "such moments," he says, "are scattered every where, taking their date from our first childhood."   In the first he tells how once riding, "while yet his inexperienced hand could hardly hold a bridle," he came upon a gibbet with a murderer's mouldering bones and chains.   This served to give emotional emphasis to an associated scene which otherwise might have remained insignificant and forgotten.

> Then, reascending the bare common, saw
> A naked pool that lay beneath the hills,
> The beacon on the summit, and, more near,
> A girl, who bore a pitcher on her head,
> And seemed with difficult steps to force her way
> Against the blowing wind.   It was, in truth,
> An ordinary sight; but I should need
> Colors and words that are unknown to man,
> To paint the visionary dreariness
> Which, while I looked all round for my lost guide,

> Invested moorland waste and naked pool,
> The beacon crowning the lone eminence,
> The female and her garments vexed and tossed
> By the strong wind.

Later, "in the blessed hours of early love," he came upon this pool again, and the early emotion returned, making the same scene now imaginative and poetical.

> And think ye not with radiance more sublime
> For these remembrances, and for the power
> They had left behind?   So feeling comes in aid
> Of feeling.

"Feeling comes in aid of feeling,"—this gives the key to the thought.   The early emotion, revived but now tranquillized, is fitted to inspire poetry.

> Oh! mystery of man, from what a depth
> Proceed thy honors.   I am lost, but see
> In simple childhood something of the base
> On which thy greatness stands; but this I feel,
> That from thyself it comes, that thou must give,
> Else never canst receive.   The days gone by
> Return upon me almost from the dawn
> Of life: the hiding-places of man's power
> Open; I would approach them, but they close.
> I see by glimpses now; when age comes on,
> May scarcely see at all; and I would give,
> While yet we may, as far as words can give,
> Substance and life to what I feel, enshrining,
> Such is my hope, the spirit of the Past
> For future restoration.

So, to give other examples, he tells in Book I how his birthplace, with its "fairest of all rivers," "sent a voice that flowed along his dreams"; how in nature he "felt gleams like the flashing of a shield"; how his song goes back to

Those recollected hours that have the charm
Of visionary things, those lovely forms
And sweet sensations that throw back our life,
And almost make remotest infancy
A visible scene, on which the sun is shining.

In school-boy days he listened to the cry of the cuckoo, and later, as he hears it again, it brings to him "a tale of visionary hours," restoring the vision of childhood.

And I can listen to thee yet;
Can lie upon the plain
And listen, till I do beget
That golden time again.

O blessed Bird! the earth we pace
Again appears to be
An unsubstantial, faery place;
That is fit home for thee!

In childhood he sees a rainbow in the sky and his "heart leaps up"; when he is a man he beholds the rainbow again with the same emotion. So feeling comes in aid of feeling, the child's imagination is father to the man's, and the poet's days are

Bound each to each by natural piety.

If we follow Wordsworth we cannot overvalue the importance for the imagination of the earliest images and the pure, strong feelings which accompany them. These feelings form at once the pattern and the source of later ones; from them descends the current which nourishes the later imagination of the poet.

Of particular importance, as the origin of the best feelings, is the influence of the mother. From her the child learns its first and best emotional lessons. "With his soul he drinks in the feelings of his mother's eye." From her embrace he learns love and pity.

Is there a flower, to which he points with hand
Too weak to gather it, already love
Drawn from love's purest earthly fount for him
Hath beautified that flower; already shades
Of pity cast from inward tenderness
Do fall around him upon aught that bears
Unsightly marks of violence or harm.

. . . .

Such, verily, is the first
Poetic spirit of our human life,
By uniform control of after years,
In most, abated or suppressed; in some,
Through every change of growth and of decay,
Pre-eminent till death.[1]

Through influences like these the poet's mind is formed. It is
stored with images from sensations and from previous imaginative experiences, and with the feelings belonging to these—this
accumulation beginning in early childhood, but continuing
through youth and manhood, perhaps in a lesser degree, with
the growth of the mind. Part of this store will be conscious, to
be drawn upon at will, part doubtless unconscious or latent.
Other things being equal he will be the best poet, who, fortunate
in the maternal influence, in his contact with nature, and in his
other experience, has gained the largest and best store.

III

How then is this store drawn upon—how are these accumulated images utilized by the imagination? One has become
linked to another by associations, slight or strong, of contiguity
or resemblance; one thus draws up another, joins and coalesces
with it; and these draw others, forming a combination. When
the mind is moved the images swarm, and the process goes on
with great rapidity. Early impressions are attracted as readily

[1] *Prelude*, Book ii, l. 245. So Alfred de Vigny, in *Samson*, finds the origin
of love in the mother's caresses; "Il rêvera toujours à la chaleur du sein."

as recent ones; at least if they come back at all, they seem to come with equal ease and distinctness. Any imaginative combination will as a rule be made up of both recent and older elements, the latter being attracted to the former in various ways, of which the following would be instances. Suppose an early scene with strong associations and emotional coloring,— for example the schoolroom in which you first went to school. The sight of this room, say upon an actual visit after thirty years, will bring back part of the old associations and the old feelings, forming a new combination of both recent and remote, in which doubtless the latter predominates. Not merely the actual scene, but any similar scene will have the same power. Image A will bring back images b and c, with feelings d and e; and image A^1, like to A, will also bring back the same series. But the second A^1 need not be very similar to A; any likeness will do, provided it is strong enough to form a link or bridge for the imagination. A^1 may look very differently, but if it has any slight resemblance—in form, color, or odor—to A, the link will serve. While I am writing this, for example, my wife asks me for a pencil. I provide one, which happens to be of cedar, and she says, "That reminds me of the cedar pencil-box I had at school," and then she goes on to reminiscences of the box and the bell and her friends, which were doubtless for her colored by the old feelings. Doubtless also the earlier images may be forgotten and only the feeling survive; that is, of the series, A, b, and c may be dropped, and A^1 will recall merely d and e. Thus a recent image may get emotional significance, as Wordsworth expresses it, by "invisible links" and by force

> Of obscure feelings representative
> Of things forgotten.[1]

This last instance, however, is so important and represents so well, as I believe, what often takes place in the working of the poetic imagination that it deserves a separate paragraph. I

[1] *Prelude*, Book i, l. 605.

have already said that of the images stored in the mind some are conscious, some unconscious; and similarly of any chain of images existing in the mind, some of the links may be conscious and some unconscious; in other words we may see one or more of the links but we do not see all or see their concatenation. This will explain imaginative combinations which otherwise would be inexplicable. Let us take a case. I suppose everyone has had the experience of looking at some ordinary scene or object and finding it suddenly and strangely poetical—of finding it clothed with a charm of imaginative coloring which does not seem to belong to it, and which can hardly be explained. At such moments "we are aware," as Shelley says, "of evanescent visitations of thought and feeling, sometimes associated with place or person, sometimes regarding our mind alone, and always arising unforeseen and departing unbidden, but elevating and delightful beyond all expression." [1] These visitations arise unforeseen and depart unbidden, of course, because they are the products not of voluntary, but of spontaneous or visionary thought. They seem to emanate from the scene before us but they in fact proceed from the mind. How are they to be explained?

Perhaps in the first place by the mental action which psychologists call "mediate association." Of this the classical example is Sir William Hamilton's, to whom Loch Lomond (A) recalled the Prussian system of education (C) because, as he found, he had once met there a Prussian officer (B) who conversed with him on this subject.[2] Between A and C a bridge is formed by B, which however does not enter consciousness. In the case in hand the scene and its emanations form the two ends of such an associative chain. For example you find a scene—say a row of apple-trees in blossom—full of a peculiar feeling of tenderness. The fact is that these blossoms (A) are linked with others of years before (B); and among these you last saw your mother or your sweetheart (C), toward whom you felt with

---

[1] *Defense of Poetry*, p. 40. [2] Ribot, *Creative Imagination*, p. 59.

tenderness (D). The links B and C are "forgotten" or unconscious; but through them D is attached to A. The trees and
blossoms are clothed again with the feeling of the first experience,
though you do not know why. The feeling may be of any
sort—one of love or fear, of awe or pity—or a "fleeting mood of
shadowy exaltation"; and it may give its tone to any subsequent scene with which it may be connected by the invisible
links. Thus

> the soul
> Remembering how she felt, but what she felt
> Remembering not, retains an obscure sense
> Of possible sublimity.[1]

Thus, as De Quincey eloquently expresses it, "Phantoms of
lost power, sudden intuitions, and shadowy restorations of forgotten feelings, sometimes dim and perplexing, sometimes by
bright but furtive glimpses, sometimes by a full and steady
revelation, overcharged with light—throw us back in a moment
upon scenes and remembrances that we have left full thirty years
behind us." [2]   But I imagine the matter is ordinarily too complex to be covered by the simple formula of the mediate association. There are many recurring scenes in nature—the colors
at sunset, the rising of the moon in a clear sky, the song of birds
in spring—scenes with which we have been familiar from childhood, which are connected, not by a mere chain but by a complex network of associations with many earlier images and feelings. Such scenes are always and for everyone poetical. And
conversely every person of sensibility, every poet, has accumulated a great number of images and feelings which, as from a
sort of reservoir, may flow in many directions through the various channels of such a network, associating first with one new
image, then with another. Thus the poet will be apt to regard
every scene imaginatively, he will always have abundant material ready for his fancy, he will live in a world of the imagina-

---

[1] *Prelude*, Book ii, l. 315.   [2] *Works*, ed. Masson, vol. ii, p. 204.

tion, and, as Shelley expresses it, "color all that he combines with its evanescent hues."

> And visions, as poetic eyes avow,
> Hang on each leaf and cling to every bough.

This network, extending ultimately to all the conscious and the latent contents of the mind, along which the countless images run, with their many emotional tones, as they are attracted by the desires, to take their place in the imaginative production, is obviously a matter so complex and intricate that it is beyond the reach of critical analysis. That is, we cannot say how or why the imaginative pictures are formed as they are. Furthermore the action will vary with each particular poet, and with each poetical moment. The network is individual, depending first upon the poet's inborn gifts; and it is alive, growing and changing with his growth and his particular experience. Thus it would be hopeless, in even a single imaginative action of the poetic mind, to try to trace the different elements to their source. Doubtless an attempt might be made—provided the poets would favor the experiment—by a process of analysis like that which psychologists have applied to dreams. But in general for such an analysis we should have to know the poet's mind, its character and growth, and its entire intellectual and emotional experience, more fully than we can hope to know them.

In comparison with this complex reticulation the end of the imaginative process is fortunately more simple. The images and feelings brought from whatever recondite source, recent or remote, conscious or "forgotten," finally combine to form one emotionalized picture, possessing the same unity and consistency for the imagination or mental vision, as an external picture has for the eye of sense. The ingredient images are not merely juxtaposed or even combined; they rather coalesce, one image, or features from it, running into another, and all growing together, by an organic action of the mind. They thus form a composite unity, related to its many constituent elements, but essentially a new creation. In this newness of course consists the value of the picture: it is the original and individual contribution of the mind, the ideal element added to the reality on which the imagery is ultimately based.

We can get a good idea of the character of this organic fusion by taking the corresponding action of the imagination in dreams. Here the imagination is more lawless and the composites are formed more boldly; but the action is essentially the same. I may borrow examples from Havelock Ellis. "I went to sleep thinking of a friend who was that night to stay at a hotel I had never seen. I dreamed that I saw the hotel in question; its façade was not unlike that of a common type of hotel, but the roof was flat, and at no very great height from the ground, so that I was able to overlook the building and see into all the windows, an arrangement that struck me as bad. My ability to overlook the building was not, however, accompanied by any perception of its diminutiveness. On awakening I remembered that my wife had received a chicken incubator the day before, and we had examined it in the evening. The image of the hotel had fused with the image of the incubator." [1] A second example: "Thus I once, as a youth, had a vivid dream of an albatross that became transformed into a woman, the beautiful eyes of the albatross taking on a womanly expression, but the bird's beak only being imperfectly changed into a nose as the bird-woman murmured 'Do you love me?'" This second example is more poetical than the first. From this it is not a long step to the pure poetry of Keats, from whom I may take one more example describing the serpent-woman Lamia.

> She was a gordian shape of dazzling hue
> Vermillion-spotted, golden, green, and blue;
> Striped like a zebra, freckled like a pard,
> And full of silver moons, that as she breathed
> Dissolved, or brighter shone, or interwreathed.

[1] *The World of Dreams*, pp. 39, 22.

> Upon her crest she wore a wannish fire
> Sprinkled with stars, like Ariadne's tiar:
> Her head was serpent, but ah, bitter-sweet!
> She had a woman's mouth with all its pearls complete.

Here many bright-colored images, doubtless from many different sources, are fused into a picture which, one is sure in reading the poem, Keats saw in imagination with the distinctness of a vivid dream.

CHAPTER XI

THE IMAGINATION: CONDENSATION AND DISPLACEMENT

I

THOUGH the action by which the component images within the poet's mind grow into the imaginative picture is very complex and obscure, it is no doubt subject to certain laws,—the discovery of which is a matter for much future investigation. As the imaginative process in poetry is analogous to that in dreams, and as the principles governing the latter have been investigated by psychologists, particularly by Freud and his followers, it is worth while to ask how far the principles thus discovered for dreams apply to the related subject of poetry. The action by which the dream is formed from the thoughts and feelings contained in the mind of the dreamer is called by Freud the "Dream work " (*Traumarbeit*), and it goes on according to laws which he has developed with considerable fullness and care.[1] If we call the corresponding action of the mind in the forming of poetic images the Poetic work (or *Dichterarbeit*), the question is how far the principles of the one are applicable to the other.

The dream picture, like the poetic picture which we have described in the preceding chapter, goes back to many antecedents in the mind. Furthermore each element of the dream picture—each object, person, or other feature—is apt to go back to two, three, or more such antecedents. Each element tends, in Freudian phrase, to be "over-determined." It may take two or three actual persons, for example, to furnish forth a single person of the dream, the composite dream person drawing some

---

[1] *Interpretation of Dreams*, ch. vi.

features from each of the different antecedents, and possessing some of the characteristics, relations, emotional attitude—in a word, psychical significance—of each. This is the reason why the dream is so full of meaning: each feature is full of the qualities and associations of its various originals. Thus a short dream which might be told in half a dozen sentences, will involve a multitude of images, impressions, or experiences, which could hardly be recorded in as many pages. It is as if a diffused and extensive body of thought were condensed and crystallized to form the dream. Indeed the term which Freud applies to this feature of the process is *condensation*.

This condensation is accomplished by the combining or telescoping of images referred to in the preceding chapter, so that the examples there given will serve here. Another simple example is as follows: "A lady who had been cooking in the course of the day and in the evening had read a scientific description of the way birds obtain and utilize their food, such as fruit and snails, dreams at night that she has discovered when out walking a kind of animal-fruit, a damson containing a snail within it, which she views with delight as admirably adapted for culinary purposes." [1]

The dream is a fusion, as is its most striking feature, the "animal-fruit." This example, however, barely illustrates the principle; it would be necessary to give a dream at length, with its analysis, to show what a multiplicity of associations radiate from it in all directions and how largely each feature is "over-determined." This condensation is most obvious when it acts upon words or names. In dreams words do not function to form language, but are treated simply as visual or auditory images which may be combined like images of other kinds. They are therefore run together with strange results. Freud tells, as an example, that, after receiving from one of his colleagues a physiological essay which he thought extravagant, he dreamed with evident reference to this essay: "That is in

---

[1] H. Ellis, *The World of Dreams*, p. 37.

true *norekdal* style." The novel formation was found on analysis to be a fusion of the names of two characters of Ibsen, upon whom the essayist had previously written a critique. The word need not, however, be a new formation; any ordinary word may be "over-determined," and this is the commonest case; that is, it may be given one significance by one of its antecedents in the dream and another significance by another, and so involve a kind of dream pun or word-play. Indeed the dream might be described as such a playing upon words or images all through, with double and triple meanings attaching to every feature.

Now the poetic work involves a similar process of condensation. Each feature of the picture which the poet beholds through his imagination tends to be a composite—to go back to many originals, and so to involve the qualities, feelings, and applications of its originals. Similarly each significant word in the language of poetry (the particles being excluded), or, we may say, each word in the poem which is definitely "poetical," will partake of this character of the imagination which inspires the poem; the poetic language in this respect truly expresses the imaginative subject matter. Or to put this differently, each word will be apt to have two, three, or even many meanings or implications, corresponding to the multiple associations of the mental imagery which it represents. The language, like the imaginative mental picture—like the vision or dream of the poet—shows condensation. Of these various meanings one may be the primary denotation, the others secondary, suggested, or connoted. One may be the apparent or surface meaning, the others latent. But often the surface meaning will be of less importance than the latent ones; the idea having true poetic significance and bearing the emotional emphasis will be not said but suggested, and the real poetry will be between the lines; the secondary meaning may be the one of prime importance. A poem will be "poetical " or "imaginative " in proportion as its language is thus overcharged with meanings. This principle of course accounts first for the brevity, and secondly for the suggestiveness of poetry.

The richness of association inherent in products of the imagination may be seen clearly in the primitive myths, which lie between poetry and dreams, or which may be called the poetic dreams of the childhood of the race. A story like that of Prometheus probably has many sources in human experience, and correspondingly it has many facets and implications. Its meaning is almost as inexhaustible as that of human life itself, though this meaning must be found beneath the surface of the story.

In the case of modern poetry it will be easiest to illustrate the principle in hand from the language of specific poems. Let us take first a line from the " Eve of St. Agnes" which has probably given the critics as much trouble as any other in Keats. It represents Madeline, in "her soft and chilly nest," as

Clasp'd like a missal where swart paynims pray.

On this Leigh Hunt comments: "Clasp'd like a missal in a land of pagans,—that is to say, where Christian prayer books must not be seen, and are, therefore, doubly cherished for the danger." This comment R. Garnett calls "entirely wide of the mark," insisting that whereas Hunt takes "clasp'd" to mean "clasp'd to the bosom," its true meaning is "fastened with a clasp." "Clasp'd missal may be allowed to suggest holiness which the prayers of swart paynims neglect," says another comment. "Missal, a prayer book bearing upon its margin pictures of converted heathen in the act of prayer," says still another. And finally M. Jusserand finds the line only "a string of beautiful words, suggesting, at most, a meaning rather than having any." I should think most if not all of the puzzled annotators were right, including the last. At least the line has all the meanings that an intelligent and imaginative reader, if not a puzzled annotator, will attach to it. The precise critic will of course note that in this line Keats first wrote "shut like a missal," and that this is final as to the meaning of "clasp'd." But the matter is not quite so simple. The fact that Keats tried this line in three different ways before he settled on the text in question shows that he wrote it, as indeed he did this whole passage, with thought and care. Why, then, did he change the original "shut" to "clasp'd"? Partly perhaps because he wanted "shut" for the last line of the stanza ("as though a rose should shut and be a bud again"), but partly also because "shut" is here a prosaic rather than a poetic word. "Clasp'd" not only says all that "shut" would say; but secondly it goes better with "missal," to fit the mediaeval character of the piece and to "suggest holiness"; and thirdly it admits the very meaning of "held closely and tenderly," which Leigh Hunt was too much of a poet to miss. "Clasp'd" was adopted by Keats, in other words, precisely because it meant two or three things instead of one, and was accordingly more suggestive and poetical. If the line as a whole "suggests a meaning rather than has any" it is in this respect precisely like many another good poetic line. And I venture to say that it never has given much trouble to any reader who reads, not by words, but by lines and stanzas, and who has had his imagination a little stirred by the context. I have dwelt on this line because it illustrates a principle which is most important in all reading of poetry, and which is inherent in its very nature —namely, that whereas in true prose words should have one meaning and one meaning only, in true poetry they should have as many meanings as possible, and the more the better, as long as these are true to the images in the poet's mind.

At the risk of being tedious I must take another example,— from Shakespeare. Hamlet's soliloquy is dramatically the expression of a mind at high tension, filled with more confused images than it can find words for, and at best fitting these images with words none too well. The broken and turbid expression itself suggests the mental situation. It is not strange therefore that this speech, when subjected to languid analysis by the verbal critics, should have given a great deal of trouble, and that it should have required ten closely printed pages in the Variorum Shakespeare even to summarize the observations that have been made upon it. Readers who wish to get an idea of what learned German criticism may do for Shakespeare should read Elze's discussion of the line

When we have shuffled off this mortal coil.

Here editors suggest "clay," "vail," "soil," and "spoil," and try to decide between the different possible meanings of "coil." Now it is well in reading Shakespeare, first to avoid emendations as far as may be, and secondly, where two or more meanings are possible and congruous with the context, not to dispute between them, but to understand them all. These two rules of course will not solve all the difficulties, but they will dispense with a great deal of the annotation. In the line just quoted Shakespeare probably had first an image of the turmoil and confusion of this mortal life, and then an image of the body as the wrapping or covering of the soul—both of which might be shuffled off in the "sleep of death." The second image is very closely related to the first, is a little more specific, and more figurative. Both can be fused and condensed in the word "coil," which kills two birds with one small stone. This line again will not bother any reader whose imagination has been awakened by the context. To such a reader the line is alive with meaning; it is not made up of dead or inert words, with definite and exclusive denotations. The real difficulty is that, as we no longer have the imagination to write poetry, we lack even the imagination to read it. The age of poetry is gone; that of sophisters, scholiasts, and antiquarians has succeeded. We must spend our time threshing over and over the remains of former harvests.

Before we take further examples, it will be well to notice also Freud's theory of wit, in which he finds the action of the mind similar to that in dreams—and so likewise to that in poetry. In wit also the mental operation involves the process of condensation that we have just been discussing, as well as other features of the "dream work" which we shall take up later. In wit the same fusion of words and images often results in a condensed or "over-determined" expression; brevity is the soul of wit. In wit, as in poetry, the fusion often unexpectedly throws together images not ordinarily associated, and brings to light unsuspected likenesses, giving thus a kind of poetical pleasure. Wit also, like poetry, often expresses indirectly and by a latent meaning what, because of some inhibition (as we shall see later), cannot be stated openly. In wit the fusion will often result, as we have seen in dreams, in new verbal formations. "Indeed, he would sometimes remark," Disraeli writes in *Lothair*, "when a man fell into his anecdotage it was a sign for him to retire from the world." The meaning compressed into the telescoped word would if expanded require a sentence. Oftener the wit will lie in an ordinary word taken in two senses, in a pun or paronomasia. Two meanings, which might be expressed separately by two unambiguous words, are fused, and this fusion represented by an ambiguity. When Wordsworth said, if he had a mind he could write like Shakespeare, Charles Lamb suggested, "It is only the mind that is wanting." Here of course a word contains two meanings, one a surface meaning which is harmless, the other a latent one which bears the point. Lamb might carry it off by looking grave and insisting on the first. Sydney Smith said of Macaulay, "He has occasional flashes of silence, that make his conversation perfectly delightful." In his mind Smith thought, "If he would only be silent for an instant." In his speech he would have had to say, without recourse to wit, "His conversation is delightful." But with the turn "flashes of silence" he can speak without being boorish on the one hand or insincere on the other. Sometimes a decorum of another kind furnishes the obstacle or inhibition which must be overcome by wit; the secondary meaning in a "double entendre" would be coarse or indecent if it stood alone. In the *Rape of the Lock* Belinda and the Baron meet in a mock-Homeric conflict of the drawing-room, in which the Baron is worsted.

> "Boast not my fall," he cried, "insulting foe!
> Thou by some other shalt be laid as low."

The case is saved here not only by the word-play but also by
the Homeric ingredient. The whole piece, like this couplet,
is double, with associations from the epic on the one hand and
from Queen Anne society on the other. In this atmosphere of
poetry and wit the point of the couplet is innocuous. It would
be hard to decide, by the way, whether the couplet is witty or
poetical,— and quite unnecessary.

In order to bring out the relationship between wit and poetry
and the ease with which one runs into the other I may quote
three related examples. The first is again from the *Rape of
the Lock*.

> See, fierce Belinda on the Baron flies,
> With more than usual lightning in her eyes:
> Nor fear'd the chief the unequal fight to try,
> Who sought no more than on his foe to die.

The word "die" is taken first in the literal sense of the Homeric
battle, and secondly in a figurative sense, which need not be
explained either to the general reader or to the psychologist.
The point is much the same in the sestet of Keats's last beautiful sonnet—only here the secondary latent meaning is not
witty, but highly poetical.

> No—yet still steadfast, still unchangeable,
> Pillow'd upon my fair love's ripening breast,
> To feel forever its soft fall and swell,
> Awake forever in a sweet unrest,
> Still, still to hear her tender-taken breath,
> And so live ever—or else swoon to death.

Some readers may doubt whether there is the latent meaning in the last word. The only real doubt is whether (as he
wrote) it was in Keats's mind consciously or only unconsciously, and whether (as he reads) the reader consciously sees
it or only unconsciously feels it. Because a poet, like a dreamer,

may use a symbol of this kind—especially an old and well
worn one—without consciously recognizing it; as a reader may
unconsciously get its effect.   Perhaps indeed the unconscious
effect is the stronger, for poetry ceases to be poetry where all
the effects are conscious and explicable, and it is precisely
through latent meanings of this kind that poetry exercises its
mysterious influence and charm.   The third example is from
the scene of Juliet's death.

Juliet. Yea, noise? then I'll be brief. O happy dagger! (*Snatching
   Romeo's dagger*)
This is thy sheath (*Stabs herself*): there rust, and let me die.   (*Falls
   on Romeo's body and dies*)

Here I venture to say, though the Shakespearean annotators
do not notice it, "die" has a shade of the latent meaning of
Pope's couplet.   I call attention to it not at all as a curiosity
but as a genuine and important poetical ingredient in the scene.
An immature or thoughtless reader will of course overlook it.
But a reader or an audience that has been carried away by the
dramatic feeling will have a sense of it, and will feel too a vague
emotional satisfaction as Juliet dies, not by the poison, but on
Romeo's dagger and falling upon Romeo's body.   The satisfaction will be of the nameless and unexplained kind that is
the truest mark of poetry: and if the point were made openly
it would be at once impossible and unpoetical.   The thoughtful
reader, however, will go on to comprehend and explain it.   He
will be familiar with the preceding examples. He will remember Shakespeare's constant word-play—sometimes coarse,
sometimes poetical—in this tragedy and throughout.   He will
note that Romeo puns in his dying speech ("O, here will I set
up my everlasting rest") and indeed falls with this same word
"die" as his last ("Thus with a kiss I die").   The word-play
here ceases to be mere pun or witticism, and becomes highly
poetical, adding greatly to the dramatic effect, though it is
perhaps a little more in the Elizabethan taste than ours.
Indeed the whole tragedy of love and death is summed up in

this last word and corresponding last action of each of the two lovers. The thoughtful reader, then, will consciously understand this effect, which I have no doubt Shakespeare consciously intended.[1]

The word-play found everywhere in Shakespeare is variously regarded. Sometimes one regrets his habit of punning and thinks of it as a half pardonable product of his playful and exuberant, somewhat boyish and primitive, imagination. This of course it is in one aspect, for boys and savages are given to playing with words. But the habit is due to the free imaginative play of the minds of boys and savages; and similarly it is inherent, as I am trying in this chapter to show, in the language of an imaginative age like the Elizabethan and in that of a highly imaginative poet like Shakespeare. Shakespeare's word-play is of the essence of his poetry. It is instructive to notice how it grows with his general poetic and dramatic growth. In the early plays it is often superficial, a bavin wit of puns and quibbles. In the later ones it becomes profoundly significant and poetical. It is of all degrees and values. Sometimes it merely adds a verbal effectiveness:

> To save our heads by raising of a head.

Sometimes it involves an expressive figure:

> The moody frontier of a servant brow.

Sometimes the meaning is not double but triple, as when Hotspur, in rebellion against Henry IV, exclaims:

> We must have bloody noses and crack'd crowns
> And pass them current too. God's me, my horse!

Here the "crack'd crowns" are first cracked coins, secondly broken heads, and thirdly royal crowns upset. Note too that the third meaning is at once the farthest from the literal, the most latent, perhaps the most unconscious (in Hotspur's mind),

[1] Compare Dryden, *Conquest of Granada*, Part I, Act III, Sc. i (Song), and Shelley, *Prometheus*, II, ii, 28.

and the most far-reaching (involving the whole dramatic action). This is almost regularly the case: the deeper the meaning is buried, the deeper its significance.

But this triple word-play is simple compared with Hamlet's. In Act I Hamlet, dressed in black, appears before the king and queen, who have cast off their mourning and are seated on their thrones in state.

> *King.* But now, my cousin Hamlet, and my son,—
> *Hamlet.* (Aside) A little more than kin, and less than kind.
> *King.* How is it that the clouds still hang on you?
> *Hamlet.* Not so, my lord; I am too much i' the sun.

In both his speeches Hamlet's feeling and roused imagination play with words. Especially in the second, addressed directly to the king and so under strongest repression, the utterance is tremendously "over-determined," charged with all kinds of meaning. It is "purposely enigmatical," Staunton observes;—"spontaneously enigmatical" would be better; and it is enigmatical not because it is meaningless but because it means so much. Besides the literal meaning borne by "clouds" and "sun" which is the starting point, Hamlet declares: 1. that, in his black, he is too much in the sunshine of royal splendor; 2. that destitute and under a cloud as he is, he is but too much in the sunshine of the king's favor; 3. that, as the "common saw" has it, he is "out of God's benediction into the warm sun" (*Lear*, II, ii, 168),—that is, out of house and home; 4. that he is "sonned" too much by the king, without a son's rights.[1] But the speech is poetry, and the meanings cannot be enumerated in prose. These, with others that my readers may suggest, are all congruous; they run into, reënforce, and harmonize with each other. The reader does not of course, as he reads, analyze and separate them; that is, to Shakespeare or to the imaginative reader, "Too much in the sun" means most or all of these things together and at

---

[1] Shakespeare's readers and printers spelled variously; his audience of course went by ear. He always plays with the sound, not with the spelling.

once, just as c-a-t means cat. It is of imagination all compact. And again the deepest meanings are the most significant.

Among these many examples we are in danger of losing sight of the principle which they illustrate,—namely that as each image seen by the poet's imagination is a complex of many images and tends to involve the associations—thoughts and feelings— of each of these constituents, so the language of any poem recording this imagination has many roots in the poet's mind; and therefore this language and even each word of it has not single, but manifold meaning and implication. Further it should not be supposed from the preceding examples that this principle applies merely to word-play in the narrow sense—to the puns and double meanings of which Shakespeare was so fond. The double meanings which can be analyzed run on into the manifold meanings which are beyond analysis, and the latter are commonest. The fact is that the imagination plays with every word that it touches, fills it with meanings and suggestions, colors and brightens it, borrowing lights and colors too from other words and from the context, until the whole expression becomes illuminated, and the glorified utterance becomes a fitting expression of the imaginative mind. The famous poetical lines and passages will regularly show this wealth of meaning.

> We are such stuff
> As dreams are made on; and our little life
> Is rounded with a sleep.

It is useless to analyze the meaning of such lines. Dreams are surrounded by sleep; and likewise our brief life is surrounded by the greater sleep, which is constantly compared by poets to the lesser one. But is life also *rounded out* and fulfilled by this sleep? And does life go on in this seeming oblivion, as dreams may go on in what seems dreamless slumber? The expression is beyond the understanding, but it goes on sounding in the imagination, as a good bell goes on ringing after it is struck, until the meaning has died away. The principle in hand, then, applies to all expressions of the imagination—to every word of poetic value in every imaginative poem. This whole matter is closely connected with the symbolical and figurative character of the poetic language which will be taken up in a later chapter.

So far the examples have dealt mainly with the language of particular passages. But the principle applies also to the poem or other work of literary art taken as a whole. A poem will not only have in sum associations from all the images of which it is made up, but taken as whole it may be double or multiple in its significance. It may have a meaning within a meaning as in the fable or allegory, or it may, like the myth, have many facets and radiations, as is always the case in the greatest poems, as in *Lear*, *The Faerie Queene*, or *Prometheus Unbound*. Poe, who defines poetry as the "rhythmical creation of beauty," includes under the beautiful what he calls the "mystical;" and this term he applies to "that class of composition in which there lies beneath the transparent upper current of meaning an under or *suggestive* one. What we vaguely term the *moral* of any sentiment is its mystic or secondary expression. It has the vast force of an accompaniment in music. This vivifies the air; that spiritualizes the *fanciful* conception, and lifts it into the ideal." The merely fanciful is thus raised to the truly imaginative by the presence of this under current. Poe gives as examples " Comus," the " Ancient Mariner," and the " Sensitive Plant " of Shelley. Poe's own " Haunted Palace " is an excellent example, in which the palace symbolizes the human body and the symbolical meaning shows through the literal one with strikingly beautiful effect. And when this poem is placed within the " Fall of the House of Usher " new and deeper currents of meaning are started, running between the poem and the story, which lend greater force to the story and more profound beauty to the poem, as the ray of a gem gains depth when it finds its appropriate setting. Indeed this beautiful poem in its perfect setting seems to me one of the best examples of the imaginative multiplication and radiation of beauty to be found in literature. And though its implications are beyond analysis it is a matter of the deepest interest to trace some of them to Poe's own mental experience, for they have many roots in the poet's mind. Though Poe was proud of his analytical powers he could never have produced this work consciously and deliberately. The intellect never produces work of this kind: the imagination, from its very nature, always does.

For a final example we may return to *Hamlet*, this time taking the play as a whole. The subject is Hamlet's revenge—that is, Hamlet has put upon him the task of securing his revenge in the face of certain obstacles. These are of three kinds. In the first place he is impeded by external and physical obstacles, thrown in his way by the king. In this aspect the play is a battle of wit and strength between the king and Hamlet. The scenes which deal with the machinations of the king and Hamlet's efforts to overcome them, like Hamlet's dispatch to England and his return, are the least interesting; and if the play were made up entirely of these it would be only melodrama. But secondly, Hamlet, in weighing his task, finds certain obstacles imposed upon him by his own mind,—which he and the audience see clearly enough and which he must strive to overcome. He must consider his duty to his father and to his country, to his mother and to Ophelia. He must not "taint his mind." These difficulties are quite numerous enough to complicate and involve the plot, and to provide great dramatic interest. If there were no more, however, the play would be only a clever psychological drama. Thirdly, however, considering the terms in which the story is told and the character delineated, we feel the presence in Hamlet's mind of further and deeper difficulties. We feel that there are obstacles, conflicts, or inhibitions, of which Hamlet is unconscious, and against which his conscious will is powerless. These of course cannot be demonstrated, first because they are hidden, and secondly because Hamlet (as we are apt to forget, so strong is the truth to life) is only a *dramatis persona* and therefore beyond investigation. But we feel that Hamlet in his soliloquies cannot explain his deepest and greatest difficulties, and that we cannot understand them, though we may sympathize with him because of them. Perhaps, if we suppose the mind of this character more than any other in the plays,—more even than Prospero's—represents the mind of Shakespeare, the mental conflict is Shakespeare's own, was unconscious also in his case, and was put into the play unconsciously. The poet himself did not comprehend this conflict, but he saw and felt it imaginatively, and therefore could suggest it in the lines which portray the character. What is beyond question is that the character is complex, many-sided, and enigmatic. Was Hamlet sane, or insane, or disordered? Was he a man of action or a helpless hypochondriac? Why did he outrage Ophelia, and why did he fail to kill the king? The questions are numerous and the answers to them infinite. But in this infinity lies the greatness of the play.

Every action of the imagination, then, produces a living complex which has many issues in the poetic mind. Every work of poetry which records it, and every feature of this work, has many meanings. Some are superficial, some are latent; the latter are most significant. Some can be comprehended, some can be felt only; the latter are most poetical. Some are consciously, others unconsciously produced; the latter are the richest products of the imagination. Some are readily expressible, others are under repression and must be veiled and hidden: the latter, as we shall see in a later chapter, are the truest subjects of poetry.

II

So far this chapter has dealt with the condensation of the "dream work." "Dream condensation and dream displacement," according to Freud, "are the two craftsmen to whom we may chiefly attribute the moulding of the dream." [1] The latter process also has some application to poetry. It may be described briefly for our purposes as follows. A matter of

[1] *Interpretation of Dreams*, p. 286.

indifference or slight importance in the mind will be represented by conspicuous and emphatic images in the dream,
whereas a matter of genuine and serious import, if it appear
in the dream at all, will be relegated to the background. The
thought as it exists in the mind, in being formed into the dream
pictures, suffers a shift or displacement of psychic emphasis—
so that what is central in the first becomes marginal in the
second, and vice versa. This accounts for the deception of
the dream; manifestly it is commonplace and innocent; only
in its latent features is it significant. For example in the dream
mentioned in Chapter X the feature of apparent importance
is that I pick up numbers of golf balls with eagerness, but it is
found on investigation that the secondary feature of the mushrooms is much more significant, has more associations, and is
more highly emotionalized. Both features indeed carry some
feeling in their origin, but the higher psychic intensity of
the second is shifted in the dream to the first. The preceding is obviously only a more explicit statement of a process we have already observed in Chapter X, by which a feeling
is transferred from an (older) significant experience to a (recent)
trivial one, and by which, through a contiguity or a resemblance, one experience is made to stand as an emotional substitute for another. This process of displacement is also closely
connected with that of condensation and multiple meanings
which we have just noticed. That is, wherever there are two
or more meanings, one obvious and apparent, the others latent,
a shifting of psychic intensity has taken place. The obvious
meaning is apparently central, the latent meaning is seen only
out of the corner of the eye. But this appearance is deceptive,
as in the dream; the apparently central meaning is relatively
unimportant, while the marginal meaning as we have seen, is
emotionally significant.

I may ask the reader therefore to reconsider the examples
given earlier in this chapter as illustrations of this new process,
and content myself here with one or two further examples.
The first, which may seem merely curious but is somewhat

instructive, is from the *Epistle to Dr. Arbuthnot* in which Pope professes to rise above hostile attack and abuse,—above

> The tale revived, the lie so oft o'erthrown,
> The imputed trash, and dullness not his own;
> The morals blacken'd when the writings 'scape,
> The libelled person and the pictured shape.

Rankling in Pope's mind as he wrote the last lines was probably the frontispiece of "Pope Alexander's " *Supremacy and Infallibility Examined*, which showed the poet in the likeness of an ape. What he ostensibly objected to was being pictured: what he really objected to was being pictured like an *ape*. The real meaning lurks and betrays itself in the choice of words and rhyme *(scape-shape)*. Pope either wittily indicates the caricature he has in mind, or he unconsciously betrays the feeling of pique he professes he is superior to. In either case there is a curious condensation and displacement. Whenever any feeling in the mind requires repression—a feeling of pique as here, or of shame or delicacy or conscientious scruple—this process of displacement will tend to come into play. The subject of repression must be considered later by itself.

Whenever in poetry or fiction an author puts himself into the story, he is apt also to include besides this character in certain aspects representative of himself, another character or other characters, not apparently to be identified with himself,—to whom, however, his most significant experiences and his deepest feelings are transferred. One character narrates the story, using the first personal "I," and in the outward incidents of his life and in his more superficial characteristics resembles the author; another character, referred to in the third person, not ostensibly autobiographical, will nevertheless represent the author's inner, deeper, and more unconscious life. This kind of transference is a variety of displacement. Often in Poe there is this mechanism—in the " Gold Bug," the " Assignation," or the " Fall of the House of Usher." In the last named story, for example, the narrator is the rational, hack-writing, work-a-day

Poe: Roderick Usher is Poe the poet, the dreamer, the victim of fear, hyperaesthesia, and neurosis. For Poe's biographer the latter is the more instructive character; it has deeper roots in Poe's mind; it reveals psychic depths which Poe would have shown reluctantly, which therefore he strives, so to speak, to shift from himself in the story. Roderick Usher suffers while the narrator only looks on and sympathizes. For another example I may take " Julian and Maddalo." The picture of the two poets talking as they ride home in the evening on the Lido is of course delightful. The remainder of the poem is more puzzling but perhaps, as far as Shelley is concerned, more instructive if we can understand it. Who is the maniac? According to Shelley himself he is "also in some degree a painting from nature, but with respect to time and place ideal." According to Dowden his confessions are probably "the idealized record of Shelley's days of misery with Harriet." If this be true we can understand why Shelley recounts trifling experiences under the thin disguise of Julian, but transfers his terrible confessions to a character much more heavily shrouded. The trifles are easily comprehensible, the confessions are confused and obscure. In poetry, as in dreams, the most confused portions doubtless often have the greatest emotional intensity. We shall return to this subject of displacement later.

The last examples here bring up the subject of the formation of characters in poetry and fiction, and as this is one of the most common and most important functions of the imagination, and as it illustrates new features of the imaginative work, I shall take it up in a new chapter.

CHAPTER XII

I

THE subject of the formation of imaginary characters covers a very wide field—as wide as the whole field of literature—and indeed wider, because, as we shall see, the imagination which forms characters for the purposes of literary fiction, forms them also for other quite non-literary purposes in much the same way. In fact the imagination in all its many employments is oftenest engaged in the imagining of persons. In the following chapter dealing with this large subject I shall be able only to attempt some classification of the processes involved, and to make some few observations on each class with examples.

The characters in poetry and prose fiction may be conceived and delineated in two ways, corresponding to the two modes of thought already explained,—that is, they may be either intellectually constructed or imaginatively created. Doubtless in practice, particularly in the ordinary novel, there is often a combination of the two faculties or methods. The character is first seen in imagination and then elaborated, discussed, criticized by the intellect. But here as earlier, the imaginative conception is what demands attention. Furthermore the intellectually constructed character will always be inferior and will betray its inferiority to the imaginatively created one—first in naturalness and truth to life, and secondly in originality and depth of significance. The imaginatively created character will delight and refresh us with its novelty; it will go on acting in our own imaginations after we have closed the book, or after we have left the theatre.[1]

The first requisite, then, for the writer of fiction, the requisite compared with which all the others are insignificant, is that he should see his characters in his imagination. As we have all so often used this expression of "seeing in the imagination" vaguely and thoughtlessly it may be better to say that the writer of fiction must see his characters appearing and acting before him with that "eye of the mind" I have referred to; or if his imagination is auditory, he must hear them speaking with his supersensory ear;—see or hear them almost as distinctly as we see and hear through the bodily senses. He may see them realistically moving among scenes of ordinary life; or more dramatically, like Stevenson, who describes "dozing off in his box seat" and watching his "little people" acting their parts "upon their lighted theatre;" or like Sully-Prudhomme, who says that in writing his plays, "I seemed to be a spectator at the play; I gazed at what was passing on the scene in an eager passionate expectation of what was to follow." But in some sense they must have to him the reality of true persons. Scott, who dictated the *Bride of Lammermoor* from his couch in illness, and who strangely after the book was written did not "recollect one single incident, character, or conversation it contained," yet conceived it with such spirit that "he arose from his couch and walked up and down the room, raising and lowering his voice, and as it were acting the parts." [2] And lest it may be thought that this kind of composition is out of date I may cite a recent American writer. Speaking of his "Minervy Anns" Joel Chandler Harris says, "I have been intensely absorbed in

---

[1] In other words the characters coming from true vision are best. This is why Mme. Rachilde preferred the characters of dream. "With one exception," she says, "all my books were first seen in dreams . . . and very often when I add chapters on my own account (de ma propre autorité) they do not turn out to be the best part of the book." Chabaneix, *Le Subconscient*, p. 57.

[2] Lockhart, *Life*, vol. vi, p. 67.

the series, more so than in anything I have ever written. There have been moments when I could hear her voice as plainly as I now hear the youngsters talking in the sitting-room." [1]

Dickens, whose characters combine originality with lifelikeness to a degree hardly equalled elsewhere in fiction, owes his success, in part at any rate, to the very vividness of his imagination. He could see a fictitious character, or by use of the same faculty, assume a fictitious part. As imagination of this kind is a gift rather than an acquirement, he possessed it long before he began to write. In an account appearing in *David Copperfield* but written first previously as fact, he tells how as a child he devoured the old English novels and impersonated his favorite characters in them. "I have been Tom Jones (a child's Tom Jones, a harmless creature) for a week together. I have sustained my own idea of Roderick Random for a month at a stretch, I verily believe . . . I have seen Tom Pipes go climbing up the church-steeple; I have watched Strap with the knapsack on his back, stopping to rest himself upon the wicket-gate; and I *know* that Commodore Trunnion held that club with Mr. Pickle, in the parlor of our little village alehouse." [2] It is not strange, therefore, that when he came to write, his characters were real to him, that he lived among them and spoke of them as real persons,—"Nancy is no more," he wrote in letter to a friend after her death in *Oliver Twist*. Forster tells us that (except in *Barnaby*) it always caused him suffering at the end to part from the creatures of his fancy.[3] He declared to Lewes that "every word said by his characters was distinctly heard by him." "When, in the midst of this trouble and pain," he writes, "I sit down to my book, some beneficent power shows it all to me, and tempts me to be interested, and I don't invent it—really do not—*but see it*, and write it down." [4] This was particularly true of the *Old Curiosity Shop* and Little Nell. "All night I have been pursued by the child," he writes on one occasion; and on another, "I think it will come famously—but I am the

[1] Julia C. Harris, *Life*, p. 403.
[2] Forster, *Life*, vol. i, p. 9.
[3] *Life*, vol. i, pp. 104, 131, 155.
[4] *Life*, vol. iii, pp. 306, 307.

wretchedest of the wretched. It casts the most horrible shadow upon me, and it is as much as I can do to keep moving at all. I tremble to approach the place a great deal more than Kit; a great deal more than Mr. Garland; a great deal more than the Single Gentleman. I shan't recover for a long time. Nobody will miss her like I shall." [1] Surely this accounts for the hold the child has on the affections of all readers; Dickens knew her, and loved her, more even than he can express in the book.

The *Old Curiosity Shop* is the marvellous product of a very rare gift—rare perhaps, however, in degree rather than in quality. George Eliot and Stevenson had the same gift, and Hawthorne and Harriet Beecher Stowe and Joel Chandler Harris; and I suppose everyone else who has written true fiction. Even outside the ranks of literature it is not uncommon.

II

The characters of fiction are imaginative fusions of the kind we have already discussed in the preceding chapters; that is, the characteristics of different persons known to the mind are abstracted and run together to form new ideal creations. The explanation already given for such fusions in general therefore applies here. Two qualifications, however, may be added. First, these fusions of character are probably more complex than others because our experiences with persons are more numerous, are more important for us, and more deeply engage our feelings than any others. Secondly, many of them involve our own characters or personalities, more fully than the ordinary fusion; the ego enters with all its implications. Evidently an author stands in a different attitude toward a character formed by a fusion of his own person with other persons, from that in which he stands, say, to a fusion of landscapes. In both the mind of the author enters, as in every imaginative product, but in a different way and to a different degree in the two cases.

Here again it will be instructive to take an example from

[1] *Life*, vol. i, pp. 184, 186.

dreams, which often show these fusions of persons in the most simple and striking way. Just as in the earlier examples the imagination formed a damson-snail or a mushroom-golfball, it will conceive a "hyphenated" character. The following from Havelock Ellis would be a simple case. "After a day in which I had received a letter from a lady, unknown to me, living in France, and later on had written out a summary of a criminal case in which a detective had to go over to France, I dreamed that some one told me that the lady I had heard from was a detective in the service of the French Government, and this explanation, though it seemed somewhat surprising, fully satisfied me. Here, it will be seen, the idea of France served as a bridge, and was utilized by the sleeping consciousness to supply an answer to a question which had been asked by waking consciousness." [1] Thus, according to Freud, the dream regularly utilizes a similarity in persons of any sort whatsoever, to justify the formation of a new unity. The unified person may be either an "identification," where an actual person appears in the dream, with features, however, drawn from other persons; or a "composition," where features are drawn from various originals to form an entirely novel dream character.[2] The elements drawn upon from the various originals may be of any sort,— their names, their visual features, their mannerisms and habit of speech, their characteristic mental attitudes and social relations. For instance, "instead of repeating A is ill disposed toward me, and B also, I make a composite fusion of A and B in the dream, or I conceive A as doing an unaccustomed action which usually characterizes B." The persons drawn upon to form the dream character may be any of those known to the dreamer, including of course the dreamer himself. Indeed— and this is a point to be particularly noted, because it may have its analogy in the case of literary fictions—according to Freud every dream treats directly or indirectly of the dreamer's own person. "In cases where not my ego, but only a strange person

---

[1] *The World of Dreams*, p. 42.   [2] *Interpretation of Dreams*, p. 297.

occurs in the dream content, I may safely assume that my ego is concealed behind that person by means of identification." This suggests the probability that every literary fiction will contain besides characters drawn from other persons, one character at least which bears the writer's ego,—in the composition of which the person of the writer himself enters, perhaps in spite of appearances, as the largest ingredient.

This suggests also, for the purposes of the following discussion, a classification of fictional characters which I believe will be found justifiable and convenient. Let us take first characters that are related closely or chiefly to the author himself, and secondly characters so related to other persons. The hero, for example, may be more or less like the author himself, in appearance, in the events of his life, in his emotional relations and mental characteristics. Or he may be more like a person or persons other than the author. The results and processes will be somewhat different in the two cases. We may have difficulty in any particular instance in telling to which class a character belongs, for the novelist, as Lamb observes, "under cover of passion uttered by another, oftentimes gives blameless vent to his most inward feelings, and expresses his own story modestly." We must remember also as before that in both kinds of characters, "autobiographical" or not, the mind of the author is a large ingredient. One is reminded of the remark of Dr. Johnson, who dreamed that he had been worsted in an argument, and was thereby much mortified. "Had not my judgment failed me," he said, "I should have seen that the wit of this supposed antagonist, by whose superiority I felt myself depressed, was as much furnished by me as that which I thought I had been uttering in my own character." [1] So in any character, whether autobiographical or not, the wit or imagination which puts it together is the author's own. But the fact remains that some fictional characters are much more autobiographical than others.

---

[1] Boswell, *Johnson*, ed. Hill, vol. iv, p. 5.

In the characters, as in other products of the imagination, there is a drawing of elements from both sources—from external nature and from the mind itself—as I have explained in Chapter IX; there is again the

> ennobling interchange
> Of action from without and from within

of which Wordsworth speaks.   And, as we have seen, sometimes one source will furnish the larger ingredient, sometimes the other.

III

Let us take first then the characters that are related closely or chiefly to the author himself, and let us begin with the simplest case,—that of the character which is quite directly and obviously autobiographical.   Examples are familiar to everyone: in *Roderick Random, Childe Harold, David Copperfield, Pendennis, The Mill on the Floss, Villette.*   In these stories the author, with more or less of his or her own appearance and external and internal experience, is represented in the hero or heroine—so directly that the story becomes an autobiography, particularly a "spiritual autobiography."   With suppressions and additions, however, and accordingly with some idealization, and here the imaginative element enters.   The hero is after all not the author as he is, but, partly, as he would like to be.   The hero is his dream and the product of his desires.   Where then does the element of the idealization come from?   From the mind of the author, of course, but not from his own actual or enacted life,—rather from his notion of what is good and great as this is abstracted ultimately from other persons whom he has known or read of.   In other words, the character is after all composite.   This is the simplest case, but typical in essentials of the more complex cases to follow.   The fictional character corresponding to the author is always a sort of dream figure, in which the author's person is modified by a composition, in a way answering to the author's desires.

In the formation of autogenous characters one of the commonest cases is where the person or mind of the author is divided, and one or more parts of it projected and personified. Sometimes only one such part—one of the author's mental qualities, faculties, or characteristics—will be objectified to form a single fictional character. Sometimes two or more such parts will be objectified to form two or more characters, parallel to each other and alike in their relations to the author's mind; that is, to employ the phrase of psychology, there will occur a "splitting of personality," resulting in multiple fictional characters. Supposing the author's mind to include various qualities—A, B, C, etc.,— one or more of these may be externalized by the imagination to form characters,—A alone, or A and B forming a pair, or A, B, and C, forming a series. And these resulting characters of course may draw additional features from other congruous external sources, so that A becomes a composite Axy, in which only the A element belongs to the author himself.

This process is common in mythology. A Greek carried away by warlike feelings and ideas to the point where other feelings and ideas are largely driven from his mind, forms an ideal conception of the warlike, which according to a well-known law of the imagination is given concreteness and life by being embodied in a person, and this ideal person becomes his god of war. When his mind is carried away by feelings and ideas of love he forms, in waking thought or in dream, a goddess of love. These conceptions, becoming common and traditional, form the divinities Ares and Aphrodite, who may be regarded as fictional characters externalizing different sides of the mind of the Greek race. The same imaginative process will account for a large share of the figures of popular myth and superstition,—for spirits as personified souls, for the angels, for the "whole brood of aerial, terrestrial, and aquatic devils;" all of these are to some extent autogenous characters. The terrors of myth and legend are largely from the mind, objective forms standing for fears within. "Gorgons, and Hydras, and Chimæras," says Lamb, "dire stories of Celæno and the Harpies—may reproduce themselves in the brain of superstition—but they were there before. They are transcripts, types—the archetypes are in us, and eternal."[1] They are most clearly understood if they are regarded as projections, in dreams or nightmare or the equivalent, from the depths of the human mind. But this process goes on also in modern fiction. Scott in Old Mortality and Irving in Diedrich Knickerbocker threw off such characters, projecting in each case a part—the traveling and recording antiquarianism—of the author's mind.

But let us take the broader case, which grows from the preceding one, of the splitting of the author's mind into two or more objectified parts—a very common one in fiction. This case is illustrated where the religious imagination first conceives a god as a person and then as a trinity of three persons with different names, and with different characteristics going back to the originating mind. The triune character is true first to the natural unity of the mind, and secondly to the natural propensity of the mind to a division in its imaginative objectifications. The type is the myth of the Judgment of Paris, which forms part of the Trojan war story but was doubtless first conceived separately. Paris is a character projecting the judgment of the mythopœic mind. He is represented as alone upon Mount Ida,—that is, the mind has the solitude required for meditation and resolution. He is to choose between power, wisdom, and beauty,—in other words he is to decide whether he shall be guided by the internal aspirations, ideas, feelings, which may be designated by one or the other of these abstract terms. But these three sides of the mind are projected by the imagination in the persons of three beautiful goddesses, Hera, Athene, and Aphrodite. Paris chooses Aphrodite, establishing a relation between these two characters which, I suppose, represents truthfully the reaction of the human judgment to the appeal of beauty. Thus four characters spring from the myth-

[1] "Witches and Other Night Fears."

making mind and carry on a veracious dramatic action. The same process is illustrated again and again in the vivid primitive imaginations of the Hebrews,—by Moses leading his flocks to the "back side of the desert" of Horeb, where the angel of the Lord appeared to him in a flame of fire out of the midst of a bush; by Elijah going a day's journey into the wilderness, where he met the angel of the Lord, or into a cave where he heard the still small voice; by Jesus driven by the spirit into the wilderness, where he remained forty days tempted of Satan, and the angels ministered unto him. The wilderness is in the mind itself, one side of the mind converses with another, and exclaims *Apage Satanas*, and forthwith is comforted by good thoughts.

This self-objectification and dramatization of our own mental experience is, according to Havelock Ellis, natural and primitive. It occurs in children, who refer to themselves sometimes in the first person, sometimes in the third, and attribute their own thoughts and actions to other persons, real or imaginary.[1] The savage or Southern negro will do the same thing. It occurs also in pathological cases, as in that recorded of a man "who attributed any feeling he experienced, even the most normal sensations of hunger and thirst, to the people around him." [2] It is not strange, therefore, to find the same occurrence in dreams. "This process," says Havelock Ellis, "by which dreams are formed through the splitting of the dreamer's personality for the construction of other personalities has been recognized ever since dreams began to be seriously studied." [3] " There are also dreams," Freud says, "in which my ego occurs along with other persons which the resolution of the identification again shows

[1] H. Ellis, *The World of Dreams*, p. 189, quotes Cooley ("The Early Use of Self-Words by a Child," *Psychological Review*, 1908, p. 339), who finds that the child distinguishes between itself as (1) body and as (2) self-assertion united with action; it refers to the former as "Baby" and to the latter as "I."

[2] H. Ellis, p. 189.

[3] H. Ellis, p. 186, citing Maury, Delbœuf, Foucault and Giessler.

to be my ego. . . . I may also give my ego manifold representation in the dream, now directly, now by means of identification with strangers." [1] This is interestingly illustrated by accounts given by Robert Louis Stevenson of waking fancies during fever, in which the action is carried on by "one part of my mind" and "another part of my mind," or by "myself" and "the other fellow." Here the process goes on while Stevenson is awake or half-awake; he is able to recognize and analyze it, and to identify his "other fellow" with "the dreamer described in his Chapter on Dreams." [2]

Now this same process which the imagination thus carries on in the formation of myths, of childish, feverish, or pathological fancies, and of dreams, it shows also in its working in literature. The simplest and most prosaic case is that of the dialogue—say one of Landor's *Imaginary Conversations* of the class Sidney Colvin calls non-dramatic, in which "often either one of the speakers or both are mere mouthpieces for the utterance of Landor's own thoughts and sentiments." [3] Landor, discussing in his own mind ideas of religion or government, which might have been put into a discursive essay, instead, by a mild effort of the imagination, throws the *pros* and *cons* into a dialogue between Melancthon and Calvin or between Washington and Franklin,—the personification giving a slight poetical interest. As Leslie Stephen remarks, "some conversations might as well be headed, in legal phraseology, Landor *v.* Landor, or at most Landor *v.* Landor and another." In the same way "the unfortunate Solitary in the *Excursion* is beset by three Wordsworths; for the Wanderer and the Pastor are little more (as Wordsworth indeed intimates) than reflections of himself, seen in different mirrors." [4] In *Sartor Resartus* Carlyle's vivid imagination shows this process of division and projection much more strikingly and poetically. Carlyle's own

---

[1] *Interpretation of Dreams*, p. 300.

[2] F. W. H. Myers, *Human Personality*, vol. i, p. 301.

[3] S. Colvin, *Landor*, p. 121.

[4] *Hours in a Library*, vol. ii, pp. 328, 287.

early life and education, his failures and disappointments, his unfortunate love affairs, which he first put into an unfinished novel, *Wotton Reinfred*, are attributed, with fantastic modifications, to Teufelsdröckh, an autobiographical character. But Teufelsdröckh is not the whole of Carlyle's mind, for Carlyle divides it, quite in the old myth-making way, assigning a part—his more individual, intuitive, mystical, and poetical side with its relations to Kant and Goethe—to the German philosopher of clothes, and another part—his social, sceptical, and literary side—to the English editor. His message comes from a synthesis of the opinions of the two characters, in which the tailor is mended, and his German ideas are adapted to English conditions. The same process is illustrated in Byron's *Cain*, Act II, in which the scene is the "Abyss of Space " (corresponding to the lone mountain or the wilderness of Greek and Hebrew myth), and a dialogue goes on between Cain and Lucifer, concerning "mortal nature's nothingness." But as usual Byron furnishes his own characters, and the dialogue, as Nichol observes, is "between two halves of the author's mind." [1]

The preceding examples are from various kinds of literature, poetry and prose, non-fictional and fictional in the popular sense, (with *Sartor* on the line between the two). It is important to see the uniform working of the imagination throughout. We may go on now to take examples from ordinary prose fiction. Stevenson's " Markheim " is the modern analogue of the primitive myth. Markheim and his mysterious visitant are the murderous instinct and the redeeming conscience which, as Stevenson intimates, are present together in every human mind, and which he doubtless found present in his own. The scene of the dialogue, as the story skillfully indicates, is in the mind itself. " Dr. Jekyll and Mr. Hyde," founded upon a dream, shows that "man is not truly one, but truly two." Indeed, "I hazard the guess that man will ultimately be known for a mere polity of multifarious, incongruous, and independent denizens." Poe's

---

[1] *Byron*, p. 142.

" William Wilson " is an earlier " Markheim "; here as in other
"Tales of Conscience," like the " Tell-Tale Heart," the conscience is objectified. Hawthorne has the same device in
" Howe's Masquerade." In Poe, however, the commonest
division is that referred to in an earlier chapter. In the " Pur-
loined Letter," the " Gold-Bug," the " Assignation," the " Fall
of the House of Usher," besides others, there appear again and
again two autogenous characters—one corresponding to the
poetical and neurotic Poe, the other to Poe the hack-writer and
analyst. It often seems to the student of Poe that the man himself was double,—that he furnished his imaginative material in
one person and worked it up for literary purposes in another.
This duplicity is constantly represented in his fictional characters;
the character who narrates the story in the first person—as, for
another example, in the " Domain of Arnheim"—is obviously
Poe, but the hero who appears in the third person is Poe just as
obviously on another side,—as any one who will read the tales
carefully, together with Poe's life, may see. If we leave out the
heroines, the characters in Poe who do not directly or indirectly
represent Poe himself are in general minor and negligible.

Other writers besides Poe and Stevenson have felt that man's
mind is not single, but double or multiple, and this feeling is
intimated in their characters. A striking example is the hero
of Flaubert's *La Morte Amoureuse*, who says:

"From that night my being became in some sort double: there
were two men in me, one of whom knew nothing of the other. Sometimes I thought myself a priest who dreamed each night that he was a
gentleman; sometimes a gentleman who dreamed that he was priest.
I could no longer distinguish dream from waking, and I could not tell
where the reality began and where the illusion ended. . . . Two
spirals entangled in each other and mingling without ever touching
will truthfully represent this bipartite life of mine."

This, however, is very much the same double life, of indis-
tinguishable dream and waking, which many writers describe
themselves as leading in their own minds, and it very likely

corresponds to a doubleness in the mind of Flaubert. But
here the doubleness of Flaubert is represented in the fiction
not by two separate characters, but by one character bipartite,
this corresponding to the ambiguous figures found in dream,
of which we say "I dreamed of a person who was either so-and-
so or someone else." In other words, the process in hand may
form either ambiguous unities or separate characters.

The most striking account I have found of this process of
division and projection describes the production of the dramatist,
F. de Curel, as follows: "He begins in the ordinary way, or
with even more than the usual degree of difficulty and distress
in getting into his subject. Then gradually he begins to feel
the creation of a number of quasi-personalities within him;—
the characters of his play, who *speak* to him—exactly as Dickens
used to describe Mrs. Gamp as speaking to him in church. These
personages are not clearly visible, but they seem to move around
him in a scene—say a house and garden—which he also dimly
perceives, somewhat as we perceive the scene of a dream. He
now no longer has the feeling of composition, of creation, but
merely of literary revision; the personages speak and act for
themselves, and even if he is interrupted while writing, or when
he is asleep at night, the play continues to compose itself in his
head. Sometimes while out shooting, etc., and not thinking of
the play, he hears sentences rising within him which belong to
a part of this play he has not yet reached. He believes that
subliminally the piece has been worked out to that further point
already. M. de Curel calls these minor duplications of personality a *bourgeonnement* or budding of his primary personality;
into which they gradually, though not without some painful
struggle, re-enter after the play is finished." [1]

Thus an active imagination will "burgeon" and throw off
characters about as freely as a young plant will generate and
sprout into leaves and flowers in the spring,—and by a process
quite as natural. The examples that have been given of this

[1] F. W. H. Myers, *Human Personality*, vol. i, p. 107, summarizing a very
instructive article by A. Binet, *L'Année Psychologique*, i, 1894, p. 124.

projection are necessarily the obvious ones; but it may be sur-
mised rather than proved that the principle applies to many
more characters than would at first appear;—that, for example,
if Dickens put himself into Copperfield, he put himself also—
his bad side—into Steerforth, and that Steerforth also, along
with externally derived features, had his archetype in Dickens's
own mind. In the bad characters the author will be harder to
identify, because they represent him with a concealment or
"displacement " due to repression. A contemporary novelist,
Somerset Maugham, shrewdly observes: "It may be that in
his rogues the writer gratifies instincts deep-rooted in him,
which the manners and customs of a civilized world have forced
back into the mysterious recesses of the subconscious. In giving
to the characters of his invention flesh and bones, he is giving
life to that part of himself which finds no other means of expression. His satisfaction is a sense of liberation." [1]

IV

We have now discussed the case in which the author divides
himself to form characters, and may go on to the case where he
forms characters by modifying his own person, by attributing
to it, in his imagination, the characteristics of other persons.
Here there is an identification or composition, in which the main
ingredient is the author himself, but with an ingredient also of
externally derived features. The two processes are not of course
exclusive, but rather go on together; they can be separated,
however, for purposes of discussion. The two may be summed
up in the happy phrase of Lamb who speaks of the author's
"making himself many, or reducing many unto himself;" [2]
this covers the whole ground as far as autogenous characters
are concerned.

The imagination of the author forming characters by attributing fancied characteristics to himself is like the imagination of
the child doing the same thing, and we may take the child first

[1] *The Moon and Sixpence*, p. 203.   [2] Preface to *Last Essays of Elia*.

as being the simpler case. The child "makes himself many" with the greatest ease. He imagines himself to be any character he "fancies"—a pirate, cowboy, or crusader. Sometimes he acts out the part, attempting to realize the composite character in play. Sometimes he makes up a story, with this character as hero. Sometimes he is deceived and takes his imagined actions for true. John Addington Symonds—a typically imaginative child, as is shown by his "night fears," recurrent dreams, and childish trances, but also a conscientious one—tells how he saw in a neighboring basement a magician "stirring ingredients in a caldron," etc., who became "a positive reality of his imagination," about which he conversed freely at home, where he was requested "not to tell lies." "The same thing happened when I arrived one evening in a state of considerable excitement at home, and declared that I had been attacked by robbers on the way. The artlessness of my narrative must have proved its worthlessness. I was soundly scolded. Yet neither the magician nor the robber are less real to my memory than most of the people who surrounded me at that time." [1]

This kind of thing is very common in the lives of imaginative children—of Dickens, George Sand, Lafcadio Hearn—but it is by no means confined to children. Even the adult imagines himself doing things, assuming parts that he fancies, with such distinctness that he takes his imaginings for truth. We have all had the experience of asking, "Did I do this or did I dream it?" "Thus Professor Näcke has recorded that his wife dreamed that an acquaintance, an old lady, had called at the house; this dream was apparently forgotten until forty or fifty hours afterwards, when, on passing the old lady's house, it was recalled, and the dreamer was only with much difficulty convinced that the dream was not an actual occurrence. When we are concerned with memories of childhood, it not infrequently happens that we cannot distinguish with absolute certainty between real occurrences and what may possibly have been dreams"—or

[1] H. F. Brown, *Symonds*, vol. i, p. 34.

other imaginings.[1] Thus Remy de Gourmont and Mme. Rachilde, adult writers of fiction, acknowledge confusing fact with
dream.

The pathological case here is that occurring most frequently
in hysteria, of the lying called by psychologists *pseudologia
phantastica*, "where the mixture of direct lying and error is so
close that the patient is no longer able to distinguish reality
from the creations of his fancy. . . . The fundamental cause
of the tendency is not so much the impulse to relate such and
such a thing, or to strive towards it, as the irresistible desire to
be, to live, to think, to feel, like some other being who is the
ideal of the patient's phantasy, in other words, to pose before
himself and the world as some one different from his real self. . . .
The true memory of the real experiences appears in the phantasy,
but only as an island, as in a misty dream. This may even result
in a double consciousness when the real and the wish form of
life course side by side, or alternately, the second form being
the dominant one." Wendt gives an example, of the kind we
have all read about in the newspapers, of a young law student,
in whom the morbid condition appeared periodically, until it
became much exaggerated and "the patient posed as a count,
conducted himself accordingly, and ultimately came into conflict with the law over money matters." [2]

Now the same process of wish, fancy, and assumption, when
not carried to the pathological extreme but used for literary purposes, is the one which produces characters in fiction. Dickens
becoming one of his own characters is analogous to the law student who becomes a count or to the child who plays pirate. "No
man," says Forster, "ever had so surprising a faculty as Dickens
of becoming himself what he was representing; and of entering
into the mental phases and processes so absolutely, in conditions
of life the most varied, as to reproduce them completely in dialogue without need of an explanatory word." Dickens himself

[1] H. Ellis, *The World of Dreams*, p. 236.

[2] E. Jones, *Journal of Abnormal Psychology*, vol. vii, p. 66, summarizing
E. Wendt.

says: "Assumption has charms for me so delightful—I hardly know for how many wild reasons—that I feel a loss of Oh I can't say what exquisite foolery, when I lose a chance of being some one not in the remotest degree like myself." [1]   Lamb also took a wild delight in assumption, and in "making himself many." In his essays he acknowledges "that what he tells us, as of himself, was often true only (historically) of another." As one of "many instances" he cites the essay on Christ's Hospital in which, writing in the first person as Elia (the name of a clerk at the South Sea House), he describes himself as "L" in the third person, attributing to himself, however, to form a fictional composite, traits drawn from his "fellow Christian" Coleridge.

Poe's case is instructive because it combines the literary with the pathological imagination—or better, illustrates that the two are fundamentally the same thing. Poe, like Shelley, was apt to confuse his fancies with fact. In 1847, his "most immemorial year," in a half delirious state he dictated to Mrs. Shew a romantic story, without basis in fact, of a voyage to France and a duel.[2]   He would imagine romantic actions that he would like to perform and then believe he had performed them,—turning the wished-for future into an actual past, just as in romance *O would that* is regularly turned into *Once upon a time*, or just as in myth the golden age of the distant future is transferred to a distant past. In his youth, like many others of his generation, Poe conceived an admiration for Byron, which affected his conduct. In Richmond he emulated Byron's feats of swimming. He "wore Byron collars and a black stock, and looked the poet all over." In early poems he was Byronic, in " Tamerlane " imitating the " Giaour," and in some of the personal pieces striking a Byronic attitude toward his "past bliss and present desolation." In 1827 he enlisted in the army under an assumed name, but he was ashamed of this episode and concealed it; so that, to account for this gap in his life, he later invented for his friends, and indeed included in sketches of his

[1] Forster, vol. iii, pp. 26, 481.

[2] G. E. Woodberry, *Poe*, vol. ii, p. 226.

own life for publication, the story of a trip to Europe, to romantic countries—Russia, Egypt, Arabia,—with variously given romantic details. This story was apparently based on accounts of
actual voyages made by his brother to Greece and St. Peters-
burg, and was perhaps inspired by a desire to go to Greece,
where Byron had died three years before, "with the wild design
of aiding in the Revolution then taking place." [1]   In other
words Poe was given to the *pseudologia phantastica*, and first
imagined and then tried to play a romantic part in which, as a
composite, Byronic features were conspicuous.

It is not strange therefore to find Poe turning this phase of
his mental experience into literary fiction in the "Assignation,"
which I ask the reader to notice particularly as a striking example of the formation of characters of the kind we are now discussing. The hero has many traits of Byron. He is a proud
English nobleman, with a mysterious past, living in a Venetian
palace; he is a poet, engaged in amorous intrigue, and a strong
swimmer. But this hero has also many traits of Poe. He has
the physical features, including the "forehead of unusual
breadth," which Poe, after looking into his mirror, was fond of
attributing to his heroes. He is proud again, and a poet—the
author of "To One in Paradise." He is a "philosopher in furni-
ture," and indeed, like all of Poe's heroes, the mouthpiece for
Poe's own stock ideas. The "visionary" of the "Assignation,"
then, is an autogenous composite, with the external ingredients
derived mainly from Byron. The ordinary literary criticism
will say that this hero shows traits derived from the life of
Byron. It is not merely this; the hero is the description in
literature of a Poe-Byronic character which Poe imagined and
lived before he put it into his story.

For another example we may as well take Byron himself
and *Childe Harold*. From Mrs. Radcliffe's romances, Beckford's *Vathek*, Scott's ballads, and other works which furnished
the atmosphere of the first decade of the nineteenth century,

[1] G. E. Woodberry, *Poe*, vol. i, pp. 26, 94, 72, 73, 365.

Byron conceived a character—romantic, mysterious, gloomy, remorseful, jaded, and as we now say, Byronic. Having formed this imaginary character, according to his own disposition and desires—this ideal picture of what he would like to be and appear —he set about living the character and playing the part; and as, unlike Poe, he had resources, he got much farther. He sailed forth from Falmouth in the Lisbon packet, with Hobhouse, his valet, and his "little page," to live the poem before he put it into a book. Indeed the actual pilgrimage, though Byron's accounts of it are doubtless somewhat pseudological, is almost more poetical than *Childe Harold*. When Byron came to write the poem he had only to describe with some further idealization, a character which he had first fancied and then lived, now adding perhaps a dash of Spenser. This was Byron's method throughout—to imagine a part, to play it in his life as far as possible, and when life failed to take refuge in poetry.

> 'Tis to create, and in creating live
> A being more intense that we endow
> With form our fancy, gaining as we give
> The life we image, even as I do now.

The Byronic literary hero changes as Byron's ideally conceived character changes—and the character changes with its two component factors— that is, first as Byron's own mind develops, and secondly as it draws in new external ingredients. In *Childe Harold*, written when he is young but wishes to be old in experience, he fancies a hero travelled and jaded; but in *Don Juan* written when he is himself old and jaded and wishes to be young, he fancies a fresh youthful hero.

It is interesting, by the way, to trace the development of human character, with the part the imagination plays in it, in its manifestations first in actual, then in fictional persons alternating—in Beckford, *Vathek*, Byron, *Childe Harold*, Poe, *The Visionary*—one in turn influencing the other—and this is the true development, rather than the purely literary one which scholars trace in parallel passages.

The examples I have given show how an author will form his hero by assuming a part,—by attributing to himself characteristics or actions of others which he fancies. The internal and external ingredients will enter in different proportions, but in general the hero will be the character that the author wishes to be and to realize in his own life. Stevenson, for example, had an adventurous and romance-loving spirit; he lived, as far as he could, a life of adventure; but he was an invalid. "I was made for a contest," he says, "and the Powers have so willed that my battle-field should be this dingy, inglorious one of the bed and the physic bottle." [1]   But he could fight his battles in the person of David Balfour, and sail the South Seas with the Wrecker. [2]

V

We have now considered the autogenous characters, in which the author either makes himself many or reduces many unto himself. We may go on to consider much more briefly the second main class of characters—those which are made up chiefly of other persons. Here the author instead of being autobiographical is objective and dramatic in his method. A case in which the method is obviously objective is that of the heroines of the masculine novelists; and I suppose the heroes we have

[1] To Meredith in Balfour, *Stevenson*, vol. ii, p. 201.

[2] In the case of minor characters it will often be difficult to apply the classification suggested in the text,—to decide, for example, whether a character is in the main internally or externally derived. Of the sisters Ione and Panthea in Shelley's *Prometheus Unbound*, Ione is the seeing one, Panthea the knowing one; Ione sees first and from a distance, and speaks first; Panthea replies,—she discerns and explains. They may be regarded therefore as representing these two sides of Shelley's mind; in fact as representing the two faculties or modes of thought of the mind in general—one seeing, the other analyzing, which I have tried to explain earlier in this book. On the other hand they are sisters of Asia, forming with her one of the familiar trinities, and may thus be regarded as emanations from the mind of Asia and so externally derived. Prometheus is clearly an autogenous character in many features.

already considered with these heroines would include most of the important characters in fiction. Byron, someone says, formed his heroes after his own image and his heroines after his own heart. The statement would apply to many other writers of fiction. Man, we may as well admit, is constantly using his imagination, both in and out of literature, to form heroines. When he falls in love, as we have seen, he glorifies his beloved object, by a composition, adding to the actual charm another drawn from his own fancy. When an object is wanting he forms an entirely ideal composite drawn from all the women he has known, or heard or read about—at least all those he has " fancied,"—

La figlia della sua mente, l'amorosa idea.

The following from Chateaubriand describes his situation. "The warmth of my (adolescent) imagination, my shyness, and my solitude, caused me, instead of casting myself on something without, to fall back upon myself. Wanting a real object, I evoked through the power of my desires a phantom, which thenceforth never left me; I made a woman, composed of all the women that I had already seen. This charming figure followed me everywhere, though invisible; I conversed with her as with a real being; she would change according to my frenzy. Pygmalion was less enamored of his statue." [1] To form a heroine of literary fiction Chateaubriand had only to describe this charming figure. In such a composite one actual woman may form the nucleus, with some elements from others, or all the elements may lack ascertainable origin. The composite may be formed by waking fancy or in dream. It will not be real, but superior to the real, in accordance with the desires. The novelist then is like Pygmalion, King of Cyprus; he forms the statue of a woman in ivory, and at his prayer Aphrodite gives it life.

The novelist forms his masculine characters, not autogenous, by an assumption similar to that already described, ex-

[1] Quoted by Ribot, *The Creative Imagination*, p. 76.

cept that here the externally derived elements are the larger ingredient in the composition, and the method becomes objective and dramatic. Thus some writers draw their characters mainly from themselves, like Byron and Poe; others draw them mainly from outside persons, like Shakespeare or Balzac. The typical method of the latter class would be that of Balzac, who describes how one evening on the boulevards he amused himself by following a workingman and his wife. He listened as they talked of the play they had just seen, then of their business, and of their household affairs. "Hearing these people," he says, "I was able to adopt their life; I felt their rags on my back, I walked along with my feet in their worn-out shoes; their desires, their wants, all passed into my soul, and my soul passed into theirs; I was like a man dreaming while he is awake." [1] Balzac observes these people and their talk closely; his imagination is meanwhile busy in filling out their lives from the lives of similar persons he has known: he may even contribute features drawn from the common human nature which he also possesses within him. Thus in his "dream" he forms composite ideal figures, which, when he takes his pen, he has only to describe.

The process by which the imagination forms characters of this objective class is quite as natural and fundamental as the processes discussed earlier, and has its analogy in the imaginative behavior of children. George Sand began to produce romances as a child at Nohant, among others a remarkable series of fictions, something between an epic cycle and a religion, in which she found expression for both her poetic and her moral life. The principal character, Corambé, and its name came to her in dreams at night. From this starting-point the story developed in waking reverie, without volition, for the dreams, she says, seemed to form of themselves. At first she was conscious of what was going on, but presently she "felt herself possessed by the subject rather than possess-

[1] *Facino Cane.*

ing it, and the dreams became a sort of sweet hallucination, sometimes so frequent and so complete that she felt herself carried away by it beyond the world of reality." She played with other children but meanwhile carried on this individual imaginative life, and the story of Corambé continued to develop, in a series of "books" or "songs"—at least a thousand, she believes—which she had no thought of writing down. "It was a continuous dream, as broken, as incoherent as the dreams of sleep, in which I should have been lost, had not the same sentiment dominated it always." It continued even after she went to the convent at the age of thirteen, and after she had composed other more ordinary romances. Corambé was a composite character, with traits from various sources, including the Bible, the *Iliad*, and *Jerusalem Delivered*. "He was pure and charitable as Jesus, radiant and beautiful as Gabriel; but he needed to have added also a little of the grace of the nymphs and the poetry of Orpheus. Accordingly he had a form less austere than the Christian God, and a feeling more spiritual than the gods of Homer. And then I had at times to complete him by giving him the guise of a woman, for the person I had up to this time loved best and understood best was a woman—my mother. In short, he had no sex and assumed all sorts of different aspects." He appeared in each song with a world of other characters grouped around him. Moreover the little girl felt each song as worship and even constructed an altar, upon which she made fanciful sacrifices.[1] In fact this childish imaginative experience not only parallels the primitive combination of poetry, myth, and religion, but illustrates the primitive and natural formation of fictional characters.

Sometimes the objective character will be a general abstract, without ascertainable antecedents. Sometimes an actual person will form the nucleus. Thus Dickens's father is idealized in Micawber, and an "Angelica" whom Dickens knew at eighteen, and who "pervaded every chink and crev-

---

[1] G. Sand, *Histoire de ma Vie*, Third part, chaps. viii, x, xiii.

ice of his mind for three of four years," is sentimentally heightened in the Dora of *David Copperfield* and comically heightened in the Flora of *Little Dorrit*. In Dora he was looking back on his youthful romance over twenty years, but "no one can imagine," he says, "in the most distant degree what pain the recollection gave me in *Copperfield*." [1] Sometimes, as in the historical novel, a historical character will form the nucleus of an imaginative accretion with contemporary ingredients. Sometimes, finally, an earlier fictional character will be taken over by the imagination and developed, as we may suppose the Hamlet character, taken over from an earlier play, served Shakespeare as a starting point, was filled in by his imagination, and was made a medium for the expression of his own mind. The final Hamlet was at once borrowed and, since it passed through his imagination, his own. We know too little of Shakespeare to be sure how much of himself he put into Hamlet, but we can be sure that Byron put himself into his Cain. Long before he wrote his drama he had identified himself with Cain; he had wandered under a curse and had sympathized with the first rebel. Of Childe Harold he had said:

> Life-abhorring gloom
> Wrote on his jaded brow curst Cain's unresting doom.

In the drama he takes the mythical character and makes it, as a kind of Cain-Byron, the medium for his own thought, and probably too, in the relation of Cain to Adah, for his own deepest feelings. Sometimes the deepest and most unconscious portions of the author's mind will doubtless be thus attributed to fictional characters, by a process analogous to that described by Anatole France, in the case of Abbé Oegger. The Abbé, a hypercritical visionary, has phantasies regarding Judas. He is obsessed with the Judas problem: was the betrayer of Christ condemned to an everlasting punishment, or was he, as an instrument necessary to

[1] Forster, vol. i, p. 73.

salvation, pardoned? To end his doubts Oegger goes one night to the church, prays for a sign of Judas' salvation and feels a heavenly touch upon his shoulder. He then resolves to go out into the world preaching God's unending mercy. Presently, however, he forsakes Catholicism to become a Swedenborgian. In other words he has been tortured by the Judas problem because he himself is a Judas, and himself wishes to be sure of God's mercy. He has transferred to the biblical character his own mental struggle, of which his phantasies were an unconscious expression.[1] By some such transfer Byron may have put himself into *Manfred* and *Cain*.

Cain and Hamlet typify a common and most important case; a character from earlier myth, legend, fiction, even history, is imaginatively re-created. It is thus a collaboration, between, two, several, or many authors: we do not know, for example, how many minds contributed to the imaginative fusions and re-fusions which resulted in the character of Hamlet, of King Arthur, of the Shelleyan Prometheus, of Don Juan, of Cleopatra. Furthermore, the characters or some characteristics are often taken over without the names, the fact of collaboration remaining the same; one character is imaginatively borrowed from another, but is still genuine if it passes through the imagination; and we see, if we follow out this line of thought that there is a network of genealogical relations among fictional characters, and that every important character is apt to have a long pedigree. It is all the better for thus being a kind of folk character. There is in strictness no such thing as folk poetry, as I have said in an earlier chapter; but since the principle I have just stated applies not only to the characters but to other features of poetry, all great poetry is in a sense folk poetry: it is produced by one man, but also by many, and this is another explanation of its human, representative, and universal character.

So much for the formation of characters. The settings in

[1] *Jardin d'Épicure*, analyzed by Jung, *Psychology of the Unconscious*, p. 37.

fiction are formed imaginatively in an analogous way. Indeed characters and settings are often formed together. Dickens saw his characters acting in their appropriate background and so described them. F. de Curel, as we have seen, perceived his characters, not *in vacuo*, but in a scene,—say a house and garden, "somewhat as we perceive the scene of a dream." Sometimes of course scenes will be imagined without characters. George Sand recalls how as a child at Nohant, when her mother read to her, she listened seated before the fire, from which she was protected by an old screen of green taffeta. Little by little she lost the sense of the words; images formed themselves before her and began to take shape on the green screen. "There were woods, meadows, rivers, cities, of a bizarre and gigantic architecture . . . . One day these apparitions became so complete that I was frightened, and asked my mother if she did not see them too." This is the faculty which makes George Sand's novels picturesque. In imagination she could picture, with the distinctness of hallucination, a unified landscape; by following its lines and reproducing its colors, she could make of it a setting in her fiction.

In closing this chapter I may repeat, what I hope is now obvious, that though fictional characters, acting in their appropriate backgrounds, draw their elements from many different originals and sources in the author's mind, these elements are not consciously assembled and combined, but are rather fused by an unobserved momentary process, to form unified and organized wholes. Just as an external scene presents itself to the eye and may be described, so these ideal scenes present themselves to the imagination, or eye of the mind, and the author has only to look and write. To form the finished novel or play he may trim, elaborate, or adjust the scenes thus furnished, by rational processes, but, as I have said, these processes require no special explanation. Indeed the whole method of fiction, in novel or drama, is suggested by the imaginative operation itself. W. D. Howells tells how he dreamed of his father appearing, wishing to greet him, and refraining. "This process in his mind, which I knew as clearly and accurately as if it had apparently gone on in my own, was apparently confined to his mind as absolutely as anything could be that was not spoken or in any wise uttered. Of course it was my agency, like any other part of the dream, and it was something like the operation of the novelist's intention through the mind of his characters." [1] The imagination creates the characters, places them all on the same footing whether they are what I have called autogenous or not, and sets them in motion in their appropriate background. The imagination does all but tell the story. Stevenson and Sully-Prud-homme, as we have seen, describe creation as assisting in the action of a mental theatre. Imaginative thought naturally takes this form. Galton, deliberately for experimental purposes evoking a merely associative or dream thought, found that the thought sequences largely "floated along on a current of visual imagery," and revealed a histrionic or dramatic talent at work,—"in which I either act a part in imagination, or see in imagination a part acted, or, most commonly by far, where I am both spectator and all the actors at once in an imaginary mental theatre." [2] The theatre as we know it, particularly for example, the primitive Greek theatre with its two or three actors and chorus, is a materialization which has its pre-existent ideal counterpart. In looking for the origins of novel and drama, then, we should finally look into the mind itself.

[1] "True I talk of Dreams," *Harper's Magazine*, May 1895, p. 841. It is strange that Howells should add: "There is no analogy, as far as I can make out, between the process of literary invention and the process of dreaming."

[2] Jastrow, *The Subconscious*, p. 181.

CHAPTER XIII

SYMBOLS AND FIGURES

I

ALL human thought proceeds ultimately through a recognition of relations and likenesses. At first the mind sees things as individual and unrelated; then it learns how to link one thing to another, and yet another. "And so tyrannized over by its own unifying instinct, it goes on tying things together, diminishing anomalies, discovering roots running under ground, whereby contrary and remote things cohere, and flower out from one stem." [1] The poet above all men leads in this progressive and constructive work.

It is especially the mark of a strong mind to be able to recognize likenesses, or in pyschological terms, to be able readily to associate ideas by similarity. The ability to do this separates man's mind from the brute's, which seems to proceed only through contiguities; and the ability to do it more readily distinguishes the higher order of human mind from the lower. Indeed, "genius is identical with the possession of similar association in an extreme degree." [2] The mind in which this mode of association prevails will be apt at reasoned thinking; and such a mind is absolutely indispensable to poetic thought. The poet above all other men is quick to see or feel resemblances, and he is sensitive to the most recondite likenesses.

The recognition of resemblances which is at the bottom of all valuable thinking is employed differently in voluntary and in poetic thought. In the former it is developed into reasoning,

[1] Emerson, "The American Scholar."
[2] James, *Psychology*, vol. ii, pp. 360, 348.

in ways explained by the psychologists,[1] which are not of interest here. In voluntary thought, however, the mind is concerned only with likenesses which are fruitful for the practical purpose which is directing the thought. It notices carefully the number of points of resemblance, and generally uses resemblances in which there are more than one of these. It notes also the quality and value of the common attributes, and disregards those that are superficial or meaningless for the purpose in hand. It sees points of resemblance which do not appear at once and are discovered only by analysis. It is not concerned, for example, with the likeness of the moon to green cheese, but it utilizes the less apparent likeness of the moon to the rings of Saturn.

The poetic thought, as we have seen, is fundamentally a variety of associative thought; and the latter proceeds merely by a free connection of one idea, object, or image, with another, according to the laws of contiguity and resemblance. Psychologists, by the way, do not agree as to these two laws, and as to which of the two is fundamental, some reducing contiguity to resemblance, others resemblance to contiguity.[2] For the purposes of the following discussion,—that is for their application to poetry—it is not very essential to distinguish between the two. It would be satisfactory to regard all the associations of poetic thought as made through resemblance. The poetic mind does not treat the two differently; it makes the same use of two images that are related, whether this relation is through contiguous position in the mind or, say, in quality. It will be somewhat helpful, however, for the classification of poetic figures, to which we shall come in a moment, to preserve the distinction. And it should be noted that of the two laws that of resemblance is much the more important for poetry, as it is for other kinds of thought. Association by contiguity goes on by a kind of mental habit which tends to routine thinking, while association by resemblance is active and progressive, and consequently is "the principal source of the material of the creative imagi-

[1] James, *Psychology*, vol. ii, p. 345.

[2] Ribot, *Creative Imagination*, p. 24; James, *Psychology*, vol. i, p. 590.

nation." [1] In what follows, therefore, we shall be concerned mainly with the matter of resemblances.

While the voluntary thought deals, as we have seen, only with likenesses of practical value in reasoning, the poetic thought is free to recognize likenesses of any kind whatever. Some of its recognitions may turn out to be of more value than others, but it is concerned merely with the recognition; and for it the likeness which appears between the moon and green cheese is as good and satisfying as any other. For it the likeness need not be extended; a likeness in any single point, to afford a link for the mind, is sufficient. Voluntary thought must see the resemblance and point out in what it consists,—that is explain it; but poetic thought is satisfied with a mere recognition of the resemblance, and may not be able at all to define it. In fact it is especially fond of recognizing likenesses which cannot be *seen* at all, but only *felt*. It is quick to feel the things that "belong together." We of course often find things like without being able to explain why. We find that two colors harmonize— that is, have some affinity, but we do not know what affinity. The color pale blue is said to have feminine and the color blood red masculine affinities. We may feel this to be true; if it is we may some day learn why; the poet, however, merely recognizes the resemblances and leaves them unexplained, but utilizes them. The recognition may be unscientific and merely individual, as for example of a likeness between the color blue and the sound of *i*, but it is true for him if it exists. Finally the recognition may be not an intellectual, but an emotional one; two images become associated, not because they are seen to be alike, but because they have a common emotional note. One sad or joyful thing will suggest another, though the two things have no other link. The poet is particularly apt to recognize resemblances which are hidden, inexplicable, and merely felt. He is quick to feel the invisible links.

Voluntary thought, then, treats resemblances in one way

[1] Ribot, *Creative Imagination*, p. 25.

and poetic thought in quite another; and therefore the results in the two cases are very different. According to William James "there are two stages in reasoned thought, one where similarity merely *operates* to call up cognate thoughts, and another farther stage, where the bond of identity between the cognate thoughts is *noticed*. So minds of genius may be divided into two main sorts, those who *notice* the bond and those who merely *obey* it." [1] The former are the abstract reasoners, the men of science; the latter are the poets, the men of intuition. "At first sight," he goes on to say, "it might seem that the analytic mind represented simply a higher intellectual stage, and that the intuitive mind represented an arrested stage of intellectual development; but the difference is not so simple as this." The reasoner gains of course for his purpose when he insists upon *noticing* the bond; but in other respects he loses. He loses all the value there is in the intuitions. The fact is, as I have tried to show in an earlier chapter, that the poetic mode of thought is an older one—more primitive perhaps it might be called—but deeper and in many respects more valuable. The poet gains much greater freedom and range by not having to *notice* the bond. He may of course notice it too.

It is worth while again to note that the poetic thought corresponds to the thought of children and primitive men. The child who sees pansies and then butterflies, and says of the latter, "The pansies are flying," is doing the same thing as the poet when he feels the likeness between a thought and a bird, and says,

> There flutters up a happy thought
> Self-balanced on a joyous wing.

The primitive Anglo-Saxon poet who, through resemblances, personifies his sword and says that "the battle-gleam was unwilling to bite," is doing the same thing as the modern poet who makes Gloster say when he has killed the king:

> See how my sword weeps for the poor king's death.

[1] James, *Psychology*, vol. ii, p. 361.

The poetic thought proceeds essentially by noting or feeling or merely obeying these resemblances in a primitive way. The poet of course in any poem will go far beyond this, and introduce more complex logical relations and even reasoning, but not *as a poet*. At least these resemblances are the poetic stock in trade. We may distinguish again between the poem and the poetic thought behind it, and insist that in the latter—in the pure poetic vision—there is only this recognition of resemblances. In this respect vision is like dream, which merely takes similar things and transforms them into a unity. Freud tries to show that the dream has means of representing various intellectual relations—those expressed by a *for*, an *if*, an *either-or* —but it will be found on analysis that all these means come down to one of two things,—either to a combination of images, or to a succession of images—from which these supposed relations are to be inferred. The dream therefore reduces to successive fusions of contiguous or similar images, and Freud states the general law when he says that the dream "does not in general think [in the ordinary sense], calculate, or judge at all, but limits itself to transforming." [1]

At any rate we shall get at the core of the matter, and the essential characteristics of the poetic thought, if we follow this subject of association through resemblance. This faculty of noting similarities and making "strange combinations out of common things," as Shelley says, is the one especially attributed the poet. "This intuitive perception of the hidden analogies of things," says Hazlitt, "or, as it may be called, this instinct of the imagination, is, perhaps, what stamps the character of genius on the productions of art more than any other circumstance; for it works unconsciously like nature, and receives its impressions from a kind of inspiration." [2] "Imagination," Leigh Hunt says, "purely so-called, is all feeling; the feeling of the subtlest and most affecting analogies; the perception of sympathies in

---

[1] *Interpretation of Dreams*, pp. 297, 402.
[2] *English Comic Writers*, p. 147.

the nature of things or in their popular attributes." [1]   So Wordsworth speaks of

> The exercise and produce of a toil,
> Than analytic industry to me
> More pleasing,

and "more poetic":

> Of that interminable building reared
> By observation of affinities
> In objects where no brotherhood exists
> To passive minds.

Through the observation of affinities Wordsworth comes to feel
that there are such bonds connecting all things and that there
is unity in all nature.

> I felt the sentiment of Being spread
> O'er all that moves and all that seemeth still.[2]

These bonds, either of contiguity or resemblance, but particularly
of the latter, exist everywhere, connecting one thing with
another, and are seemingly infinite in number, so that the poet,
instead of having to search for resemblances, is overwhelmed by
the number and variety of them.   "The feat of the imagination," Emerson says, "is in showing the convertibility of everything into every other thing."   It is this infinity of relation that
has led poets and philosophers from the earliest times, like
Wordsworth, to feel the unity and homogeneity of nature, and
of mind as answering to nature.   Lucretius, for example, quotes
Anaxagoras, "ut omnibus omnes res putet immixtas rebus
latitare," [3]—everything is latently involved in everything else,—
or as Emerson expresses it,

> A subtle chain of countless rings
> The next unto the farthest brings.[4]

---

[1] *Imagination and Fancy.*
[2] *Prelude*, Book ii, ll. 378–418.
[3] Book i, v. 876.
[4] "Nature."

The poet, then, is the man who above all others can follow this chain, from ring to ring, connecting the nearest with the most remote, and his work is obviously constructive and unifying.

The way this work is carried on and its results, in the particular case of the novelist of genius, are well suggested by Ward's criticism of Dickens. "But in the power of his imagination— of this I am convinced—he surpassed them [his contemporaries], one and all. That imagination could call up at will those associations which, could we but summon them in their full number, would bind together the human family, and make that expression no longer a name, but a living reality. Such associations sympathy alone can warm into life, and imagination alone can at times discern. . . . But more than this. So marvellously has this earth become the inheritance of mankind that there is not a thing upon it, animate or inanimate, with which, or with the likeness of which, man's mind has not come in contact, . . . with which human feelings, aspirations, thoughts, have not acquired an endless variety of single or subtle associations. . . . These also, which we imperfectly divine or carelessly pass by, the imagination of genius distinctly reveals to us, and powerfully impresses upon us. When they appeal directly to the emotions of the heart, it is the power of pathos which has awakened them; and when the suddenness, the unexpectedness, the apparent oddity of the one by the side of the other, strike the mind with irresistible force, it is the equally divine gift of humor which has touched the spring of laughter by the side of the spring of tears." [1]

II

A consequence of the recognition of resemblances is the symbolism which is constant in poetry. If two things are felt to be alike, one is for the mind, to that extent, an equivalent and so a substitute for the other. If a and b resemble each other, a becomes a symbol for b, and vice versa. The body, for example, as the dwelling-place of the soul, is commonly felt to be like a

[1] Quoted by Forster, *Dickens*, vol. iii, p. 319.

house; the latter may therefore take the place of the former, as a symbol,—as when Shakespeare says,

> This mortal house I'll ruin.

And conversely a house may be regarded as a body, as in Shakespeare again,

> But stop my house's ears, I mean my casements.

Of the two things resembling each other one will usually be more familiar than the other—one will be material, the other immaterial; one physical, the other mental; one concrete, the other abstract. The more familiar thing will then generally be treated as a symbol for the less familiar, the concrete, for example, as a symbol for the abstract, as the anchor is a symbol of hope. Sometimes, however, the abstract will stand for the concrete, as in Gray,

> Through verdant vales and Ceres' golden *reign*.

And, as I have said, if *a* and *b* are similar they are potentially interchangeable as symbols.

Sometimes, as in the case of *house* and *body*, the resemblance is generally recognized, and the symbol is therefore common and traditional. The use of *house*, *temple*, or other *building* as a figure for the body is accordingly very common in literature,—as in *Macbeth*,

> Most sacrilegious murder hath broke ope
> The Lord's anointed temple, and stole thence
> The life o' the building.

There are thus many very widely recognized or universal symbols,—like *fire* for love, which is more widely current than the anchor for hope, or the cross for religious feeling. On the other hand symbols are often entirely individual, because they arise from peculiar associations. A person, for example, who has learned his alphabet from colored blocks, may find the letter *A* a symbol for the color red,—but this will be entirely individual unless some one else has the same association. Thus A. W.

Schlegel found a symbolism in sounds, and regarded *a* as suggestive of bright red, and as conveying youth, joy, or brightness (as in the words *Strahl*, *Glanz*). He may in this way have got genuine effects of "tone color" from poetry, which others, lacking the same associations, cannot share.[1] Between such individual symbols and universal ones there are all degrees.

Symbols may be valid for certain groups or periods. The middle ages, sensitive to resemblances between material and immaterial things, were extremely fertile in symbols. "All the members of the body are symbols, the head is Christ, the hairs are the saints, the legs are the apostles, the eye is contemplation, etc." The cathedrals gave rise to endless symbolism: "the towers are prayer, the columns are the apostles, the stones and mortar the assembly of the faithful; the windows are the organs of sense, the buttresses and abutments are the divine assistance; and so on to the minutest detail." [2] This explains the difficulty in the interpretation of symbols; it arises because they often rest on individual or unknown associations. For this reason the symbolism of poetry often gives difficulty, as it does in Blake. But the poet will presumably use symbols which are generally recognized or readily interpreted from the context. So the symbol *house* for the body is in such general use as to be included in the definitions in the dictionary, and other symbolical uses of the same word are easily understood,—as in "the dark *house* and the long sleep." The *house* is used in an extended and

---

[1] Guest also thinks the sounds of letters in themselves suggestive of ideas; for example the trembling character of *l* suggests trepidation, as in "Double, double, toil and trouble." Butler doubtless lacked this association when he wrote the lines, with which Dr. Johnson makes Minim (*Idler*, June 9, 1759) ridicule effects of this kind,

> Honor is like the glossy bubble
> Which cost philosophers such trouble.

But some sounds are without doubt universally symbolical. The liquids are pleasing, and the word *pleasure* is pleasant in both sound and meaning.

[2] Ribot, *Creative Imagination*, p. 230.

detailed symbolism in the *House of the Seven Gables* and in the *Fall of the House of Usher*. In the latter, for example, the house is first the literal house which falls to pieces, then the family or line of Usher and then the body of Usher, which go to pieces also. For the house is then substituted the "haunted palace," with its "two luminous windows" and its "door," etc. Finally the "red-litten windows" no doubt go back to the eyes of the author himself. Thus upon the basis of a familiar object may be raised an extended symbolical construction, which, however, is readily interpreted by the imagination.[1]

In the examples we have just discussed there is an essential symbolism between objects without reference to the words which denote these objects. The object *house* is a symbol for the object *body*. Since the relation between symbols and language, however, is close, and since also it is impossible to speak of symbols without employing the words which denote them, we had better analyze this relation of symbols to language before going further. Suppose two objects, *a* and *b*, resembling each other; then, as I have said, each may stand for the other as a symbol. If both *a* and *b* have their own proper words to denote them, say *A* and *B*, then *a* may be called by the name of its symbol *b*—that is, by the name *B*. And vice versa. That is, the names of the objects, like the objects themselves, are interchangeable. The object *body* may be called by the name *house*, and vice versa. When a word is so used to designate, not its own proper object, but another similar—when *a* is called *B*, when a body is called a *house*—it becomes a trope or figure. It often happens, however, that one of the two objects, resembling each other, has no proper word to denote it. Fortunately, then, for

[1] It is not strange, therefore, to find *house* employed in the same symbolical way in dreams and neurotic fancies. Scherner noted this symbol, among many other common ones, in dreams. Compare Freud, *Interpretation of Dreams*: p. 319: "I know patients who have steadily adhered to an architectural symbolism for the body . . . to whom posts and pillars signify legs (as in the *Song of Songs*)," etc. This symbolism is common in the Bible.

language, this nameless object can be called or expressed figuratively. Otherwise it would be nameless and inexpressible, unless a new word were coined to express it. It is always easier, however, instead of coining a new word, to extend figuratively the meaning of an old one. Such extensions, therefore, make for economy, and also greatly increase the facility and expressiveness of language. Now the poet, since he is constantly seeing new resemblances, and uncovering new objects or ideas, which, because they are new, lack words to express them, is constantly forced to make such extensions. By using figures he gains greatly in power of expression; indeed he is enabled to express ideas which would otherwise remain inexpressible. The poets, therefore, are the great builders of language.

Indeed most extensions of language, and the growth of language in general, are the result of a poetic exercise of the mind. This is familiar ground, but I may give some examples. If *a* is seen to be like *b*, then *b*, lacking a word of its own, may be called *A*. If the erect posture of a man is seen to be like an honest mental carriage, then an honest man may be called *upright*, an expressive addition to the vocabulary. Physical qualities and actions are often felt to be like mental ones,—it would perhaps puzzle us to say why. Thus we speak of a *sweet* or *bitter* disposition, an *iron* will, *cool* courage, or a *hard* heart. Let us take the last example. The heart was by the old philosophers supposed to be the seat of feeling, that is of mental feeling, so-called because it is like the feeling of the body. Feeling was therefore once associated with the heart itself, and continues to be expressed by the word. Furthermore lack of feeling was thought of as having a quality like the physical hardness of, say, a stone. We thus speak of a hard or stony heart. We use these expressions so constantly that we forget the associations and figures they imply. But we could not possibly express ourselves without them or without equivalent figures. If we speak instead of obduracy, we only use a Latin figure instead of an English one. For this facility of expression we may thank the poetic mind which first saw the resemblances and used the figures.

Before going on to consider particularly the figures of poetry
we must notice one other point which is in fact of great importance. We have spoken hitherto as if two objects, a and b,
were simply juxtaposed in the mind and compared. This is
not at all the case in imaginative thought, as I hope has been
shown in earlier chapters. The imagination does not merely
see or even feel, that two things are alike, but it throws these
two things together, and fuses them. It makes a new compound of a and b—that is an ab which is an ideal object. Or
to be more exact, since in the composition certain features of
each thing are suppressed which may be called x and y, it makes
a compound which may be represented by the formula $(a—x)$
$(b—y)$. Let us take an example. The heart is first felt to be
like a stone. Then certain features of the heart are suppressed,
leaving say its shape and position in the body. Certain features also of the stone are dropped, leaving its texture, weight,
and certainly its hardness. Of the two, thus abstracted, a
composite is formed, and the body is thought by the poetic
mind to contain a heart of stone— that is not a heart and not
a stone, but an ideal composite of the two. This, then, is the
imaginative action of the mind, when, for example, Dante
says, "I did not weep, I was so turned to stone within." Features belonging to the heart (or the interior of the body), a,
are fused with features belonging to the stone, b, to form an
image, which is expressed by the word *stone*, B,—with the
addition, however, of words, I, *within*, which point to *heart*,
A. Thus a composite is formed, ab, which is called by one
of the two words A and B, belonging properly to its two ingredients, or by a compounding of these words,—just as in the preceding chapter we saw that a fictional character is formed by
the compounding of two actual persons, m and n, with the
name either M or N, or a "hyphenation" of both. In other
words, we are dealing here merely with the naming, or desig-
nation in words, of the compounded images and characters
which we have discussed in earlier chapters. This point of
the imaginative fusion is ordinarily overlooked; and we are

therefore now in a position to treat the subject of symbols and figures more clearly than do the ordinary books on this subject. A symbol is literally a "throwing together" of two things. A metaphor has been defined as a "rapid confusion" of two objects, and it is exactly this, the word confusion being employed in its literal sense. In what follows this imaginative confusion should be kept in mind.

The subject of symbols and figures is of course a very extensive one. Its difficulties, however, perhaps arise, as has been suggested, from the infinite number of possible associations which they may represent, and from the peculiarities of each individual's associations, and are therefore difficulties of interpretation.[1] I believe that the theory as given above covers the essential points and will go far toward explaining symbols and figures, at least as they appear in literature. It will at any rate explain the difference "between those metaphors which rise glowing from the heart," as Goldsmith calls them, "and the cold conceits which are engendered in the fancy."

The metaphor is the commonest figure in poetry and the most poetic. It is so, first because it is a figure of resemblance, and resemblances are for poetry the most important if not the most numerous associations; and secondly, because instead of comparing two objects, it names an imaginative fusion which has already taken place in the poet's mind. It is therefore strictly the language of the imagination. When Shakespeare, for instance, speaks of the sun as the "eye of heaven," we feel sure that his imagination has made the fusion. The metaphor, originally in primitive thought always the expression of such a fusion, may of course now-a-days be used to condense a mere comparison. This is apt to be the case in "mixed" metaphor, which is proper if a "mixed" fusion is to be ex-

[1] Underestimating these difficulties has, I surmise, sometimes led the psychoanalysts into error. Though right in their theory of *Traumdeutung*, they cannot with the analytic intellect follow the imaginative flights. Bottom cannot catch Puck.

pressed, as in Hamlet's soliloquy, but improper if it represents an ununified picture or series of mere conceits, as

> I *bridle* in my struggling muse with pain
> That longs to *launch* into a nobler strain.[1]

The simile on the other hand, which connects the names of two objects with the word *like* or its equivalent, is the language of prose. It puts two things side by side and deliberately compares them with the understanding; it does not fuse them in the imagination. It notices the bond instead of merely obeying it. This at least is the mood of the simile. Sometimes the simile will be truly poetical because it represents a true imaginative fusion, as in *Lear:*

> That she may feel
> How sharper than a serpent's tooth it is
> To have a thankless child.

This, however, is less imaginative in statement than Cleopatra's metaphor:

> Dost thou not see my baby at my breast
> That sucks the nurse asleep?

The distinctions ordinarily made between simile, "implied simile," and metaphor rest largely on mere form of expression. The metaphor will sometimes be prosaic, the simile often poetical. The real question is whether the expression results from a fusion of the visionary imagination, or is a mere comparison of the directed thought; and it can be said only that the fusion expresses itself most naturally in metaphor, the comparison in simile.

It is sometimes stated in school books that the metaphor is a "condensed simile." If this means that the poet first makes a conscious comparison and then compresses this into a meta-

[1] This and some other examples are taken from Gummere, *Handbook of Poetics.*

phor, it is of course not at all true. It might rather be said that the simile is an analyzed and expanded metaphor. The metaphor is the older and more fundamental figure. The primitive man who speaks of the fire "eating" or "devouring" the wood has no notion of a conscious comparison, which would be beyond his ability. He merely feels the likeness between two processes, identifies them, and calls one by the word belonging to the other which is more familiar to him. Later analytic thought may deliberately compare the two. The modern poet thinks in the same primitive way. When Shakespeare speaks of

> Sleep that knits up the ravell'd sleeve of care,

he obeys a series of bonds and expresses in a metaphor a fusion of images which he might have difficulty in identifying in order to express them in the simile form. When he makes Kent say "I have years on my back forty-eight," it is not to be supposed that he first formed a simile and then condensed it into a metaphor. This mistake, however, would be only a little worse than many made—not by the readers of poetry, who have no difficulty—but by the critics and rhetoricians who attribute to the poet the habits of ordinary prosaic thought and do not understand the working of the poet's mind.

Personification is merely a variety of metaphor, though a very large and important one. Ordinary metaphor represents a fusion of objects with objects; personification a fusion of objects with persons. This kind of fusion was particularly natural to the primitive imagination. A tree was fused with a female person to form a dryad, and by the same processes all things in nature, and all the faculties and qualities of the mind itself were given life. Furthermore the persons thus formed were fused with each other—as Isis with Aphrodite—by the processes for the formation of fictional characters explained in the preceding chapter. The imagination thus gave rise to all the shifting and interrelated figures of mythology. It has been said that in primitive times "the poet believed, now he as-

sumes, animism in nature."[1] It is true that the belief of
the modern poet is half-hearted,—at least he can never believe
with the full faith of the primitive man. The true poet, however,
must still believe, and not merely assume, that nature is alive.
When Lear exclaims, "Blow, winds, and crack your cheeks,"
his strong feeling leads to a genuine imaginative fusion, and
when Wordsworth addresses the daisy,

> In shoals and bands, a morrice train,
> Thou greet'st the traveller in the lane,

he believes quite as sincerely as the primitive poet, in his own
way, that nature is alive.

The figures just spoken of are based on resemblance.
Other figures—"tropes of connection"—the synecdoche and
metonymy, represent a fusion of contiguous objects. If we
except the figures like hyperbole and irony which are to be explained on different principles, these two classes—the figures
of resemblance, of which metaphor is the type, and the less
important figures of contiguity, of which synecdoche is the
type—cover the whole field.

But we have not yet got to the bottom of this subject. I
have spoken so far as if two things only were fused and represented by figures. In fact three, four, or more things are
often so fused, and the expression strives to represent the resulting complex image. Image a suggests image b by resemblance, and this in turn image c; and from these results a compound image abc, which is expressed by some choice from the
terms A, B, and C. This compounding of three images occurs
in Shakespeare's sonnet (where the third image enters in l. 4):

> That time of year thou mayst in me behold
> When yellow leaves, or none, or few, do hang
> Upon those boughs which shake against the cold,
> *Bare ruined choirs*, where late the sweet birds sang.

[1] Gummere, *Handbook of Poetics*, p. 97.

Another sonnet in which Shakespeare uses the word *state* three times, with shifting meaning, closes

> That then I scorn to change my *state* with kings.

Here the word *state* might mean "condition," "estate," or "royal splendor," and probably means all of these—not successively, but all at once. In other words the three meanings are fused in the mind, and the word *state* is a kind of triple figure. Sometimes the different meanings are not thus definitely assignable. Shakespeare in writing

> When to the *sessions* of sweet silent thought
> I summon up remembrance of things past,

has probably first in mind legal sessions, but this calls up other associations and the word therefore has other meanings—which are not to be defined, and are for this reason all the more poetical. This is perhaps the place to note that the associations in the mind of Shakespeare may not be the same as the associations in the mind of the present-day reader. This matter of associations is largely individual at best. From this fact flow several consequences. First, it is useless to try to determine Shakespeare's meaning in its finer points, though critics waste time in this effort. Secondly, since every great object with which the poet deals is connected with others by "countless rings" of thought and feeling, it may have many suggestions for other minds of which the poet is unconscious. Shakespeare always meant more than he intended, and of the poets generally it may be said, "They know not what they do." Thirdly, it is not only legitimate but inevitable for readers to read poetry in their own way—that is, to find in it their own associations of thought and feeling. And as a matter of fact great works of literature are thus always developed and enriched from age to age with the growth of thought. Shakespeare's works therefore mean something less, something different, and something more to us than they meant to him or to his contemporaries.

The point here, however, is that the word *sessions* is a many-sided figure. Thus from a different direction we again reach the conclusion of the last chapter but one, where we found that, on account of the imaginative process of condensation, each image and so each word in poetry has manifold meaning and implication. The conclusion may be stated here in the following form: any figurative word will have, besides its literal meaning, various other meanings, for the poet and for his readers. The value of such a word will not be limited to any one assignable likeness which could be expressed in a simile, but will involve many likenesses, depending on the links, sometimes visible, often invisible, formed in the mind of the poet or his readers. The poet's language will thus have a wealth of figurative meanings. Goldsmith rightly calls the metaphor " the muse's caduceus;"—it is "a kind of magical coat by which the same idea assumes a thousand different appearances."[1] Or, since the process of condensation works both ways, he might have said, " by which the same appearance stands for a thousand different ideas." This magical character of the metaphor, which Goldsmith was poet enough to see, but which is not properly noticed in the ordinary books on the subject, constitutes its greatest value in poetry.

III

The poet is constantly recognizing likenesses, and finding pleasure in their recognition. This fact also perhaps gives a key to peculiarities in the form of poetry, in which there constantly recur similarities which are recognized with pleasure. The similarity of two rhyming words, like *weep* and *deep*, is at once an instance and a symbol of the satisfying resemblances which it is the work of the poet to recognize. We should note, however, that as the poet is always conscious of resemblances, so he must be conscious of differences also: the two go together. The associated images are always seen to be not identical, but only similar; and the likeness and the unlikeness are therefore

[1] "Essay on the Use of Metaphors."

both a part of the mental experience. Thus the poet is confronted with endless differences as well as endless resemblances. From this results the principle insisted upon by the nineteenth century critics, of "similitude in dissimilitude " or "variety in uniformity,"—which indeed goes back to Plato. Wordsworth speaks in the Preface of 1800 of "the pleasure which the mind derives from the perception of similitude in dissimilitude. This principle is the great spring of the activity of our minds, and their chief feeder. From this principle the direction of the sexual appetite, and all the passions connected with it, take their origin: it is the life of our ordinary conversation," etc.[1]

The form of poetry is constantly illustrating and symbolizing this similitude in dissimilitude. Two lines, alike in metrical pattern but unlike in wording and modulation, closing with two rhyming words, like but unlike, form a pleasing pair that are first matched and then married. Two stanzas, different in substance and in music, are seen to be similar in form. In blank verse two "patterns," to use Stevenson's phrase, the verse pattern and the sentence pattern, first contrast and then combine, like the parts in music, to "reach their solution on the same ringing note." In a line two members of an antithesis are pleasingly alike, yet pleasingly unlike:

Have eyes to wonder but lack tongues to praise.

The same principle explains the repetition and parallelism of the ballads, with its imitation in Coleridge and Poe; and why

[1] Compare Coleridge, *Biographia Literaria*, ed. Shawcross, vol. ii, p. 232 ("multeity in unity"); *Table Talk*, Dec. 27, 1831 ("multitude in unity"); *Anima Poetæ* (Boston, 1895), p. 129: "Now poetry produces two kinds of pleasure, one for each of the two master-movements or impulses of man,— the gratification of the love of variety, and the gratification of the love of uniformity." Compare also Leigh Hunt, *Imagination and Fancy:* "Modifying its language on the principle of variety in uniformity;" and Plato, *Phaedrus,* 261–269.

Poe for example, was so fond, both in prose and verse, of repetition, but of repetition with variation.

> In the misty mid region of Weir,
> In the ghoul-haunted woodland of Weir.

The uniformity and variety of the poetic form make it symbolic of the content of the poet's mind.

CHAPTER XIV

THE IMPULSE AND THE CONTROL

I

THE close of the last chapter brings up the form of poetry, which hitherto we have not much considered. So far we have attended mainly to the poetic vision which is the antecedent ideal pattern of the finished poem. We have discussed the inspiration of poetry to the neglect of the poetic art. This of course leaves the theory incomplete, because both inspiration and art are necessary to poetry. These two things, the impulse and the form, are very closely related, but distinct in their origin in the mind, and due to different mental causes. They are indeed more or less opposed to each other and originate in a mental conflict. To understand their relation, however, and the nature of their opposition, we shall have to begin with more fundamental considerations.

The poetic impulse, as we have seen, lies in the poet's desires, wishes, or aspirations. The desires of the individual mind, if it stood alone and untrammelled, would presumably all be satisfied.

> Real are the dreams of Gods, and smoothly pass
> Their pleasures in a long immortal dream.[1]

But this gratification, the privilege of pure spirit, is denied to the poet. As a consequence of the mind's material embodiment, its desires meet physical obstacles, which often result in their denial. Furthermore the poet does not stand alone but in the presence of other men; he is an individual but also a member of society. His desires are met by the demands of what sociol-

[1] Keats, "Lamia," I, 127.

ogists call the "herd." Evidently the poetic thought, motivated by the desires, will be influenced by these two circumstances—the physical obstacles, and the control exercised by society. Of the two influences, however, the second is by far the more important. The poetic art, for example, belongs mainly to this social control.

Our conduct, in action or expression, even our thought, is largely a resultant from two factors, the native individual impulse on the one hand, and the demands of society on the other. The individual has certain impulses, desires, accompanied by their appropriate feelings and by the thoughts calculated to promote their gratification. These impulses are met by the opposing claims of society in the form of custom, "common" sense, fashion, traditional rule or habit, law—in a word authority in all its various forms. Sometimes these claims are exercised from without, as in law or custom; sometimes they are adopted into the mind itself, and operate from within, as in duty and conscience. Conduct is largely the result of a series of compromises or adjustments, more or less satisfactory, between impulse and authority. In dress, for example, we express our own taste within the limits of fashion, and that is the best compromise which best expresses the individual character on the one hand and the social demand on the other. In manners we act as we like so far as our training will allow. In moral matters we follow the devices and desires of our own hearts, so far as moral obligations will permit. In writing we give utterance to our own thought and feeling, but in accordance with the traditions and usages in the prosaic and poetic styles. In all these cases—and every expression will be found to involve a similar adjustment—following the individual impulse is felt to be freedom and privilege, the social claim obligation and limitation. But as has always been recognized in civil relations, true liberty—at least the only liberty possible in this world of the individual and society—lies in freedom controlled by obligation.

Our impulses are primary and innate, our regard for external opinion secondary and acquired. The savage is a man of un-governed passions; civilization is a long training in self-govern-ment; civilized man has come to feel his obligations sensitively and to respond to them by second nature. This response, how-ever, never becomes better than second nature, our first nature being always to follow our own desires. The child likewise is morally still in the savage state. He is born completely an individual. He satisfies his desires selfishly, and expresses him-self naturally and lawlessly in acts and speech. Soon, however, he begins to feel the force of authority, and to learn from parents and playmates the meaning of obligation, manners, duty. His education is a long training in the government of the impulses, in repression,—a conservative and conventionalizing process undertaken by society in its own interest. "The years bring the inevitable yoke." Youth is subdued by age until youth be-comes age; the young man becomes not merely an individual, but a member of society, helping in turn to impose the authority of society upon others. Thus the progressive and life-giving energy of youth is gradually overgrown by authority and con-servatism, until finally it ends in age and death. *Nascendo morimur:* as soon as we are born we begin to die. The spirit first animates our mortal clay and then is quenched by it. The thought of this—the thought of Wordsworth in the "Intimations of Immortality," the fact that we find pleasure in following our own impulses and pain in the social inhibitions, the fancy that the impulses partake of the freedom of the spirit, while the authority is one of the fatal consequences of the spirit's fleshly embodiment, lead us to be impatient—lead poets in particular to attempt to throw off the restrictions. But in this world at any rate there is no escape from this dualism with its conflict.

The life and poetry of Wordsworth would furnish forth a treatise on this subject. As a young man, indeed always, Wordsworth rejoices in the life of the spirit, but as he grows older he becomes thankful for "the rich bounties of constraint." He lives through the conflict and feels the strength of both claims. The balance is struck in the greatest of his "poems of reflection": happy is the man who can "rely upon the genial sense of youth," upon the innate impulse, his first nature; but happy also is he who, when this "unchartered freedom" fails, can fall back on a "second will more wise." In the sonnet "Nuns fret not," he has come, at the age of thirty-seven, to feel "the weight of too much liberty," and he is ready to subject his inspiration to the most exacting of literary forms.

This sonnet will suggest how the two opposing principles I have explained apply to poetry, and how in poetry also true liberty comes from a freedom under restraint. Poetry is a resultant from the same two factors: the individual impulse provides the motive and inspiration of poetry; the authority has for one of its consequences the poetic art. The art is a social element; it embraces not only the proprieties of language, form, and style demanded of the poet by his present audience, but also all the poetic forms, laws, customs that are traditional, that are imposed upon the poet from the past—poetic authority in all its aspects. For his inspiration a poet must be born a poet; for his art he must of course go to school. If the old adage is not usually completed—*poeta nascitur et fit*—it is presumably because the inspiration is the peculiar and important, or perhaps preferable element. The poet himself is, so to speak, naturally on the side of the inspiration, and leaves it largely to the critics to enforce the authority. Indeed the poet is constantly breaking the poetic law, throwing off form, making new forms, justifying them, and so creating new law which may be enforced by the critics.

But if the two functions of divine law-giver and judge are thus in some degree specialized in the poet and the critic, the poet himself is after all human and must recognize both claims; both factors will operate in the poet's own mind. His first nature is to express his individual desires; but he must cultivate a second nature, a "second will more wise,"—the desire to conform and to express himself within the limitations of the poetic art. Without the inspiration his work is mere artistry, satisfying only to the critic intent on laws; but without the art it is merely individual, eccentric, incomprehensible to other men, to society, which must insist that some law be observed. "In poets," Lowell says, "this liability to be possessed by the creations of their own brains is limited and proportioned by the artistic sense, and the imagination thus truly becomes a shaping faculty, while in less regulated organizations it dwells forever in the Nifelheim of phantasmagoria and dream." [1] The true poet, as Lamb says, is not merely "possessed by his subject, but has dominion over it"; he is mad, but there is a "hidden sanity which still guides him in the widest seeming aberrations." [2] "Thus poetry, in its metrical form as well as in its substance, would seem to be deducible from two great instinctive necessities of our common nature—the same to which it was long ago referred by Aristotle; the need for some vent for absorbing or exciting thoughts, which he calls imitation or expression; and the need of so controlling that expression, as that the presence of reason, subduing and ordering it, shall be felt, and make itself discernible throughout; which in this case becomes what he calls the instinct of harmony and of rhythm." [3]

These two factors, then, long recognized as determining the character of the poetic product, I am going to refer to as the "impulse" and the "control." The principles are clear enough, and the claims insistent: the difficulty is in making the adjustment. Just as in trifling everyday matters of dress we must compromise between personality and fashion, or in moral matters between desire and obligation, so the poet must make an adjustment between his inspiration and the traditional requirements. An individual poet, like Shelley or Walt Whitman, makes one adjustment; the conventional poet, like Pope or Tennyson, another. One expresses himself at any cost, almost lawlessly; the other is easy within the bonds of form. The critics discuss the satisfactoriness of the adjustment—in the

[1] *Prose Works*, vol. ii, p. 321.

[2] "The Sanity of True Genius."

[3] John Keble, *British Critic*, vol. xxiv (1838), p. 436.

case of Shakespeare for example or Shelley or Walt Whitman—particularly whether the demands of art have been satisfied. Shakespeare, according to Dryden, "wanted art." The same question arises about the latest writer of free verse; and the answer, as always, depends on the force with which the two opposing claims are felt.

Of the two factors, the poetic impulse is the inventive one, furnishing, so to speak, the raw material of poetry; the poetic control is the shaping one, in the broadest sense,—giving form to this raw material, not merely (1) to the structure, language, and verse of the finished poem, but even (2), as we shall presently see, to the antecedent poetic vision itself. Let us take these two formative processes in turn.

In one of his critical essays John Keble "proposes by way of conjecture" the following definition: "Poetry is the indirect expression in words, most appropriately in metrical words, of some overpowering emotion, ruling taste, or feeling, the direct indulgence whereof is somehow repressed." [1] In this definition the emotion, or as he calls it on another page, the "desire or regret," is the impulse; the repression arises from the social control. There is no poetry in the direct indulgence or expression of feeling. It is only when this indulgence or expression is impeded that poetry arises. Thus, to summarize Keble's examples, a speech which wittily contrives by association or allusion to expose a hidden feeling, or a face which by a sudden and fleeting play of feature conveys a forbidden and otherwise incommunicable motion of the heart, is felt to be "expressive" and "poetical." It gives pleasure by obviating the repression. A wink is often better than a word—more expressive and pleasurable. Similarly in poetry a direct expression is improper or impossible; a veiled or "poetical" one is the recourse. The motive impulse in poetry is supplied by the poet's desires. But these cannot give themselves free expression. They are met by the repressive forces of authority—regard for appearances,

[1] *The British Critic*, vol. xxiv (1838), p. 426, reprinted in *Occasional Papers and Reviews*, 1877. See also Keble's *De Poeticæ Vi Medica*, 1844.

convention, morality—which conflict with and control them. The result is an indirect or veiled expression, which we call poetry.

This may be illustrated most readily first in the verse form of poetry, its rhythm and metre, which gives utterance to both elements, the impulse and the control, and is produced by their conflict. Coleridge is on the right track when he finds the origin of metre in "the balance in the mind effected by that spontaneous effort which strives to hold in check the workings of passion." [1] The poetic passion is a form of energy,—or to be exact, it is a kind of mental friction resulting from an expenditure of energy. Apparently all energy in nature—in light, heat, etc.,—comes not constantly, but in recurrent movements, or waves,—in other words, rhythmically. The movements of the body are rhythmical. So strong and unrestrained emotion inevitably expresses itself in waves, with a throbbing or pulsation, in recurrences of voice or gesture, which constitute a natural rhythm; and poetry, as an emotional expression, has this rhythm. These natural waves are not exactly regular, but only roughly so—like the waves on a body of water, to which the word rhythm etymologically refers—or like the waves on a field of grass in the wind to which Walt Whitman compared his natural rhythms. The recurrent beat of verse is therefore not a superadded ornament, but a vital and inevitable accompaniment of the poetic feeling, going back, we may imagine, to the poet's heart. The poet's feeling starts this rhythm, and the rhythm in turn will arouse feeling in the hearer, as the heart is aroused at the beat of a drum. Just as Shakespeare's words convey his sense, so his rhythm conveys to us his feeling; and it is one of the miracles of language that not merely his thought but his very emotion is thus reconstituted for us after three centuries. Now in a free expression of feeling this rhythm would be bound by no law but that imposed by the feeling itself. In poets of a primitive or strongly individual kind, like Whit-

---

[1] *Biographia Literaria*, chap. xviii.

man, it is felt in something like its native wildness and force.
Usually, however, it is restrained and modified by regard for the
traditions and conventions of the poetic style. In Tennyson, for
example, it has become conventionalized in metre, in regularly
measured or metrical beats, by its subjection to prosodial law;
it has been adapted to recognized forms of line and stanza. In
free verse the conventionalizing is slight; in the sonnet, for
example, or the heroic couplet, it is much greater. It is well
therefore to distinguish thus between rhythm and metre.

The nature and cause of this metrical restraint are well stated
by Keble. "The conventional rules of metre and rhythm . . .
may be no less useful, in throwing a kind of veil over those strong
and deep emotions, which need relief, but cannot endure publicity. The very circumstance of their being expressed in verse
draws off attention from the violence of the feelings themselves,
and enables people to say things which they could not venture on
in prose. . . . This effect of metre seems quite obvious as far
as regards the sympathies of others. Emotions which in their
unrestrained expression would appear too keen and outrageous
to kindle fellow feeling in any one, are mitigated and become
comparatively tolerable, not to say interesting to us, when we
find them so far under control as to leave those who feel them at
liberty to pay attention to measure and rhyme, and the other
expedients of metrical composition. But over and above the
effect on others, we apprehend that even in a writer's own
mind there commonly exists a sort of instinctive delicacy, which
finds its account in the work of arranging lines and syllables,
and is content to utter, by their aid, what it would have shrunk
from setting down in the language of conversation; the metrical
form thus furnishing, at the same time, a vent for eager feelings,
and a veil of reserve to draw over them." [1]

This figure of the "veil" is a common one. Goethe, writing
to Schiller about tragic scenes in Faust first done in prose in
which they were "quite intolerable," says: "I am, therefore, now

[1] *British Critic*, Vol. xxiv, p. 435.

trying to put them into rhyme, for there the idea is seen as if under a veil, and the immediate effect of the tremendous material is softened." [1] "Rhythm," Nietzsche says, "casts a veil over reality"; just as "Art makes the aspect of life endurable by the throwing over it the veil of obscure thought." [2] "Embodied in the mystery of words," Wordsworth says,

> Even forms and substances are circumfused
> By that transparent veil with light divine,
> And through the turnings intricate of verse,
> Present themselves as objects recognized,
> In flashes, and with glory not their own. [3]

This, however, takes us a little beyond the verse form of poetry; we shall return to this matter of the "veil" in a moment.

The form of poetry is the product of two forces—the rhythmic impulse, and the control represented by metre, line, stanza, and the like. The natural rhythm of unrestrained emotion would be unpleasing to a hearer as wanting in regard for this hearer—as wanting art; it must accordingly be reduced to recognized forms. It must not, however, be lost in this reduction, but must be felt constantly behind and through these forms giving them animation. In a poet like Shelley, in whom the poetic impulse is strong, the natural rhythm is always so felt; it even constantly threatens to break through the bonds of form and secure its freedom. In Pope, in whom the poetic impulse is weak, or at any rate in some of the followers of Pope, in whom native impulse is wanting, the form is everything, and the "echo of the eternal music" is entirely lost. The old question, whether or not metre is essential to poetry, must be answered formally, as the best critics from Aristotle to Wordsworth have answered it, in the negative; in every

[1] Translated by F. B. Gummere, *The Beginnings of Poetry*, p. 73.

[2] *Human, All too Human*, (1910), vol. i, p. 157. "Real thoughts of real poets always go about with the veil on, like Egyptian women."—vol. ii, p. 249.

[3] *Prelude*, Book v, l. 601.

tolerable literary expression, however,—even in that other
harmony of poetical prose, which has not only its rhythm but
its laws no less exacting than those of verse—there must be, or
will be, not only the element of inspiration but the element of
control, which in poetry employs metre as one of its commonest instruments.

The two opposing principles which thus determine the verse
form of poetry, determine also the language, which I shall
discuss presently, and even the substance; indeed it is to the
substance that they first and most fundamentally apply. The
figure of the "veil" which Keble applies to the form, he employs again in describing the substance of poetry. "In the
prose romances of Sir Walter Scott," he says for example,
"and in all others which would be justly considered poetical, it
will be found, we believe, that the story is, in fact, interposed
as a kind of transparent veil between the listener and the narrator's real drift and feelings." Scott's ruling passion, his
desire to live in the past and to make the past live again, met,
as Keble shows, various checks; it could, however, be freely
expressed in the guise of a story. This case is typical; every
creative poetical work is such a veiled representation. The
feeling of the poet cannot have a direct, but only an indirect
or repressed expression, through the medium of what Keble
calls "associations more or less accidental."

It is a fact worth noting that any object in nature is more
beautiful if thus "veiled." A landscape is more "poetical"
if it is seen *through* a foreground in glimpses, or in the semi-
obscurity of haze or distance. A beautiful human figure is
only the more beautiful if it is half seen, or similarly veiled or
softened. So in poetry Poe finds the greatest beauty in the
"mystical," "in which there lies beneath the transparent
upper current of meaning an under or suggestive one,"—in
which, therefore, the deepest meaning is seen *through*. This
is partly to be explained on the principle already stated in
Chapter V: that poetry lies always where the known verges
upon the unknown. But it is connected also with the present

subject. Carlyle finds a "wondrous agency" in symbols, and it is because "in a symbol there is concealment and yet revelation."[1] A full explanation of Carlyle's meaning would clear up much in poetry. In poetry also, which is symbolic, and indeed, as we shall see, because it is symbolic,—because it expresses its true feeling only through what Keble calls "associations more or less accidental"—there is concealment, yet revelation; in fact Carlyle's expression is a complete description of poetry from the present point of view. I may preface the following discussion by saying that the poetic impulse is satisfied by the revelation, while the concealment is due to the control.

II

The poet is naturally an individualist and an enemy of convention. Shelley, for example, was at war with society. Even Shelley, however, had to make his own one-sided adjustment with the social demands in moral matters. And so in his poetry he had sometimes to ask consciously and deliberately whether this or that expression was within the bounds of poetic art—at the risk of losing all hearing and recognition in eccentricity. This open and conscious regard for the social demand, however, is not different from that of the ordinary man and needs no explanation. The important influence of the control on the poet lies much deeper. The poet is an individualist partly because he is a dreamer. In practical life, and in ordinary directed thought, the social demand is strongly felt; in our second mode of thought—in abstraction, vision, or dream—which as we have seen in Chapter III is in its nature more individual—the social demand falls away to some degree, leaving a life of impulse. The poet and dreamer in a way return to childhood and the individual life. But even in the second mode of thought both the impulse and the control are still operative, and they in fact conflict to form the poetic vision itself. To understand this we shall have to consider

[1] *Sartor Resartus*, Book iii, chap. iii.

carefully the poetic desires and what Keble calls their repression.

Those "desires of the mind," as Bacon calls them, to which the poet "submits the shows of things," and which form the motives for the poetical activity, are not different, except in their elevation and refinement, from the desires of other men. Sometimes, for example, the poet's desire is the common one of love. Every man may be thought of as made up of the desires which ultimately motivate his thought and action, and which therefore form his basic character—of those "cravings," to use Nietzsche's phrase, which "constitute his being," [1] and which call for "sustenance." These cravings are of all sorts from the personal and immediate bodily desires, like those for food and drink, to the most elevated aspirations, like Scott's wish to make the feudal past live again. The main desires are those which serve the preservation of life and the propagation of the species. Perhaps about these all the others gather; the others are these main desires extended, specialized, and diffused. Man's desires set in motion his activities, these being calculated to secure the appropriate gratification. Of the whole number of desires, however, only a part are gratified by action; others in seeking or contemplating gratification, encounter obstacles and are denied.

These obstacles arise ultimately from external circumstances in various forms. The obstacle may be an actual external hindrance, as where a man desires something, acts in order to obtain it, and finds it actually snatched from him by another. Or it may arise from a realization in the mind itself, antecedent to action, that action and gratification are impossible or inexpedient. Thus the hindrance becomes a mental one,— that is, both the desire and the impeding thought exist in the mind itself. Here again there are two cases: the mind may realize first that its desire is physically impossible of attainment, as to bring back a dead friend; or secondly, that it is impossible or improper in the light of social obligation, this

[1] The Dawn of Day, p. 116.

last word being employed in the broadest sense to include all the demands made by society upon the individual which the mind may recognize. That is, the obligation may be of any sort,—regard for law, morality, custom or use, "appearance," artistic propriety or fashion; if it is recognized by the mind it influences the thought. There arises a conflict between impulse on the one hand and propriety or authority on the other.

Now in all the cases just mentioned,—wherever the desires are denied actual and full gratification, they may take refuge in a substitute fictional gratification. In all these cases then poetry may arise. The first case, however, in which there is merely physical hindrance, is relatively unimportant; the desire here is free of obligation, and can therefore find vent through the imagination untrammelled. The resulting thought and poetry will show revelation without concealment. The last case in which the hindrance is moral, is perhaps most frequent, certainly the most important, and is the one requiring explanation. The moment the social obligation is felt the case is complicated. There are now two factors, first the primary individual desire, secondly the acquired and secondary desire to conform to the social demand. There is the wish, but also a "second will more wise." The first is the impulse, the second the control. The two are still in conflict: the primary desire is impeded and repressed by the secondary one. The poetic thought or vision is a result of this conflict; the imagination must now supply a fictional gratification of both primary and secondary desires at once. Here then lies the explanation of the veiling or concealment. When the primary desire is free the imagination pictures a direct image of the gratification. When, however, the primary desire is met by the secondary one, when the impulse is controlled, the imagination affords not a direct image, but an equivalent associated one, which, however, is accompanied by the same feelings and supplies a similar gratification. The secondary desire is in turn also gratified by this substitution of the associated image, for the very reason that the substitution makes for concealment or palliation, and, so to speak, keeps up appearances.

Before we go on with this, however, we shall have to consider another peculiarity of the mind. When the primary desires are met and repressed by the secondary ones, particularly where both are strong, instead of remaining before the conscious mind they are apt to be driven from it into unconsciousness. This happens for one or both of two reasons. In the first place they are dropped as useless. Just as attention is the concentration of the mind upon one point of interest (desire) and the rejection by an antagonism of all the matters of less interest or value; so the conscious thought depends upon the retention of matters of practical value, having to do with present or contemplated action, and the relegation of other matters, useless or indifferent, to unconsciousness. The primary desires, when found incapable of satisfaction, therefore become unconscious, and perhaps with them the secondary ones also for the same reason.[1] Or in the second place the desires, when denied, become painful and are therefore, by a defensive operation, driven out of range of the conscious attention, into unconsciousness. This is the explanation of Freud, and it agrees with Bergson, who intimates that our mental health depends on the constant elimination of such matter alien to our sane attention to life.[2] These two reasons, however, as appears in the preceding statement of them, are related or identical. An impracticable and unsatisfied desire is painful: dissatisfaction and pain are the same thing. When finally incapable of satisfaction, then, the desires are driven back into unconsciousness. I believe that the primary and the opposed secondary desires may thus be both conscious, or both unconscious, or even one conscious and the other unconscious: in all four cases. It might happen, for example, that the primary desire had dropped to unconsciousness, while the secondary one remained before the mind. The cases

[1] See James, *Psychology*, vol. i, p. 685; and *ante*, pp. 92, 115.

[2] *Revue Philosophique*, 1908, II, p. 573.

where one or both of the instances have become unconscious would be the most important for poetry—certainly those most requiring explanation.

These hidden impulses still originate imaginative presentations, and are also still under hidden control. Here in fact, just because the impracticability and consequent repression are due to the social inhibition, the control is strongest and the conflict most violent. Here, therefore, the revelation is accomplished with greatest difficulty, and the concealment is greatest, amounting through a complex working of the associations, to complete substitution and distortion. The substitution, however, may arouse the same feelings and afford the same gratification.

The mental operation throughout is complicated and obscure, and simplified statement is difficult and no doubt misleading. I venture, however, for the sake of clearness to formulate it as follows. A wish, arousing certain thoughts calculated to direct action, along with certain feelings, has its normal end in action and gratification. If, however, the wish is denied, it parallels this series in the imagination. If a conscious wish is merely denied then this wish, v, arouses certain appropriate images, a, b, accompanied by appropriate feelings, c, d, and secures a gratification, g. If, secondly, it is inhibited by the control, the wish v arouses, not $a\,b$, but other substitute images, $a'\,b'$, by association, accompanied, however, by the same feelings $c\,d$, and securing the gratification g. But here, unless the associations are followed, $a'\,b'$ does not seem appropriate to either v, or c, d, and g. Thus $a'\,b'$ is a veiled or concealed representation of the wish. If, thirdly, the denied wish becomes unconscious, it gives rise through more "mediate" or remote associations, to still stranger substitutes, $a''\,b''$, etc.; stranger, too, because the wish v, being unconscious, the images simply spring into the mind without apparent motivation, along with feelings not felt as particularly belonging to the images, and inexplicable pleasure.

Poetry may correspond to each of these three cases. In the

first case the poetic vision is fictional in the sense that it directly represents an ungratified desire as gratified. In the second and third cases it is doubly fictional, because it goes on to do this indirectly by a kind of allegory or symbolism (since a' b' stand to a b as symbols). The direct representation might seem more satisfying than the indirect, veiled, or symbolical one. It is not so; the veiled representation both liberates the individual and "squares " him with society, and is thus doubly grateful. In any case the veiled representation is more poetical, and is the regular mode of the deeper and more unconscious mind from which poetry mainly proceeds. "Poetry," Shelley says, "arrests the vanishing apparitions which haunt the interlunations of life, and veiling them or in language or in form, sends them forth among mankind, bearing sweet news of kindred joy to those with whom their sisters abide—abide, because there is no portal of expression from the caverns of the spirit which they inhabit into the universe of things." [1] This from Shelley is poetical, but perhaps clearer for most of us than the prose formulation above. The "interlunations " and the "caverns " are the deeper or more unconscious portions of the mind; the "apparitions " are the imaginative creations; the "veiling " constitutes the concealment; the "sisters " represent the corresponding imagination of the reader, which finds no expression, but answers readily to the imagination of the poet. The apparitions of the poet's mind are gladly received and their language readily comprehended by the reader, in spite of the symbolic veils they wear.

The operation of the poetic imagination just explained finds illustration in imaginative operations of other kinds. The unconscious wishes of the poet, with their accompanying thoughts and feelings (v ab cd), are parallel to the *souvenirs traumatiques* or *idées fixes* of the school of Janet,[2] which break up the coherence of the sane personality and lead to hysterical imaginative presentations; and to the "complex " of the Freudians, par-

---

[1] *Defense of Poetry*, ed. Cook, p. 41.

[2] P. Janet, *Les Médications Psychologiques*, vol. ii, pp. 204, 209.

ticularly of the Zurich School,—the "complex of ideas of marked emotional accentuation which has been repressed into the unconscious." [1] The imagination in pathological cases works like that of the poet in surprising ways, which space will not permit to be detailed here. In the poet too an *idée fixe* or complex— that is, an unconscious network of desires, thoughts, and feelings, perhaps of early or childhood origin—will inspire the poetic vision, and furnish the poetic material. The examples given by Wordsworth at the end of Book XII of the *Prelude* of "passages of life," "taking their date from our first childhood," and revealing "the hiding places of man's power," represent such emotionally accentuated ideas.[2] We may suppose then either that the poet shows a healthy and normal working of the imagination which in the hysteric becomes pathological; or that the poet's case is to some extent pathological also. Poets have always been thought mad; they are among the *hystériques qui mènent le monde*. This alternative we shall consider in the next chapter.

The poetic vision is also here again parallel to the dream as described by Freud. It represents wishes, particularly early wishes and unconscious complexes. "The formation of dreams," according to the Freudians, "is brought about by the working of the two psychic forces (streams or systems), one of which forms the wish of the dream, while the other exerts its censorship on this wish and thus produces the distortion." [3] The censor, standing "at the gateway of consciousness," repressing certain ideas, but in nocturnal relaxation allowing others to pass in the grotesque concealments of the dream, corresponds to the control of the preceding pages. The censor, as it is described in the Freudian theory, though amply supported, seems a little factitious, until it is traced back to the social control, which fully explains it. The conflict between the wish and the psychic censor is only one phase of the conflict, omnipresent in human thought and action, between the individual and society.

The concealment explained above corresponds to the dis-

[1] A. A. Brill, *Psychanalysis*, p. 142.   [2] See *ante*, p. 159.
[3] Brill, *Psychanalysis*, p. 37.

placement of the dream-theory, which is the work of the censor. As this displacement in its application to poetry has already been explained in Chapter XI, the examples there given are pertinent here. And as this displacement occurs through the substitution of associations, that is, symbols, the theory of the preceding chapter should be connected with this one. Displacement occurs when the desire is represented not directly but through some trifling association, to which the original emotional emphasis is shifted; the trifling association stands as symbol. In other words the displacement affords revelation with concealment.

The painting of Félicien Rops used somewhere by Freud to illustrate the emergence of repressed material in dream and morbid fancy, is also an excellent example of what occurs in the formation of the poetic vision. The picture shows Saint Anthony kneeling in ecstasy before a cross glowing with heavenly light, glowing, however, in the nude form of a woman of ideal beauty. Here the woman answers to the individual's mortified desire; the cross to the demands of religious duty. The first is due to the impulse, the second to the control or censor. The saint's vision is a composite, representing both and compromising between the two. We can imagine this vision as shifting— first showing the cross more distinctly, then the woman, as one or the other of the conflicting desires is more strongly felt; first inclining toward revelation, then toward concealment. Thus the poet's vision will be a shifting composite, variously satisfying both demands.

This Carlylean principle of revelation with concealment is so fundamental that it will be found constantly applicable in literature—in poetry and allied expressions. It applies to wit. If I say for example: "The English army loses all its battles but the last," I at first appear to mean: "The English army almost always loses;" but the concealed meaning is nearly the opposite, and is the more effective for being concealed. In irony, through the surface meaning, the concealed meaning is revealed with access of pleasure. In poetry, as has already been explained, where there is double or multiple meaning, the most veiled meaning is deepest and most significant. In general the stronger the feeling and the repression and the greater the conflict, the greater is the displacement, the heavier the veil, and the more poetical the effect.

One other feature of the poetic process must be included here, because though it is distinct from those just discussed it shows the influence of the social control. The poetic vision is probably subjected to a modification similar to that described as taking place in dreams under the name of "secondary elaboration." This shows the action of the censor, and arises "from the activity, not of the underlying dream thoughts, but of the more conscious mental processes. . . . When a dream is apprehended in consciousness [that is, recollected on waking], it is treated in the same way as any other perceptive content, and is therefore not accepted in its unaltered state, but is assimilated to pre-existing conceptions. It is thus to a certain extent remodeled so as to bring it, so far as is possible, into harmony with the other conscious mental processes." [1] So when the poet brings his vision out of the region of inspiration into the everyday world, when he comes consciously to recollect and record it, he naturally modifies it to bring it into harmony with his ordinary waking thought. Trelawny tells of finding Shelley alone in a wood near Pisa, with the manuscript of one of his lyrics: "It was a frightful scrawl, words smeared out with his fingers, and one upon another, over and over in tiers, and all run together in the most admired disorder. . . . On my observing this to him, he answered, 'When my brain gets heated with a thought, it soon boils, and throws off images and words faster than I can skim them off. In the morning when cooled down, out of the rude sketch, as you justly call it, I shall attempt a drawing.'" [2] When Shelley recorded his vision in this frightful scrawl, made almost in the moment of rapture, he doubtless lost something of his original inspiration and modified it. And

[1] E. Jones, *American Journal of Psychology*, vol. xxi, p. 297.
[2] J. A. Symonds, *Shelley*, p. 166.

when the next morning he made from the rude sketch a finished drawing he modified still more. He had to find words for his vision in the language of this world, to mould it into a conventional metrical form, to give it local habitation in a world of prose. There was more poetry in Shelley's heart than could find expression in the finished lyric. "The most glorious poetry that has ever been communicated to the world," says Shelley himself, "is probably a feeble shadow of the original conceptions of the poet." [1] At best parts of poems are faintly animated by the authentic poetical inspiration. The impulse is again grievously controlled. Life animates the mortal clay and is in turn quenched by it. The poetic spirit finds its incarnation and partial expression in the fictions and conventional forms which we call poetry. In poetry the word is made flesh. [2]

III

We have been considering mainly the individual poet. We may perhaps regard man as a microcosm of mankind, and the larger life of mankind as the resultant from the same conflict of opposing forces,—between the individual and society, between men taken separately and men taken together as a unit. We may perhaps regard imaginative literature as a whole—the literature, for example, of a period or a nation—as determined by these same opposing forces.

The terms *classicism* and *romanticism* have been common in literary history and criticism. They have been often abused and often used vaguely. Every student of literary history, however, knows that they serve to name, if not to explain, certain observed facts and tendencies in literature. The difficulty is not with the terms, but with the definition or explanation of them. Accounts of the so-called "romantic movement," for example, give instances and characteristics which everyone feels

[1] *Defense of Poetry*, ed. Cook, p. 39.

[2] The rest of this chapter is reprinted from my *Poetry and Dreams*, 1912; see Preface. Some paragraphs in the following chapters are substantially from the same source.

to be somehow "romantic" and related, but do not amount to satisfactory explanations, because they do not unify the phenomena by bringing them under a cause or principle. The principles which best explain romanticism and classicism are well stated in two words by Walter Pater, as "the principles of liberty, and authority, respectively." These principles, Pater says, are not mutually exclusive, but rather complementary. "However falsely those two tendencies may be opposed by the critics, or exaggerated by artists themselves, they are tendencies really at work at all times in art, molding it, with the balance sometimes a little on one side, sometimes a little on the other, generating, respectively, as the balance inclines on this side or that, two principles, two traditions, in art and in literature." [1] Literature, in other words, is the result of a conflict between the individual impulse, the life-giving and progressive principle, on the one hand, and the power of authority, the controlling and conservative principle, on the other. Both of these forces are always at work; but according as one or the other has in any period the upper hand, we call that period romantic or classical.

The literature of England and generally of Northern Europe is romantic; that is, in the northern literature the vital impulse has always more than held its own against the force of authority. The conflict, however, has been strenuous. The northern genius expressed itself characteristically in the Gothic architecture of the Middle Ages. We can understand this expression if we think of the northern peoples as they first appeared in history, full of youth and life and energy, with strong bodies and strong emotions; if we think of them subjected, in a comparatively brief time, through their introduction to civilization and Christianity, to the control of older laws and the ordinances of a religion which placed the main emphasis on the mortification of the flesh. Their pent energy expressed itself in this architecture, the product of great genius under unwonted pressure; it was forced up into the points and pinnacles, broken into the colors of

[1] *Appreciations,* "Postscript."

the windows, tortured into the grotesque forms and monstrous figures of the decorations. It subjected itself to form—to a form, however, which it seems to tolerate uneasily, which it threatens to throw off in order to secure its liberty. This is characteristic of the northern art and literature, which retain a wildness, grotesqueness, and freedom to the present day.

We may be sure that the human creative energy, like energy in other forms, comes not constantly but intermittently, or in waves,—waves century long, however, so that we can look back over only a small number of these in our literary history. The Elizabethan period felt such an influx of energy. It was a time of individualism, of youth, of progress, and therefore, as we should expect, a time of initiative, activity, curiosity, invention, imagination. "To vent the feelings, to satisfy the heart and eyes, to set free boldly on all the roads of existence the pack of appetites and instincts, this," says Taine, "was the craving which the manners of the time betrayed." [1] In the world of action it produced men like John Smith, a kind of great boy, as fresh, active, and adventurous as Ulysses. In the world of letters it produced men like Christopher Marlowe, the type of genius fresh and uncontrolled,—a man who

> Had in him those brave translunary things
> That the first poets had. [2]

Its writers were full of passion, originality, and imagination; they were impatient of form as form, having a natural rather than a traditional art; as artists they were naïve, even boyish, playing and experimenting with literary forms and with language, fond of the verbal conceits and jingles that boys delight in. Shakespeare is a good representative of this remarkable time.

While Shakespeare lived, however, the wave began to recede, and in the Jacobean writers passion grew pale and imagination

[1] *History of English Literature*, Book ii, chap. i, sec. 3.
[2] Drayton, "To H. Reynolds."

feeble. The force of authority asserted itself. Ben Jonson and his classical followers were not satisfied with Shakespeare's natural art; to them Shakespeare wanted art. "Sufflaminandus erat," said Jonson,—[1] "he ought to have had the brakes put on him"—and this sums up the attitude of authority toward Shakespeare and its hostility to the romantic spirit. Dryden's expression, however, may be added. Representing the adult and Frenchified criticism of the Restoration, with the air of a man who has grown and traveled, he says of the boyish exuberance of the Elizabethans—"Their wit was not that of gentlemen," and "it frequently descended to clenches."

The classical critics found standards for judging the Elizabethans where they are usually found—in the past. The effort of authority is always to bind the present by the past. Modern writers, it should be noted, may return to the classics for two purposes,—some, like Marlowe and Keats, to stand "up to the chin in the Pierian flood," and to live with those first poets who "are yet the fountain light of all our day"; others, like Jonson and Pope, to find laws and precedents. The former go generally to Homer and the Greeks, the latter to the Latin poets, particularly to Horace. The main characteristic of the writers in our so-called classical period was not that they returned to the classics, or that their work is marked by traits conspicuous in the classics, but that they made authority the guide of life and sought authority in Homer and Virgil, Aristotle and Horace.

> Hear how learned Greece her useful rules indites,
> When to repress, and when indulge our flights.

> Learn hence for ancient rules a just esteem;
> To copy nature is to copy them. [2]

---

[1] Jonson, *Timber*, and Dryden, *Dramatic Poetry of the Last Age*. Both Jonson and Dryden, in speaking of Shakespeare, more often acknowledge their kinship and admiration; but then they are not speaking with the voice of authority.

[2] Pope, "Essay on Criticism."

The period from the Restoration to the end of the eighteenth century is best explained by this key idea. It was social, frowning upon individuality—a time of rigid conventionality, when one man was expected to be like another in dress, manners, language, and style. It was sophisticated and cynical,—as if age had come upon it since the time of Shakespeare,—"a decrepit, death-sick era," Carlyle calls the latter part of it. It was reflective and critical rather than progressive and creative. It was strong in its common sense, which recognizes the demands of society. In literature it was an age of prose and reason; it produced satires and novels; it perfected the heroic couplet. It produced men like Pope and Chesterfield and Franklin, sane men, who saw no visions and had no illusions. A very valuable period this no doubt was too; not to be underestimated, but rather to be seen for what it is; for, if man cannot live by bread alone, in this world at any rate bread is necessary; man must think as well as dream; art is necessary as well as inspiration; and we may suppose the eighteenth century well spent in criticism and reflection.

The nineteenth century, however, broke the bonds of authority and reasserted the power of the individual. Rousseau had sounded the new note in the first page of his *Confessions:* "I am not made like any one else I have ever known; yet if I am not better, at least I am different." These words introduce another era of creative energy:

> Bliss was it in that dawn to be alive;
> But to be young was very heaven. [1]

We need not stop to characterize this "romantic movement," with its rejuvenation of English life and literature, except to note that one of its traits was a strain of melancholy, morbidity, and madness, which hardly finds its parallel in the earlier romantic era. The author of *Hamlet* must have sounded the gloomy depths of the human mind, but he always kept up

[1] Wordsworth, *Prelude*, Book xi.

appearances. The abandonment of Rousseau, of Werther and René and Childe Harold, is new in the nineteenth century. There is an apparent difference in mental constitution between the men of letters of this period and those of the eighteenth century. The latter—Addison, Steele, Pope, Fielding, Johnson, Goldsmith, Burke—whatever their bodily infirmities, were pre-eminently sane in mind. Even Swift, whose insanity was probably due to physical causes, could look at life clearly. The romantic writers, with the exception of Scott,—Chatterton, Cowper, and Blake; Wordsworth,[1] Coleridge and Southey; Byron, Shelley, and Keats; Hazlitt, Lamb, and De Quincey— all these were in some way mentally eccentric or abnormal. For one reason or another they would have seemed "strange" to a belated observer from the polite and sensible eighteenth century. It would seem—if a conclusion can be drawn from evidence like this—that something in the romantic temper, with its individualism, its passion, its fondness for solitude and hatred of society, were conducive to mental aberration. Perhaps an explanation for this will be found in the following pages.

[1] Some readers may object to the inclusion of Wordsworth here, and I have no objection to omission.

CHAPTER XV

THE POETIC MADNESS AND CATHARSIS

I

IN taking up the poetic madness I must first note that it has been the subject of much confused and even foolish opinion, largely because of its extreme complexity,—partly also because of illogical procedure, particularly in the employment of terms. The question of the normality or sanity of this madness is at once raised; the words *abnormal* and *insane* are used, and here, as often elsewhere, they are abused. The term *abnormal* can never be employed safely if the norm to which it refers is vague or arbitrarily established. If it be taken to mean departing from a norm set by the common or average run of persons, then the poet is in many of his characteristics always abnormal. He cannot be normal with reference to an average struck from lawyers, stockbrokers, carpenters, etc. And as most of us, by the way, including the scientific observers, belong to the common run, we are apt to look with distrust, even with reprehension, on the strangenesses of the poetic character. If again abnormal be taken to mean departing from a norm of mental stability, or if insane be taken to mean falling below a minimum of mental health, then mental stability and health in turn must be carefully defined. This is difficult because there is no clear line between health, either mental or physical, and disease, the latter growing out of the former by a continuous gradation. Disease is not a distinct principle disputing with health for the possession of the organism, but a disproportionate development of one or more mental features as compared with others—an anharmony, greater or less, in normal phenomena. Insanity means literally only lacking in mental health. In no person is the mental health perfect; in some it is so far from being so that their minds are clearly, even hideously distorted. The lack of health may appear in all degrees, from a trifling temporary indisposition to a violent, permanent, and incurable derangement. What then is the mental harmony or perfection which is to be taken as a standard? Is it established again by the common average? Or by an abstract conception of the specialist? Or in the case of the poet, by his ordinary moments, to which his mad ones are to be referred? Again what degree of departure from the standard do we find in the poet?   And when does this departure become so great that it must be called abnormal or diseased?   Is it, in the case of the poet, when his passion or illusion interferes with his rational thought? —or his practical action?   Is it when they so interfere only temporarily? or permanently?   Is it when the poet becomes— either temporarily or permanently—unfit to discharge the ordinary obligations of society?   Or to note further possible standards, is the anharmony to be called abnormal or diseased only when it becomes objectionable from the point of view of the good, either first of the individual concerned, or secondly of the race?   Would the poet have been on the whole better off without some of his strange mental features, so that he might wisely have wished them absent?   Even if he would have been better off individually would a change have meant loss or gain to the race?—because individual suffering may mean racial profit. We should note that we are inclined to question the poet's sanity, but not generally his beneficence. Obviously this analysis raises very large questions. It shows, I believe, that the standards of normality and sanity must be clearly established,—and established not arbitrarily but with due regard for all the factors entering into the complicated question.

Again observers have noted in poets a deviation from type and have called this a deterioration; Nordau and Lombroso have found in poets a degeneration. They again arbitrarily assume a type; and they assume that the departure is a deterioration. May it not be an improvement? May not men of poetic genius, as Myers suggests, be rather *progenerates*? May not "their perturbation mask an evolution which we or our children must traverse when they have shown the way?"[1] There are reasons for supposing this. There are other reasons for supposing in the poet a reversion to a primitive type of thought. Evidently the question is not to be decided off hand. Observers like Lombroso have displayed a great number of "morbid symptoms of genius." They find, for example, in the insane hallucinations and confusions of fact with fancy. They jump to the conclusion that hallucinations are necessarily "morbid symptoms;" and they illogically throw the great poet and the common lunatic into one class. They find that Shelley and Poe, for example, had an unusual keenness of sense often found in derangement; they call this hyperaesthesia—which to the layman may have a bad sound and give the dog a bad name. They do not show that this unusual keenness of sense is inseparable from derangement, or that, in the race of life, it was on the whole disadvantageous to Shelley and Poe—or to their readers.

These difficulties raised by the terms, together with those inherent in the subject, are so great that for the present chapter I must try to simplify them as much as I can. It would perhaps be best, if it were possible, simply to describe the phenomena in the poet, without trying to decide whether they are within or without the imaginary line between health and disease—whether they are pathological or not. This would require a new terminology; judgment on the point of health is largely inseparable from the ordinary terms—which I must employ. The psychologist or alienist would have to consider this point more fully than is necessary here. I shall try not to raise it where it can be avoided; but even for the present pur-

[1] *Human Personality*, vol. i, p. 56.

pose it must be considered. We may agree at once that the poet has a mental development different in degree and proportion from that of the ordinary man; that his moments of vision and "madness" are different from his ordinary moments, and are not devoted to rational thought. But we may ask how the poet stands with reference to other men of similar ability and surroundings. We shall have to inquire particularly whether his peculiar mental constitution is good or bad in its consequences for himself and for the race. Avoiding the word *abnormal*, I shall use the word *insane* to designate a prolonged mental derangement, clearly incapacitating a man for rational thought and action, particularly in the view of his contemporaries—that is, in something like its most common sense. I shall use the word *pathological* somewhat vaguely for a condition characterizing or tending toward mental unhealth or insanity. In particular I ask the reader to regard the word *madness* as colorless, not good or bad in its connotation, not necessarily designating anything pathological, and not to be identified with insanity.

Though the poetic madness has been recognized from the earliest times, the descriptions of it in literature are not usually definite enough to be of great service. It apparently applies to different kinds of disturbance, or to the same disturbance in varying degrees. If madness can be attributed to Scott we may suppose it to have amounted only to a genial glow— like his ruling passion mild, prolonged, and diffused. With Shelley it may have been a higher but temporary disturbance— a rapture or even a fine frenzy. With Coleridge, De Quincey, and Poe it may have taken peculiar forms because complicated with the effects of alcohol or opium, resorted to perhaps for alleviation. With Blake it was perhaps equivalent to an almost uninterrupted and lifelong ecstasy. Where poets have been attacked by a recognized insanity, as in the case of Cowper, we cannot be sure what connection there was between the poetic madness and the insanity. In the case of Swift, where the insanity seems to have been due to physical causes, we may feel that there is no connection; in the case of Lamb we may feel that the connection is close. Perhaps a typical case would be that of Byron, who says in *Childe Harold:*

> I have thought
> Too long and darkly, till my brain became,
> In its own eddy boiling and o'erwrought,
> A whirling gulf of phantasy and flame.

Or, as he says in his letter, after speaking of this poem as his favorite: "I was half mad during the time of its composition, between metaphysics, mountains, lakes, love unextinguishable, thoughts unutterable, and the nightmare of my own delinquencies." [1] We do not know definitely, however, what Byron means by this half-madness. In general even the recent cases furnish interesting suggestions, but insufficient data for satisfactory analysis.

The madness is different in character or degree in different poets; but in some sense and in some degree, the true poet will always be mad. We have it on the authority of a long line of poets and critics, reaching back to the oldest. The primary *locus classicus* is the well known passage in the *Phaedrus* in which Socrates is made to divide madness into four kinds.[2] Of these the first and the fourth belong to the prophet and the lover. The second is less familiar to us; it is a madness which "purges away ancient wrath," to which I shall refer at the end of this chapter. Then comes the poetic madness. "The third kind is the madness of those who are possessed by the Muses, which taking hold of a delicate and virgin soul, and there inspiring frenzy, awakens lyrical and all other numbers; with these adorning the myriad actions of ancient heroes for the instruction of posterity. But he who, having no touch of the Muses' madness in his soul, comes to the door and thinks he will get into the temple by the help of art—he, I say, and

---

[1] *Childe Harold*, III, vii; Letter to Moore, Jan. 28, 1817.

[2] Jowett's translation, vol. i, p. 450; compare *Ion*, vol. i, p. 502.

his poetry are not admitted; the sane man disappears and is
nowhere when he enters into rivalry with the madman."

Aristotle's expressions are in substantial agreement with
Plato's, though he is more liberal to the poets of art. According to the *Poetics* a poet must be εὐφυὴς ἢ μανικός; poetry
"implies either a strain of madness or a happy gift of nature."
Poets are thus of the two classes, as we have seen in the first
chapter.   The second class, however, is derivative; the primary poet must be mad.

Other expressions to the same effect are common in classical
writers, and doubtless go back to Plato and Aristotle. "Poetam
bonum neminem," says Cicero, giving as authorities Plato
and Democritus, "sine inflammatione animorum existere
posse, et sine quodam afflatu quasi furoris." [1] Plutarch explains verse as arising from this madness: "But above all, the
ravishment of the spirit or that divine inspiration which is
called *enthusiasmus*, casteth body, mind, voice, and all far beyond
the ordinary habit; which is the cause that the furious raging
priests of Bacchus . . . use rime and metre; those also who
by a prophetical spirit give answer by oracle, deliver the same
in verse; and few persons shall we see stark mad, but among
their raving speeches they sing or say some verses." [2] Seneca
attributes to Aristotle the saying, "Nullum magnum ingenium
sine mixtura dementiae fuit.[3]

The English poets in turn have taken the idea from the
classics. Dryden, for example, translates from Seneca, "Great
wits are sure to madness near allied." [4] Pope, probably on
classical authority, attributes to Spleen "the hysteric or poetic
fit." [5] The idea is not, however, native only to the classics.
Our old word *wood*, meaning mad, is etymologically related
to *woð*, a song, and to Latin *vates*, a seer or poet,—suggesting

[1] *De Oratore*, ii, 46; compare *De Natura Deorum*, ii, 66.
[2] *Morals, Symposiacs*, i, 5,—Holland's translation.
[3] *De Tranquillitate Animi*, xv, 16.
[4] "Absolom and Achitophel," i, 163.
[5] "Rape of the Lock," iv, 60.

that recognition of the poetic madness is widespread and older than Plato. So when Drayton writes of Marlowe,

> For that fine madness still he did retain
> That rightly should possess the poet's brain,[1]

and when Shakespeare speaks of the "poet's eye in a fine frenzy rolling," these writers are not necessarily indebted to Plato for the idea. The respect shown by primitive peoples, like the American Indians, for their priests and poets, and similarly for their madmen, suggests a nearly universal recognition of the poetic madness and its value.

The famous passage in *Midsummer Night's Dream*, taken with similar lines in other plays, shows that Shakespeare apprehended the truth in this matter.[2]

> Lovers and madmen have such seething brains,
> Such shaping phantasies, that apprehend
> More than cool reason ever comprehends.
> The lunatic, the lover, and the poet
> Are of imagination all compact, etc.

The lover, as we have already noted, is in many respects parallel to the poet; he has the poet's unsatisfied desire, his passion, his inspiration, his ecstasy, and his madness. The lover often sings and becomes a poet. Love is often spoken of in literature as a "madness most discreet," even as a disease. Ophelia in *Hamlet* goes mad for love, and her songs are the appropriate expression of her thwarted love and consequent madness—a natural poetry.[3] Ordinary love can hardly be regarded as a pathological

---

[1] " To H. Reynolds."

[2] The passage occurs in the most fanciful of Shakespeare's plays, entitled a dream, and having many dream-like qualities. Shakespeare undoubtedly wrote on the "dream power" of the poet from his own mental experience. See the play, V, i; and for other passages M. Luce, *Handbook of Shakespeare*, pp. 31-45.

[3] Mrs. Jamieson suggests that Ophelia is here recalling snatches of ballads heard in infancy; but the expression or hysterical discharge is a poetic one,

aberration, and similarly the poetic madness need not be so regarded. Both the lover's madness and the poet's, however, like other natural states, may run on into a pathological condition,—indeed as we shall see, from their essential nature, are particularly liable to do so. The ordinary condition of the lover and the poet even displays certain phenomena which come out sharply in mental disease. Shakespeare was not wrong, therefore, in bracketing the lover, the lunatic, and the poet. We shall find also that the poet's madness is not peculiar to him, but like the lover's, is shared, though in lesser degree, by all men—just as we found earlier that all men are in some degree poets. With these prefatory observations I may go on to suggest a partial explanation of the poetic madness, which, I hope, will agree with the quotations just given, and with the facts as we find them not only in the poet but in the lunatic and the lover,—and agree also with the theory of the preceding chapters.

We must return again to the "desires of the mind," which we have found to be the fundamental motives of poetry—as of all thought and action. Of the whole number of desires some are satisfied and thus ended. This satisfaction, we may presume, provides our comfort and happiness, and conduces to our sanity. That man would be completely happy whose desires aroused the appropriate thoughts and activities, and whose activities attained their end in gratification,—between whose desires and experience there was perfect correspondence. Complete satisfaction and happiness, however, are denied us. Many desires, conflicting with physical fact or authority, are incapable of satisfaction. These give rise to feelings of dissatisfaction, to unpleasant or painful feelings, to some degree of emotional disturbance,—if this disturbance is severe, to what we call passion. This is what we have in mind when we say we have a

and, being doubtless in part extempore, it represents just that fusion of elements from childhood and recent experience which is found generally in the poetic expression. Hamlet is in love, and thought by Polonius to be "from his reason fall'n thereon." He has also other thwarted desires, and his madness and poetry are excellent illustrations of the text above.

"passion" for a thing, or are "passionately fond" of it; we have a disturbing desire for it. The word *fond* connotes folly; and the reason why we say we are "mad" or "crazy" about a thing will appear in a moment. When the desires are violent and the dissatisfaction prolonged—when strong desires are repressed or dammed up—the result is a condition of tension, inflammation, a disturbance of higher intensity. "A violent desire," Swift says, "is little better than a distemper"; this statement elaborated would be almost an explanation of the madness in question. The poetic madness is a high degree of the emotional disturbance arising from unsatisfied desire. As the desires may be of all kinds and degrees, strong or weak, violent and insistent or mild and diffused, temporary or persisting, conscious or unconscious, and as the denial may be strongly or weakly felt, so the resulting emotional disturbance will be of all kinds, and degrees of intensity—from a fleeting unpleasant feeling to a prolonged and violent madness. This disturbance always causes some uncertainty or suspension of rational thought and action. The emotion, passion, or madness leads, as we have seen in earlier chapters, to a spontaneous imaginative thought, to vision. The irrationality, then, may be temporary or prolonged, mild or violent. Here again there is no clear line between health and disease. But the irrationality is so common, often so temporary, so much like that of the lover, and in many ways so beneficent that we must consider it in large part a natural and healthful condition of the human mind.

A complete explanation of the poetic madness in all its appearances, with their complications from other mental and physical disturbances and perhaps from alcohol and drugs, would cover much ground and many details. No true explanation, however, I am confident, will be found out of harmony with the fundamental principle I have just stated: that it is an equivalent to, or an aggravation of the emotion or passion arising from the poet's unsatisfied desires.

The word *passion* is commonly applied to one of our main or fundamental desires, the sexual one. The passion is the result of the desire, and only when the desire is impeded; the lover separated from his mistress is consumed by passion, but when satisfied is of course no longer so. It may be thought that this passion is pleasurable, but observation will probably show, as a consideration of its nature would suggest, that, as in hunger, its main element is one of dissatisfaction and displeasure—or rather that it is wholly unpleasurable except as it is modified by preliminary and partial, or imaginary satisfactions. The desire of love is universal; and as, especially in civilized life, it often conflicts with fact or authority, and is thus denied or repressed, it leads to an inflammation akin to the poetic one. The lover often breaks into verse, and the poet is often inspired by the desire of love in its various forms. Indeed a large part of imaginative literature—poetry, plays, and novels—is inspired by this desire (and satisfies this desire in its readers)—a larger part indeed than we commonly suppose, in the first place because in civilized life the desire ramifies and conceals itself in countless forms; in the second place because it often expresses itself through the imagination, by means of recondite associations, in symbolic fictions not readily identified with their inspiring motive. The love literature is unquestionably very large. We see then that the poet and the lover are often identical. And their cases are always parallel; the poet's desire may be other than sexual; it may be a love truly Platonic or any other desire; but it works in a similar way.

We must consider also the lunatic of Shakespeare's line. Unsatisfied desire may lead to a serious and permanent disturbance—to a lunacy, hysteria, or neurosis. When a strong desire is strongly repressed it is forced into unconsciousness; various forms of sexual desire are especially subject to such repression. With its associations it becomes what Freud calls a complex or what Janet calls a *souvenir traumatique*—that is, it constitutes a mental wound or sore. The resulting inflammation is clearly noxious and pathological. The unconscious desire now expresses itself through the imagination in hysterical manifestations—dreams, hallucinations, even involuntary speeches and actions. The working of the imagination is here parallel—in its concreteness, symbolism, displacement, character formation, etc.—to that of the ordinary poetic imagination, as it is described in the preceding chapters. The hysterical imagination is a kind of insane poetical one. The hysteric indeed is what the poet often becomes when he goes insane. Ophelia's songs, for a convenient example, are a kind of natural poetry, but also the manifestation of a neurosis. In Ophelia, and likewise in Hamlet, Shakespeare exhibits the combination of lunatic, lover, and poet. The discussion of Hamlet's madness presents all the difficulties suggested at the beginning of this chapter. Was Hamlet insane? Was the author of this largely autogenous character insane? It is better instead of answering these questions point blank as is so often done, to elaborate them and make them intelligible. They can be answered only with endless explanations and qualifications. Lamb insists on the control or "hidden sanity" of true genius, and finds it "impossible for the mind to conceive a mad Shakespeare." [1] Heine in form gives the opposite answer: "Oder ist die Poesie vielleicht eine Krankheit des Menschen, wie die Perle nur der Krankheitsstoff ist, woran das arme Austertier leidet?" [2]—but he insists on the beauty and value of the product.

II

The emotion and tension accompanying dreams, which we have found to be a product of the desires, we may probably identify with the poetic madness. We may go back once more to the parallel between poetry and dreams to introduce a new phase of the subject—namely the function of poetry in its relation to the poetic madness. Let us take first the function of dreams. Dreams have been thought to afford the mind relief, refreshment, recuperation. "The dream," Novalis says, "is a bulwark against the regularity and commonness of life, a free recreation of the fettered phantasy, in which it mixes together

---

[1] "The Sanity of True Genius."   [2] *Die Romantische Schule*, II, iv.

all the pictures of life and interrupts the continued earnestness of grown-up men with a joyous children's play. Without the dream we should surely age earlier." [1] The analogy here to play must be considered in the next chapter. "I have had times in my life," Goethe said to Eckermann, "when I have fallen asleep in tears, but in my dreams the loveliest figures come to give me comfort and happiness, and I awake next morning once more fresh and cheerful." "Dreams," Byron says, "take a weight from off our waking toils." [2] This dreaming accomplishes by affording an imaginary satisfaction for the desires and a discharge for the accompanying emotions. It secures mental repose and is thus "the guardian of sleep." So day dreams come when, in slang phrase, we are "sore," suffering from a mild *souvenir traumatique*—and afford relief and comfort to the mind overburdened by a lack of correspondence between desire and reality.

The function of poetry is analogous. Just as Daudet calls dream a mental "soupape " or valve, so Keble says: "Here, no doubt, is one final cause of poetry: to innumerable persons it acts as a safety-valve tending to preserve them from mental disease." Or as Cardinal Newman expresses it: "Poetry is a means of relieving the overburdened mind; it is a channel through which emotion finds expression, and that a safe, regulated expression." It accomplishes "thus a *cleansing*, as Aristotle would word it, of the sick soul." [3] The poetic expression is thus a natural antidote for the poetic madness.

The testimony of poets supports this view. Goethe speaks of his habit "of converting whatever rejoiced, or worried, or otherwise concerned me into a poem and so have done with it, and thus at once to correct my conception of outward things and to set my mind at rest." "Sing I must," he makes Tasso say, "else life's not life." Schiller, of some of his lyrics says: "They are too true for the individual to be called poetry proper;

[1] Quoted by Freud, *Interpretation of Dreams*, p. 69.

[2] "The Dream."

[3] *Essays Critical and Historical*, "John Keble."

for in them the individual appeases his need and alleviates his burden." [1] "I kittle up my rustic reed," Burns says in a poem, "it gies me ease;" and to the same effect in a letter: "My passions raged like so many devils till they got vent in rhyme; and then conning over my verses, like a spell, soothed all into quiet." [2] Wordsworth found relief in poetical expression:

> To me alone there came a thought of grief;
> A timely utterance gave that thought relief,
> And I again am strong. [3]

Poetry, Byron says, "is the lava of the imagination whose eruption prevents the earthquake. They say poets never or rarely go mad . . . but [they] are generally so near it that I cannot help thinking rhyme is so far useful in anticipating and preventing the disorder." [4]

The relief of poetry is afforded in two ways closely connected with each other but separable in analysis. Poetry is a safety valve, first merely in providing an expression. Whatever the state of mind, there is what Keble calls the "instinctive wish to communicate," which is gratified by utterance. "The man is only half himself," Emerson says, "the other half is his expression." [5] Man is a social being to whom communication is necessary, isolation terrifying. Merely to "open one's mind " is healthful and comforting. But this is particularly true in

[1] Quoted by Hirsch, *Genius and Degeneration*, pp. 45, 50.

[2] "Epistle to W. Simson;" letter to Moore August 2, 1787.

[3] "Intimations of Immortality." Compare Tennyson, *In Memoriam*, v. 2, of a relief of another sort—mechanic rather than poetic?

> But for the unquiet heart and brain
> A use in measured language lies;
> The sad mechanic exercise,
> Like dull narcotics numbing pain.

[4] Compare Byron to Moore: "It comes over me in a kind of rage every now and then . . . and then, if I don't write to empty my mind, I go mad."— Carpenter, *Selections*, p. xxxii.

[5] *Essays*, "The Poet."

passion or mental tension. The lover is relieved by confessing his passion. The criminal is often instinctively driven to relief in confession. The man in anger must "speak his mind," or "have it out." "He often finds present help who does his grief impart." [1] On the other hand the repression of emotion is painful and dangerous. "That way madness lies."

> Give sorrow words: the grief that does not speak,
> Whispers the o'erfraught heart and bids it break. [2]

Where there is the wish to communicate or any other wish, utterance also is a kind of action—often an outlet for energy that might be expended in action of a different kind leading to gratification, for which utterance becomes a surrogate. Moreover where an impulse is in conflict with authority poetry, through its veiled or "censored" representation, provides, with wit and other veiled utterances, the only means of expression. Thus an interdicted or shameful impulse is relieved. Kipling writes of the narrator in the "Phantom Rickshaw ": "When he recovered I suggested that he should write out the whole affair from beginning to end, knowing that ink might assist him to ease his mind. When little boys have learned a new bad word they are never happy until they have chalked it upon a door. And this also is literature." [3] Only in literature the expression is commonly veiled.

This leads, however, to the second and more important reason why poetry secures relief. For the desire, giving rise to passion, repression, and madness, the poetic vision and the poetry afford a fictional gratification which tends to allay the desire and the emotional tension. The desire may not be removed; a thirsty man who dreams of drinking will be thirsty when he wakes; but he has perhaps avoided disturbance of his sleep. A poet when his vision is over may still feel his desire, but as we shall see in the next chapter, even the fictional gratification puts the

---

[1] Spenser, *Faerie Queen*, II, i, 46.   [2] *Macbeth*, IV, iii.

[3] The last two sentences are omitted in some editions.

desire on the way to its ultimate actual satisfaction; and at
any rate it is robbed of its noxious effect. To this the poets
testify as we have seen. Poetry is therefore broadly a safeguard
for the individual and for the race against mental disturbance
and disease. Shakespeare, if not mad, prevents madness by
writing *Hamlet*.

Shakespeare also secures the sanity of his readers, because
we must remember that the poet provides expression also for
his readers. One who reads, not as a student or a connoisseur
for an ulterior purpose, but for the true pleasure and satisfaction
which poetical reading affords, finds in poetry the expression
not so much of the poet's feeling as of his own. He regards the
poet as his spokesman,—even imaginatively identifies himself
with the poet and the hero, and lives through the poem. He
thus finds needed outlet for his pent emotion,—for what otherwise would remain repressed and inexpressible. In the fiction
his desires too are satisfied. For the reader also, then, poetry
is a "safe, regulated expression." This is particularly obvious
in the fiction of novel and drama. Men are fatigued by the
business of life, preyed upon by unpleasant feelings, under a
tension that requires relaxation. They read a novel or go to a
play and find supplied in fiction what is wanting in reality. They
feel what Keble calls the *vis medica poeticae*, and after living
in this imaginary world they

> With peace and consolation are dismissed
> And calm of mind, all passion spent. [1]

I must quote once more from the *Prelude* a passage which
also bears on the preceding and following chapters but is a
particularly eloquent defense of fiction in the aspect considered
here:

> The tales that charm away the wakeful night
> In Araby, romances: legends penned
> For solace by dim light of monkish lamps;
> Fictions, for ladies of their love, devised

[1] Milton, *Samson Agonistes*, last two lines.

By youthful squires; adventures endless, spun
By the dismantled warrior in old age,
Out of the bowels of those very schemes
In which his youth did first extravagate;
These spread like day, and something in the shape
Of these will live till man shall be no more.
Dumb yearnings, hidden appetites, are ours,
And they must have their food. Our childhood sits,
Our simple childhood, sits upon a throne
That hath more power than all the elements.
I guess not what this tells of Being past,
Nor what it augurs of the life to come;
But so it is; and, in that dubious hour,
That twilight—when we first begin to see
This dawning earth, to recognize, expect,
And in the long probation that ensues,
The time of trial, ere we learn to live
In reconcilement with our stinted powers;
To endure this state of meagre vassalage,
Unwilling to forego, confess, submit,
Uneasy and unsettled, yoke-fellows
To custom, mettlesome, and not yet tamed
And humbled down;—oh! then we feel, we feel,
We know where we have friends. Ye dreamers, then,
Forgers of daring tales! We bless you then,
Imposters, drivellers, dotards, as the ape
Philosophy will call you: *then* we feel
With what, and how great might ye are in league,
Who make our wish, our power, our thought a deed,
An empire, a possession.[1]

In mental disease of the kinds to which, as we have seen, the
disturbance or madness of the poet leads, the hysterical dreams,
illusions, and actions afford a similar fictional expression,
gratification, and relief. The law student referred to in Chapter
XII who imagined himself a count and acted the part until
prevented by the police, found, we may presume, a kind of
poetic pleasure in acting his imaginary part. By a shrewd

[1] Book v, ll. 496–533.

extension and application of the principles I have just been discussing, psychopathologists have found a cure for such cases in what they refer to as a *cathartic* method. The essential feature of this method is that it secures complete expression, confession, and clearing up of the repressed desires and emotions; it makes what Wordsworth calls the "dumb yearnings, hidden appetites "—what the psychologists call the "complexes "—conscious. It thus robs them of their traumatic or noxious character and effects a cure. Unlike the doctor who, when Lady Macbeth is "troubled with thick-coming fancies," declares that the "patient must minister to himself " these doctors can

> minister to a mind diseased,
> Pluck from the memory a rooted sorrow,
> Raze out the written troubles of the brain
> And with a sweet oblivious antidote
> Cleanse the stuff'd bosom of that perilous stuff
> Which weighs upon the heart.[1]

The catharsis is accomplished by a psychological "analysis," to which Stekel likens poetry, except that in poetry the patient ministers to himself. Poetry is "ein Heilungsprozess durch Autoanalyse "—a natural curative process through the clearing up of the hidden emotions.[2]

The Greeks had a cathartic method for the treatment of morbid emotional states. Persons afflicted with madness or "enthusiasm" were treated by music which accomplished an emotional cleansing. Persons so treated, says Aristotle, "fall back into their normal state, as if they had undergone a medical or purgative treatment." With this is to be connected Plato's second kind of madness, which "purges away ancient wrath," or "blood guiltiness." "He who has part in this gift and is truly possessed and duly out of his mind, is by the use of

---

[1] See P. Janet, *Les Médications Psychologiques*, II, iii, "Les Traitements par la Liquidation morale."

[2] W. Stekel, *Dichtung und Neurose*, p. 12.

purifications and mysteries made whole and exempt from evil." [1]
Madness drives out madness by a homeopathic method. So in
popular belief a person possessed of the devil could be cured
by charms—*carmina*.[2] Evidently poetry has long been regarded as a disease and as its own cure.

This leads to Aristotle's famous definition, according to which
the function of tragedy is "to effect through pity and fear the
catharsis or purgation of these emotions." This effect is related
to the *vis medica* I have explained. Tragedy has a moral value,
not in the puritan sense but in a much broader one. It is a
psychic cleansing, or curative process, aimed at an unwholesome
condition of the mind. "Catharsis" is a medical term; in "the
language of the school of Hippocrates it strictly denotes the
removal of a painful or disturbing element in the organism, by
the elimination of alien matter." "Applying this to tragedy,"
says Butcher, "we observe that the feelings of pity and fear in
real life contain a morbid or disturbing element. In the process
of tragic excitation they find relief, and the morbid element is
thrown off. The curative or tranquilizing influence that tragedy
exercises follows as an immediate accompaniment of the transformation of feeling." Thus among the Greeks a dramatic
representation was doubtless to the popular mind only a "play"
and means of amusement, though with poetic and religious
significance; but to the thoughtful mind it was also a great
public and sacred rite of purification.

Poetry in general "cleanses the sick soul," and, in its various
forms of poem, novel, drama, should be recognized as a hygienic
and curative agent of the highest value. Apollo has for his
province both poetry and healing—not only the healing of the
body but the more important cure of the mind—the two being
thus intimately related as means to end.

[1] See Butcher, *Aristotle's Theory of Poetry*, chap. vi; Jowett's *Plato*, third
edition, vol. i, p. 450, p. 13.

[2] In the recent war the neurosis called "shell-shock" has been treated by
music.

CHAPTER XVI

THE USES OF POETRY

I

WE have just noted one use of poetry. There is another larger use presently to be brought out, to which this one is merely subordinate and preparatory. This is a negative use in preventing madness, but leads to a positive one of the highest value to the progress of the race. There are doubtless many uses of poetry which we may hope eventually to discover, and may find clearly related to each other. Poetry, in the broad sense, is a human activity having many sides, manifestations, relations, and values. No one can at present hope to describe, trace, and estimate them all. I may repeat what I said in the introduction that I have by no means attempted to present an exhaustive theory of the poetic operation, certainly not a theory which will cover all the possibilities and difficulties at each particular point. I have tried only to present in outline a tentative explanation which will be in agreement with the main facts and at the same time coherent within itself. I may now recall this explanation, as it has been developed, by way of summary.

The desires are the fundamental motives, standing at the beginning of the poetic process. These when impeded arouse emotions, which are the "ferment without which no creation is possible,"—the passion which poetry always implies. The feeling gives rise to a thought different from our ordinary purposive thought—in being free, spontaneous, effortless, and dreamlike. This thought is visionary and imaginative in that it presents concrete images to the "eye of the mind." It is the older, primary thought; it can be called primitive and childlike. It draws from the deeper unconscious mind, and consequently has a character of universality. The imagination, in the thought formation the master faculty, creates a new subjective reality, parallel to the objective reality because it derives ultimately from nature; but above it because it is a making over of nature in accordance with the desires of the mind. To these desires the imagery, drawn partly from recent, mainly from older sources, affords a gratification:—usually a veiled gratification, however, because the imagination, drawing upon associations of contiguity or resemblance and fusing them, forms a merely symbolical representation, doubly fictitious. The best in this kind are but shadows, and the worst are no worse if imagination amend them. Accompanying the fiction, however, is the actuality of the emotions, and behind all the fundamental desires. The poetic passion is at best a disturbance of the ordinary tenor of the mind; when it arises from strong feelings under repression it becomes the poetic madness,—a condition threatening peace of mind, which is allayed by the poetic catharsis as we have just seen.

The theory thus barely outlined is made up of old elements, as the reader will recognize, and is new only in their systematization—of which I hope the reader will approve. It is supported by old quotations, many of which, I hope, get new light when read in the connection I have given them. It is an ordering and correlation of the best information to be got on the subject from literature. I ask the reader to prove it by the test of its agreement with literature. I have myself tried to test it in my reading, so far as this has gone, in literature classical, modern, and contemporary. If the reader will prove it by keeping it in mind in his reading I believe he will find it in the main confirmed. I believe he will find the statements of the poets and other imaginative writers,—their formal and deliberate statements as well as their most casual ones—in substantial agreement with it. He will find the words I have had to repeat so often—vision, dream, imagination, desire, passion, fiction, and the rest— almost always used, even in chance expressions, in consonance with the relations I have given them here. He will find particular works in literature showing a character and development in accordance with the principles I have set down. That there are errors and especially gaps in the explanation I have no doubt: these can be corrected and supplied if the main outline—with which I have been concerned rather than with the details—be found correct.

II

We may get further light on the uses of poetry by considering the prophetic and mantic character that has always been ascribed to it, as also to dreams. The belief that dreams are prophetic is very old and widespread, prevailing among all peoples, civilized and uncivilized, and leaving its traces in all literatures.[1] "I will pour out my spirit upon all flesh," says the Lord to Joel, "and your sons and your daughters shall prophesy, your old men shall dream dreams, and your young men shall see visions." We may say of prophecy in dreams, as Dr. Johnson said of apparitions: "All argument is against it, but all belief is for it." Here, as so often, I surmise that the argument is wrong and the belief is right; and that the denial arises from mis-understanding. There is the same traditional and universal confidence in the prophetic power of poetry. Apollo was the god of poetry and of the oracles. "The oracles of Delphos and Sibylla's prophecies were wholly delivered in verses"; as those of Mother Shipton and the present fortune-teller are in jingling rhymes. The same is true of "the dreamer Merlin and his prophecies." To the seer, the bard, and the prophet have always been attributed the same character and inspiration. The belief is not yet out of date. After noting that in earlier epochs poets were called legislators and prophets, Shelley says: "A poet essentially comprises and unites both of these charac-ters. For he not only beholds the present intensely as it is, and discovers those laws according to which present things ought to be ordered, but he beholds the future in the present, and his

[1] See E. B. Tylor, *Primitive Culture*, index.

thoughts are the germs of the flower and the fruit of latest time." [1]
Emerson believes that poets are still inspired to prophesy, as
in "Merlin":

> There are open hours
> When the God's will sallies free,
> And the dull idiot might see
> The flowing fortunes of a thousand years.

Obviously a universal belief of this kind is true in some profound
sense.

The poets sometimes seem to show a strange power of foretelling future events inexplicable to us, and elusive and fas-
cinating to us, as divination has always been to the popular
mind. Shelley seems in his poetry almost to have foreseen the
manner of his own death. Of Alastor, who is what I have called
an autogenous character, for example, we read:

> A restless impulse urged him to embark
> And meet lone death on the drear ocean's waste;
> For well he knew that mighty shadow loves
> The slimy caverns of the populous deep.

This thought recurs so often that Shelley seems almost to have
had beforehand an image of the event and to have

> heard the sea
> Breathe o'er his dying brain its last monotony. [2]

Shelley, it may be said, had a great fondness for the water,
which would account naturally for both the images and for his
death. This is true; but both the fondness and the poetic images
thus in a sense naturally forecast his death. Blake, taken by his
father to Ryland's studio, said after leaving, "Father, I do not
like the man's face; it looks as if he will live to be hanged,"—
as he was twelve years later. [3] Perhaps we had better leave this

---

[1] *Defense of Poetry*, p. 6.

[2] See "Adonais," last lines, "Ode to Liberty," "Stanzas Written in Dejection."

[3] Gilchrist, *Life*, vol. i, p. 13.

kind of fortune-telling unexplained. The poetic prophecy, however, is not entirely inexplicable.

To the Greeks the mantic art was twofold, one kind being sane and rational, the other ecstatic and enthusiastic; these correspond to the two kinds of thought, the practical and the visionary, earlier explained. The poet like all of us, or more clearly than most of us—may foresee the future in the ordinary way. He is a man of wide learning and observation, and of comprehensive thought; by employing an imagination of the merely practical order, akin to that of the merchant forecasting the coming year in business, he may "behold the future in the present." Thus Symonds calls certain sentences in Shelley's *Proposals for an Association* in Ireland "prophetic," and says that the Catholic Emancipation "has since his day been brought about by the very measure he proposed and under the conditions he foresaw." [1] This kind of prophecy, however, needs no explanation, and we may turn to the other ecstatic one.

We found in Chapter VII that the unconscious mind, from which poetry largely proceeds, has a wider view than the conscious one;—and that this to some extent frees the poet from limitations of time and space and gives to poetry a universality which the productions of ordinary thought do not possess. A simple illustration of this wider view is found in the fact, observed by Aristotle and many others, that a pathological condition of the body is often noted by the unconscious mind and revealed in dream before it is noted consciously. Villeneuve dreams he is bitten in the leg by a dog; a few days later his leg is attacked by cancer. A man sees in dream an epileptic, who turns out to be himself, for a short time afterward he becomes an epileptic. [2] Similarly from dreams of unconscious origin may come the first self-acknowledgment that one is in love, or in moral danger. Such dreams are of course premonitions only to the conscious mind; monitions to the unconscious one. The point, however, is that the unconscious mind has means of

[1] *Shelley*, p. 62.   [2] Ribot, *Diseases of the Personality*, p. 24.

arriving at knowledge beyond the ordinary one; and we do not know how far this wider view may extend. The ordinary mind looks a little into the future; the unconscious mind, and so poetry, may look much further. Some readers may regard this as "transcendental;" but transcendental or poetic truth is largely what we are trying to get at in this book. Instead of carrying this discussion further here, however, I may refer to Myers, who represents the frontier of investigation in this subject. He believes the evidence sufficient to show that visionary thought has precognitive powers, and concludes: "As is the memory and the foresight of a child to that of a man, even such, I suggest, is the memory and foresight of the man's supraliminal self as compared with the retrocognition and the precognition exercised by an intelligence unrestrained by sensory limits." [1] This view may be held quite independently of Myers's belief in disembodied spirit. It may be justified by future investigation. In any investigation of the prophetic nature of poetry, however, I believe we must always ask what is the precognitive power not of the ordinary thought, but of the visionary thought; not of the conscious mind, but of the deeper and wider unconscious poetic mind. Here again we must beware of considering the poet's prophecy as merely our ordinary limited conscious foresight raised to a higher power.

There is another explanation of the prophetic character of poetry, not inconsistent with that just referred to,—fundamental enough indeed to include this one,—which is less debatable and more intelligible in our present state of knowledge. The wishes that inspire our dreams are often reasonable, seldom preposterous or inconceivably attainable. "In the attempt to realize our dreams," as Havelock Ellis says, "lies a large part of our business in life,"—indeed, in the broad sense, all of it. Where there is a will there is a way. In waking we look toward and sometimes succeed in getting what we have longed for and dreamed of getting. Every dream subsequently real-

[1] *Human Personality*, vol. ii, pp. 262–274.

ized is at the time of dreaming prophetic. To take the simplest example, if a thirsty man dreams of drinking and upon waking drinks, his dream is prophetic of his waking action. Let us take a prophetic day dream. Goethe tells how, as he was once riding to Sesenheim after visiting Fredericka he saw his own double riding toward him. "I saw myself coming," he says, "along the same path on horseback toward me, dressed as I had never been, in pike-gray and gold. I shook myself out of the dream, and the figure was gone." The hallucinatory vision prophesies its realization. "But it is singular," he continues, "that eight years later, not at all by choice, but only by chance, I found myself riding over the same path in the very direction my visionary self took, and clad in just those clothes, being again on my way to Fredericka. Whatever the explanation of these things may be, the wonderful phantom gave me at that moment of separation some alleviation." [1] Even the suit of pike-gray and gold is realized, though this will not seem remarkable after a moment's consideration. The return and the dress were by conscious chance, but unconscious choice. The wish was father to both vision and action.

So the poet's vision when it is realized is found to be prophetic. If the poet, like Ezekiel, longs for his people's liberation, his song, which may help to bring it about, is seen to be prophetic when the liberation is accomplished. The theory is indeed particularly applicable to the poet's visions and songs. The true poet expresses primarily his own desires, but through his well-known representative character, the desires of others— of his class or country, of mankind. He is a spokesman. A great poet is great partly for this reason, that his writings give some shadow of satisfaction to the desires of all men. And what all men desire they strive earnestly to obtain, and will obtain eventually. Our individual desires—including even our trifling ones—taken all together constitute our common desire, the desire of all men. This common desire is not irresponsible

[1] Quoted by Hirsch, *Genius and Degeneration*, p. 93.

and divorced from nature, but as a part of nature ordered and
significant. It arises from the present reality and reflects the
coming one. By a preëstablished harmony it looks toward
that universal or purified or perfected nature of which Aristotle
speaks. "The desire of all nations shall come." As Lowell
says,

> The dreams which nations dream come true
> And shape the world anew.[1]

Sometimes the poet must communicate his desire to others,
who are inert and heedless. He stands

> Like a poet hidden
>   In the light of thought,
> Singing hymns unbidden,
>   Till the world is wrought
> To sympathy with hopes and fears it heeded not.[2]

Shelley, who was both poet and prophet in the old traditional
sense, speaks of his poems as "visions which impersonate my
own apprehension of the beautiful and the just." "They are
dreams," he says, "of what ought to be, or may be." [3] When
they become dreams of what *is* their prophecy will have been
fulfilled. The poet's imagination sees

> lovely apparitions,—dim at first,
> Then radiant, as the mind, arising bright
> From the embrace of beauty (whence the forms
> Of which these are the phantoms) casts on them
> The gathered rays which are reality.

The forms which become reality are

> the progeny immortal
> Of Painting, Sculpture, and rapt Poesy,
> And arts, though unimagined, yet to be.
> The wandering voices and the shadows these
> Of all that man becomes.

[1] "Ode to France."   [2] Shelley, "To a Skylark."
[3] Dedication of the " Cenci."

Thus the connection between poetry and prophecy, so often thought mystery and superstition, becomes comprehensible and explicable to us. The poet, through his high desire and vision, sees the future in the present. We must remember that the prophecy is always delivered in a symbolic picture difficult of interpretation. We must be careful also not to cheapen the prophetic power. It is never fortune-telling in the vulgar sense. The oracles, Emerson says, "do not answer the questions which the understanding asks. . . . The understanding seeks to find answers to sensual questions, and undertakes to tell from God how long men shall exist, what their hands shall do, and who shall be their company, adding names and dates and places. But we must pick no locks." [1] The oracles of poetry come from an unconscious visionary thought tending to transcend time and space. The poetic vision sees a future event symbolically as already present; it sees it indeed without time; it cannot therefore establish dates according to our ordinary calendar.[2] It cannot, as Emerson says, "wander from the present, which is infinite, to a future which would be finite." But by disregarding time it commands it. The range of the poetic prophecy is as great as that of human desire or aspiration. There is no marvel if it tells "the flowing fortunes of a thousand years." The Hebrew prophets saw the need of their people for liberation—a liberation from physical captivity in a lower sense, a liberation of the spirit in a higher one. They longed for, saw in

[1] "The Over-Soul."

[2] So the true mantic character of dreams is prostituted. The ancients recognized this character and apparently established some principles of dream interpretation. Finding that with some regularity certain dream images symbolized certain desires and so foretold their realization, they prepared authentic manuals. When these were handed down, translated from one language to another—say from Greek or Arabic to Latin and English— and were made dogmatic, without reference to the variableness of symbols due to the variableness of associations, which would be different for different times, countries, and languages, they became the vulgar "dream books" of the present day.

symbolic vision, and so prophesied the coming of a Savior.
They sang of his coming in songs still read by countless readers.
They could not for the importunate fix the date of his birth.
Their dream of liberation in the lower sense was hardly realized;
the higher one was partly realized in the coming of Christ—not
wholly, or their songs would not still be so eagerly read. Christ
when he came had still to prophesy a coming salvation. The
beautiful vision of John, who was carried away in the spirit and
saw the new Jerusalem, symbolized as a great city, the street
whereof was pure gold, as it were transparent glass, will one
day, we may hope, be realized.

"Among the Romans a poet was called *vates* which is as much
as a diviner, foreseer, or prophet, as by his conjoined words,
vaticinium and *vaticinari*, is manifest; so heavenly a title did
that excellent people bestow upon this heart-ravishing knowledge." [1] The poet and the prophet are one,—and the priest
also, because the best of religion is poetry and prophecy of the
highest kind. The true priest sees truth by subjecting the shows
of things to the desires of the mind—to our highest desires or
aspirations. Or if the function of the priest is specialized he is,
like Aaron as compared with Moses, the interpreter between
the seer and his people. At the present time when prophecy
is no longer believed in, when poetry is too often regarded as
mere versifying or art for art's sake, and when religion is so
much in need of inspired ministers, it will help us to recognize
the common character in these three things, which the men
of old joined together and which we have put asunder. Poets
like Wordsworth, Shelley, and Emerson still represent the
common character.

III

Before going further with the prophetic side of poetry let us
turn for a moment to the analogy between poetry and play.
"Fiction," Stevenson says, "is to the grown man what play is
to the child." Fiction does not belong exclusively to the grown

[1] Sidney, *Defense of Poetry*, ed. Cook, p. 5.

man because children have their imaginative stories, and play does not belong exclusively to the child but continues into maturity. The two are hardly coincident, though in the broadest sense of the two words, all poetry might be called play, and all play regarded as fictional, imaginative, and poetical. At any rate the two have many close connections and analogies. The primitive festival, perhaps religious, of music, song, and dancing, was playful; it probably gave rise to the drama, which is still called the "play." What are the uses of play, and what light do they throw on the uses of poetry? Play, like poetry, is a many-sided activity, having various functions. To say that play affords amusement, and that poetry may be regarded as amusement, and that novel and drama are regularly so regarded, does not help us much, except that we may notice that the word *amusement* is connected with the verb *muse*, and that this in turn doubtless means turning to the muses. Musing—in other words the visionary thought—has a general character of restfulness and relaxation.

The theories of play are at least three. Play is regarded as an outlet for superfluous energy; as a mending or recuperation of strength; and (by Groos) as "an apprenticeship, a preliminary exercise for the active functions of life and for the development of our natural gifts." [1] These three theories are not mutually exclusive, but rather probably all true but partial, and related to each other. Let us consider briefly how each applies to poetry.

According to the first poetry would have "its beginning in a superfluous, bounding activity, useless as regards the preservation of the individual, which is first shown in the form of play,"—for instance in the Bacchic festival. "Then through transformation and complication play becomes primitive art,—dancing, music, and poetry at the same time, united in an apparently indissoluble unity." [2] This theory is right in substance, wrong in statement. Poetry does not—and I should say that play does

---

[1] Groos, *The Play of Man*, pp. 361, ff.

[2] Ribot, *Creative Imagination*, pp. 46, 97.

not—proceed from a truly superfluous activity, or from an activity useless as regards the preservation of the individual or the race, as I hope to show in what follows. It proceeds from an activity superfluous in the sense that it might conceivably be devoted to work or what we call serious effort,—though even this is not always true because, as we can still play when we have not strength for work, so we can fall into the imaginative thought productive of poetry when we are unfit for the other thought—and indeed are particularly apt to do so. The fact is that the desires, and the energy at their disposal may be expended, first in reasoned thought and action; and secondly in imaginative thought producing fiction. We have already considered the circumstances under which they will do one or the other. Both expenditures may occur when the spirits and energy are high or low. Both are thoroughly natural and universal. Neither is superfluous or useless, as we shall see.

Play and poetry, according to the second explanation, may be regarded as restorative and recuperative. This may seem inconsistent with the first or "bounding activity" theory; but is not so because activity of one sort, however vigorous, is rest from another. Thus there is recuperation in the change from the directed thought to the visionary, as there is even in the change in the opposite direction, though a greater one in the first case because the visionary thought is comparatively effortless. Much more important, however, is the fact explained in the preceding chapter, that poetry, and so all imaginative play, provides relief for a burdened mind in its fictional gratification, and prevents mental disturbance. The evidence and conclusions of the preceding chapter fit in here.

The third theory of play, that of Groos, is best worth considering for our purpose. "Play offers an apprenticeship, a preliminary exercise for the active functions of life." Poetry also is a preliminary exercise. As it is a substitute for present action, so it provides an ideal pattern for future action. Play, I presume, may be divided into two classes; that, like throwing a ball, which is mainly a mere rehearsal of physical activities, and that which is rather a mental apprenticeship, and which is therefore more highly imaginative and fictional. Poetry of course would correspond to the second class. The child who plays and imagines himself a soldier is a primitive little poet; he satisfies a primitive instinct or desire; he dreams his dream; but the point here is that he also forms a conception, partly by developing his instincts, partly by imitating others whom he has seen or read about, of the part of a soldier,—a conception which prophesies the actual soldier and is of indispensable service to him when he comes as a man to play the actual part. So in playing solitaire I learn to extricate myself from difficulty, and in playing golf I am schooled in enduring defeat; and perhaps unconsciously I store up patterns for future conduct. The child's conception of the soldier is partly mental, partly physical in a training of nerve and muscle, but of whichever kind it goes very deep into his being; it is a training of the instinctive and unconscious, as well as of the conscious mind. Behold the child, Wordsworth writes,

> See, at his feet, some little plan or chart,
> Some fragment from his dream of human life,
> Shaped by himself with newly-learned art:
> > A wedding or a festival,
> > A mourning or a funeral;
> > > And this hath now his heart,
> > And unto this he frames his song.

The song is his poem, and also his intellectual and emotional "chart" for later action. Or his chart may be a little drama.

> > Then will he fit his tongue
> To dialogues of business, love, or strife;
> > But it will not be long
> > Ere this be thrown aside,
> > And with new joy and pride
> The little actor cons another part;
> Filling from time to time his "humorous stage"

With all the Persons, down to palsied Age,
That Life brings with her in her equipage;
    As if his whole vocation
    Were endless imitation.[1]

The grown man likewise records his dream in a fiction or play,
in which he himself always takes a part—a part which, when
sooner or later he is called upon to play it, he has fortunately
already conned. And in this novel or drama a reader or spectator may likewise find not only amusement and recuperation,
but also, as he imagines himself acting in the characters, a deep
culture of the intellect, and particularly of the desires, emotions,
and imagination, preparatory to his own future action.   He
even finds a chart for conduct in particular cases. Poetry is
then not only an outlet and a solace, but a means of education,
and the poet is the best teacher. When the fiction is realized
in future action the poet is recognized as prophet.

The child, even after his birth in a sense still embryonic in
body and in mind, is brought to both physical and mental
maturity by his play. This development, particularly on the
mental side, is continued in the adult by play and poetry until
he is too old to enjoy either. The absence of play is the characteristic of and recipe for a dull boy, as the absence of poetry
is for a dull man. In play the child by exercising his innate
impulses learns his individual lesson; by imitating others he
learns the traditional lessons of the race, and secures an inheritance which does not come through his physical birth. In
poetry the poet and his readers learn the same lessons in much
the same way, particularly in youth, but even to the end. The
poet thus secures our spiritual inheritance. There is an ideal
continuity in the race as well as a physical one, a birth and
propagation of ideas as well as a physical birth and propagation.
The poet is always present at this birth of ideas and in the
broad sense is their only begetter. The poet is rightly named a
maker or creator.

[1] "Intimations of Immortality."

What we call our serious activity, as Schiller observed, is partial and one-sided. It leaves many desires unsatisfied, many regions of thought and feeling unexplored. Our play and our poetry open and gratify these, and thus by "widening and deepening human perception tend to preserve and improve the race." [1] Schiller's saying that man is fully human only when he plays is justified by all our feelings,—by the gladness with which we turn from work to play, from the business to the poetry of life—a gladness surely not delusive; by the fact that from first to last we spend most of our time, and, as our hearts testify, our best time in playful or poetic enjoyment—surely not in vain. Play then is not a "superfluous activity"; and I must insist more strongly than on anything else in this book that poetry is not "an activity useless as regards the preservation of the individual," or the race.

IV

From this analogy between play and poetry which we may now leave, and from the preceding discussion of the prophetic nature of poetry, we can perhaps go on to form a more definite conception of the final use of poetry. The individual man has at any moment certain desires, which if the way is open he may plan and act to satisfy; this leads to what we call his serious and useful activity. But if action and satisfaction are for the time denied he is forced to take refuge in a second alternative,— to dream of an imaginary action and satisfaction. Such dreaming, comparing it with action, we regard as idle and useless, but in the sequel it turns out to be most valuable in prophesying his future action,—in other words in furnishing an ideal form or pattern which later may be filled up. This statement, however, needs revision because most of our desires, the larger and higher ones particularly, are at first incapable of satisfaction, and even a logical plan is indiscernible; the dreaming is therefore at first the only available activity. A man thus first desires, then dreams, then forms a logical plan, and finally, if possible, acts.

[1] Quoted by Groos, p. 379.

Or in the larger life of mankind, the race first feels a large need and aspiration. It then dreams through its mystics and poets and the effect is poetry, a symbolical prophetic pattern. It next rationalizes this poetry in philosophy: "history shows," Hartmann says, "that philosophy has done nothing but transform ideas of mystic production, substituting for the form of images and undemonstrated statements the form of assertions of a rational system." [1] This rational system is the plan for final possible action. In this process the most important feature— the idealist at least will feel—is the poetic engendering of the idea. At any rate without poetry philosophy and science would not come into being, and action would be impossible.

The individual's present denial and dissatisfaction, his passion and suffering, his poetic madness, are the natural means, and only means, to his future satisfaction and happiness. Most often, however, in the large view the individual will experience the suffering, and others, his people or race, will reap the benefit. "Most wretched men," Shelley says,

> learn in suffering what they teach in song.

The poet suffers; his teaching is for the profit of others. Thus Prometheus suffered for mankind. Thus Moses saw from Pisgah the promised land which not he but his people were to occupy. Thus, in the greatest example, Christ was crucified— not in vain unless poetry be valueless, for as he felt the highest and most nearly universal aspirations known to man, so he left as the result of his vision or revelation,—in his parables, in his Sermon on the Mount, in his transmission to the ten disciples of the Holy Spirit, in his instruction: "Go ye and teach all nations "—the highest pattern,—a pattern we shall long be engaged in filling in. In his passion and sacrifice he became the highest human—and indeed, if the word ever applies, divine—exemplar and means to salvation. He is the greatest poet and prophet. So many a later poet passes through

[1] Quoted by Ribot, *Creative Imagination*, p. 233.

a suffering which might be symbolized as a Calvary or a Geth-semane. His material desires are denied by poverty, his higher desires by an unfriendly world. His highest desires are incapable of satisfaction except in a world to come. He takes refuge in dreams and visions which are ridiculed. He is driven to mad-ness, perhaps to strong drink, which cause his further estrange-ment. But often, for the good fortune of others, he "writes his vision, and makes it plain upon tables, that he may run that readeth it;" [1] and henceforth, save perhaps in his own time and country, he is not without honor. Shelley's life illustrates the fate of the poet as an individual, and his teaching the value of the poet to the race. Shelley's Prometheus, partly an autog-enous character, partly a traditional one going back to the earliest imaginings of the race, is first man as poet, suffering for mankind, and in the final act man enjoying the realization of his vision. The poetic passion and madness may thus be immediately a disadvantage, and even by this test a patho-logical disturbance to the individual; but they are ultimately a blessing to the race. "From insanity," Plato said, "Greece derived its greatest benefits."

If poetry is of inestimable value, and has been accordingly esteemed in all ages and countries, it has been depreciated too, from antiquity to the present,—thought visionary by philos-ophers, idle by practical men, wicked by puritans, and many charges have been brought against it. The poet has often been called upon, like Sidney and Shelley, to write a Defense of Poetry. This depreciation is an error, though a natural one for several reasons. In the first place poetry often satisfies trifling, selfish, or base desires, and such poetry will seem rep-rehensible. We do not see that all human desire and vision, like all human action, is to be taken together, the evil with the good, and perhaps the evil as necessary to the good. The un-conscious vision, morally considered, will at least be better than the conscious action. Poetry again provides a symbolical,

[1] *Habakkuk*, ii, 2.

fictional, and concealed plan of action; the concealment prevents our seeing its true value. Or, though poetry is a necessary preliminary to action, we are too intent on the end in action to see the value of the means. The philosopher does not see that poetry must come first; the man of action is absorbed in his final but special part of the whole process; even the teacher does not see that poetry is the first and fundamental requisite to education. We are all practical in a narrow sense, and too short-sighted to see that poetry is indispensable to practice. Finally, though poetry is perennial, it is always tending to lose its inspired and prophetic character, and to become empty form and artistry. It then ceases to be poetry, and to have the value of poetry, but it has the form, and charges against its emptiness seem charges against poetry itself. I shall not engage in a defense of poetry, which has always taken care of itself as far as it is true poetry. I am only trying to explain the reasons for its universally recognized value, and also for its almost as general depreciation.

The universality of Shakespeare, the Shelleyan Prometheus, representing, as we have seen, not the individual man but mankind, the person of Christ in his representative character, and other examples of the same kind, urge us to rise above an individual to a generalized conception of the poetic process—to the conception of man universal as poet and creator. Science, which generalizes tardily, must still look upon such a conception as speculative and transcendental; poetry, always first in the unifying and constructive work which constitutes human progress, not only suggests but enforces such a conception. Poets, from Plato to Wordsworth and Emerson, have recognized that "there is one mind common to all individual men,"—a common human mind, finite perhaps, but affording our natural approach to a conception of the divine and infinite. "There is no bar or wall in the soul, where man, the effect, ceases, and God, the cause, begins." The poets see all our human needs, desires, aspirations growing into one as they approach the will of God. They speak, like Wordsworth, of a "human soul of universal earth," or like Shakespeare of a "prophetic soul of the wide world," and of this soul as "dreaming on things to come." They regard this vision as a divine revelation. They regard the universal mind as creative, for in its dream are born the "phantoms " which are "the shadows of all that man becomes." The creation is still a finite one, but "a repetition in the finite mind of the eternal act of creation in the infinite *I am*." The poetic dream and creation are our nearest approach to "the vision and faculty divine." They produce "the progeny immortal of Painting, Sculpture and rapt Poesy;" and form "that great poem, which all poets, like the coöperating thoughts of one great mind, have built up since the beginning of the world." The creative process is complete when the mind casts upon the phantoms "the gathered rays which are reality." When all the aspirations of the universal human soul are realized, the divine volition, as far as we are humanly concerned with it, will have been accomplished. Thus "poetry redeems from decay the visitations of the divinity in man."

INDEXES

INDEX OF AUTHORS

CITED OR REFERRED TO

INDEX OF SUBJECTS